SCOTLAND 2021

Edited by Simon Barrow and Mike Small

SCOTLAND 2021

EDITED BY SIMON BARROW
AND MIKE SMALL

A BELLA CALEDONIA / EKKLESIA PUBLICATION

First published in 2016

Ekklesia
3/3 Kirk Street
Edinburgh
EH6 5EX
www.ekklesia.co.uk

Bella Caledonia
Creative Exchange
29 Constitution Street
Leith EH6 7BS
bellacaledonia.org.uk

Ekklesia

BELLA CALEDONIA

Production and design: Bob Carling (www.carling.org.uk)
Cover design: Stewart Bremner (www.stewartbremner.co.uk)
Managing Editor: Simon Barrow

ISBN: 978-0-9932942-3-5

A Catalogue record for this book is available from the British Library.

Contents

Preface and acknowledgements

If you want worthwhile change, un-expect the expected, someone once suggested to me, in somewhat elliptical terms. They were right. When this book was originally conceived, the idea was that it would be published in June 2016, on a few weeks' turnaround, as a set of immediate responses to the Holyrood elections in May. Then a number of things happened, the most significant of which was undoubtedly a (largely unexpected, at least among the professional political class) referendum vote for leaving the European Union.

The upshot is that while much of the content you have in your hand was conceived six months ago, and written to a remarkably tight deadline, a range of changes and additions (within and outwith *Scotland 2021*) have reshaped the project somewhat. The editors are grateful for the forbearance of contributors and prospective readers in this regard. If you have been waiting and wondering, we hope and trust that it will have proved worthwhile as you work you way through the riches within!

A few comments on what is and is not contained within this collection are in order before we proceed. First, we have retained the focus on visions of Scotland through to 2021 (just under five years), and have not asked people to re-write everything on the basis of speculation – for that is what it would still be – about whether Brexit means Brexit or something rather different, not least for Scotland. That means, among other things, that the chapters that deal with Europe are largely retained in the shape that they were presented (before 23rd June) in order to provide an expected/unexpected comparator on the EU question. It's often better to re-read history before attempting to re-write it.

Second, there is no dedicated chapter on 'the constitutional question', for similar reasons. Instead, we asked people to dream dreams about Scotland, or their portion of it, and to link those to practical ideas for change. Some have done that with a sharp focus on policy, others have looked at the conditions and politics that shapes those choices and decisions.

Third, we have sought to include both well-known names and (perhaps) lesser-known voices in this volume. But we won't be attempting to define which is which – you can decide, if you want or need to! Most of our authors, all of whom contributed on the understanding that there is likely to be very little if any remuneration from a venture like this (thank you, one and all), fall broadly into the Yes camp as far as the independence question is concerned. But some do not. Again, no further clues. Read what they say, not what you think they should say. Similarly, there are voices who would identify as humanist, Christian, Muslim, 'none of the above' and more in a book which puts 'believing in the future' to test in Scotland and beyond – also those from different national and cultural backgrounds and those with direct experience of what they write about: not least questions of poverty, (dis)ability, racism, racism, sexist, homophobia, transphobia and classism.

As far as the gender balance is concerned, the outcome is less than satisfactory. We have a chapter on the need for 50:50 representation in politics and society. Our own ratio is 32 men and 26 women as far as direct and indirect contributors are concerned. The challenges presented in this volume are, forthrightly, to ourselves as well as those we address.

Last but not least, I would like to thank Mike for being willing to agree to this collaboration before we'd even finished our first cup of coffee together. We knew that kind of craziness made us kindred spirits! Thanks also to Stewart Bremner for his striking cover, Alison Phipps for her poem, Bob Carling for working miracles with the production, the good people at IngramSpark, colleagues at both Ekklesia and Bella Caledonia, Carla Roth and Virginia Moffatt for being beyond the call of duty as ever, Jordan Tchilingirian for his thought and wisdom, and anyone else we've unforgivably forgotten and who will therefore be expecting a drink from us. Un-expect the expected, perhaps...

Simon Barrow, Ekklesia
November 2016

Introduction: politics with imagination

After the madness of Brexit the reality is that "the UK Scotland voted to stay in doesn't exist any more". Those who vowed to 'take back control' appear to have lost it, as efforts to resist contagion will quickly reveal. The chaos of Anglo-British political manoeuvring may have destabilise the economy for years but it has also given claims for constitutional change within Britain a jolt of new energy.

But while independence or otherwise remains a central defining issue of power for our generation and beyond in Scotland, the temptation to focus all energy to this end to the exclusion of all others can leads to a disempowering lethargy, a political *ennui*.

The contributors to this collection, originally assembled in the immediate aftermath of the Holyrood 2016 elections, are alive to the need to engage the national question and routes to self-determination but also to confront the pressing social, economic, and ecological crisis we face, and to connect all together. Our writers step beyond posturing into a liberating space of innovation and ambition exploring deeper issues in an attempt to find richer solutions.

If the referendum campaign of 2014 brought us within reach of independence and caused panic in the London government, the fallout has been a botched and partial settlement, a strange patchwork of devolution leaving us in control of some policy but not others. We are ruled both by a government we elect but also by one we do not.

We exist now in a space 'in between' – a *Liminal Land,** somewhere between expectancy and doubt, pride and shame.

It is into this messy, creative space that these brave writers step.

The book is structured into three parts. In part one, **Landscapes and Futures,** our contributors take the longer view, exploring the deeper structural problems and opportunities we face. Emily St Denny asks where next for participatory democracy and the Greens? Adam Ramsay and Alyn Smith discuss that rare thing, Scottish foreign policy – though Smith makes the important point that the EU policy isn't 'foreign'. It's an area taken up later in the third section where Michael Marten asks: what might a postcolonial approach from the current

---

* http://www.qub.ac.uk/cecpa/liminal_lands.html

Scottish parliament through to 2021 look like? In the same zone Khuloud Alsaba examines the issues of human rights and the refugee crisis as helps Scotland mop up the disaster of British foreign policy failure and fallout.

Ian Dommett then takes a forensic analysis to the Holyrood elections and a wider view of where this leads our parties and our politics. The driving force of Common Weal, Robin McAlpine, meanwhile berates the weakness of our 'collective thinking infrastructure' and has some solid ideas on how to renew it.

David Gow also looks at Scotland, Europe and the implications of Brexit, one of several contributions to put Scotland in wider international context. The Greens' Maggie Chapman sees a positive future for the next five years but detects a challenge for the SNP: "Scotland is facing an onslaught of austerity from Westminster; deep cuts to Holyrood's budget, potential decimation of public services, increasing inequality. The ideologically driven neoliberal agenda of the Conservatives is going to prove difficult for the SNP to explain: why they are cutting public spending rather than using the new powers they will have over income tax to raise more revenue. So, will the SNP simply stagnate, or will the hegemonic party use it's position to deepen democracy, to change the structures of power to improve people's lives, to change our politics and create a better Scotland?"

Alistair Davidson asks some penetrating and necessary questions of the Scandic model and Joyce McMillan reminds us that: "whoever is in power, only strong grassroots social movements, campaigning for social justice, for equal rights, for a sustainable future, and for a constant progressive redistribution of power in our society, can ensure that our elected politicians remain servants of the people, and not mere front-men and women for a global system that increasingly seems interested only in ensuring that the many are made to pay, for the folly of the few."

Connor Beaton and Bill Gilby examine what some see as the carcass of Labour and the Scottish left, while Irvine Welsh asks us to shrug off the "dire consequences of being tied to the UK's debtor economy, within a neoliberal, pro-austerity economic orthodoxy". He writes: "The succession of Scotland from the UK is going to alter the rest of it. We should not only recognize that, but embrace it from a perspective of opportunity, not threat. We should be making a common cause with radical forces in England, to look at how we can work together to break up the centralist, imperialist, elitist UK state. It shouldn't be based on a 'we're alright – that's England's business' mentality. I'm personally pro-independence as I'm an anti-British imperialist, and not a Scottish (nor English) nationalist. I see as many possibilities in the decline of the UK for England as I do for Scotland. I believe in dissolving the antiquated, elitist chains of UK government and letting smaller, more localized democracies breathe."

In the following section, ***Policies and Perspectives,*** the writers get more specific, and we get down and dirty with ideas and innovation. Anuj Kapilashrami, Sara Marsden and Tony Robertson lay out a challenging health manifesto. Neil Cooper maps a cultural future that takes the local seriously in a wider setting. Paul Holleran examines the death throes of the media industry and the constitutional aspect of broadcast decline.

Talat Yaqoob and Lesley Orr then discuss women's representation and the crucial issue of gender justice, while Jamie Szymkowiak discusses practical proposals for the increased participation of disabled people in politics. Sara Marsden, Lee Bunce and Hamish Allan explore what for urban land reform can mean for a renewed Scotland.

Moving on, Doug Chalmers examines the potential – and the potential is huge – for successfully democratising universities and higher education so that they can be fit for the twenty-first century. Vonny Moyes demands a new cultural norm as we step towards a better childcare system based on equality and respect, connecting once again to the issue of gender politics.

Wendy Bradley begins with the old joke about asking directions, if you were designing a rational tax system you "wouldn't start from here". She poses the rhetorical question: "Is Scotland going to double the complexity of the UK tax system by adopting all the UK tax structures but with its own thresholds and tweaks and administrative improvements to the underlying structure but leaving the underlying structure intact?"

Kirsty McAlpine writes that "It is no coincidence that as the number of LGBTIQ+ MSPs in Scotland has grown, Scotland has become a better place for LGBTIQ+ people to live. This correlation will undoubtedly be the same for other under-represented or minority groups too. The next Scottish Parliament, and all political parties, need to move forward with this now."

Tim McGuire, Matthew Ross and Richard Frazer all explore questions of belief and values, from humanism to religion, in a changed landscape of worldviews and life stances. So does (in a different way) Mary Lockhart who looks at the potential in reimagining cooperative practice in a chapter that places economic and social democracy centre stage and incorporates some practical ways forward. Next Mark Smith and Trisha McCulloch look at vales in terms of a fresh approach to criminal justice and the penal system.

Jan Bebbington, Iain Black, Katherine Trebeck and Deirdre Shaw then throw a large gauntlet down to the Scottish parliament. Being 'greener' isn't good enough any more. Post-Paris it's time to step up and create actually coherent sustainable and joined-up environmental policy: "the Greens and the SNP want 50% of *all* energy coming from renewables by 2030, so we should expect that target to be adopted. The question can be posed – why not be bolder? It needs to be and countries like Germany, Denmark and Costa Rica show us it is possible."

This is a section pulsing with ideas, plans, fresh perspectives and new possibilities, and – if the politicians can be accused of endless triangulation and 'safety first' – this isn't an accusation that can be made here.

In our final section, **Nation and Imagination,** fresh possibilities are explored from the micro of Jane Denholm and Tam McTurk's look at what a campaign on the ground feels like (and fails at) in 2016, to the wider vista of Milja Radovic's view of 'nation' from the Balkans. Bernadette Meaden then takes a hopeful a view of Scottish politics from south of the border, while Jamie Maxwell looks at the issues of class, identity and independence.

Gerry Hassan, drawing from Tom Nairn's classic 1968 essay 'Three Dreams of Scottish Nationalism', asks what is the story of modern nationalism today, and how do the SNP measure up? Hassan casts a critical eye, but writes: 'The 2014 indyref was a watershed in Scotland's political maturity. The forces of the union won the vote 55:45 but in the longer perspective, the forces of change shook the British establishment to its roots, disorientated the Labour Party, and came close enough to winning to make sure the status quo and union were not strengthened."

Doug Gay then provides a fascinating philosophical (and even theological) reflection on 'the vision thing', imagining Scotland's future, and different ways we might go about it.

Stuart Fairweather looks at the longer-term consequences of the Holyrood vote back in 2106, with the 2017 council elections on the horizon. He points to the disaffected (and again absent): "All these parliamentary parties would do well to remember that almost two million Scots did not vote; many poor, many young. Those seduced by the 'both votes SNP' strategy were pushed towards 'wasting' their votes. If the objective was to elect the maximum number of pro-independence MSPs, then this tactic was futile."

In two final flourishes, first Alison Phipps, herself no stranger to dense discourse, moves us out of the real of the prosaic and into the imaginative and liberating zone of poetry, courtesy of her verse 'New Leaves'. Then Simon Barrow rounds the volume off, picking up and probing some themes from the collection as a whole, and looking at what the often misused word 'radical' can mean in positive theory and tangible practice, for both Scotland and for the changing world of which it is part. He also includes thoughts from others we engaged with during the production of this book: Catherine Harkin, Paul Goodwin, Polly Jones, Maureen McGonigle and Moni Tagore.

This is just a flavour of the rich content within, which tries to make sense of the landscape ahead utterly altered by the continuing insurgency of Scottish politics. All of this is given further impetus by the consequences not just of the Brexit result in the June 2016 EU referendum, but the toxicity of the campaign. As John Lanchester has written elsewhere:

> The mendacity of the Leave campaign may represent a recalibration of our system along American lines, where voters only listen to people whom they already believe, and there are in effect no penalties for falsehood, especially not on the political right.

The need for us to resist a decline into the form of political dialogue characterised by the Brexit campaign becomes vital, as the perpetual need for consistency of ends and means returns.

So here is a remarkable snapshot of the continuing energy of the Yes movement, now acting as a centrifugal force, engaging and inspiring in a wider arc a range of thinkers and activists with much more in common than the sometimes strained world of social media would let us believe – as the sheer variety of contributors, including a couple who take a different view on the national question, illustrates.

All in all, the will to change manifested in this book is palpable, as we present just a small cross-section of people with ideas, vision, and the long-view. It seems 'another Scotland' is still possible. In fact, in a world where the far right is in ascendancy and has become not just normalised but institutionalised, another Scotland and another world isn't just possible. It's essential.

Mike Small, Bella Caledonia
November 2016

Landscapes and Futures

Chapter 1

Reasons for progressives to be cheerful or not

Joyce McMillan*

Can we cast our minds back beyond the EU referendum vote and to the Holyrood elections in May 2016? Yes and no. Brexit will impact everything, but we should not lose sight of the underlying political and parliamentary landscape, which provides the basis for where politics will go at the end of 2016 and beyond.

Let's start with the reasons to be cheerful. First, despite huffing and puffing about the electoral system, in Scotland we now have a parliament which pretty accurately represents the views of the people as expressed on 5th May 2016. That is something that can almost never be said of Westminster, and I remain proud of the system agreed by the Constitutional Convention to which I contributed, back in the 1990s.

There is always room for debate about refinements to the present Additional Member system, which is based on the one created for the German Bundestag by the allies after the Second World War, and is still used there today. We could change the balance of constituency and list MSPs, making the parliament less or more proportional. We could give voters the chance to vote on the order of list candidates in the party of their choice, although that would introduce an additional layer of complexity to a system which is already attacked for being too hard to understand. Or we could once again consider moving to a more perfectly proportional Single Transferable Vote (STV) system in multi-member constituencies – although huge constituencies would be required, in Scotland's rural and Highland areas, to give the same degree of proportionality as the Additional member System (AMS).

What no-one except a tiny minority of diehards seems to want to do, though, is to revert to the Westminster system, which would, given current voter preferences, have replicated at Holyrood in 2016 the SNP's near clean sweep of Scottish Westminster seats on May 2015,

---

* This chapter is an expanded version of a short response to the election result published on the Bella Caledonia website on Friday 6 May 2016. It also contains material previously published in the election opinion section of *The Scotsman*, on Saturday 7 May 2016 and a couple of post-Brexit updates.

achieved with just half of the vote.

The lack of an overall SNP majority in the 2016 parliament both reflects voters' views, and should lay to rest the irritating and inaccurate "one party state" talk of the UK media, largely based on ignorance. The Westminster system, by contrast, is deliberately designed greatly to exaggerate the strength of the largest party, so that (as in the 2015 general election) a party with barely two-thirds of the popular vote can win a clear working majority of seats, and, if it chooses, use that majority to undermine the entire historical and financial basis of the main opposition party, as the Cameron government is now seeking to do. That looks to me like a far more dangerous situation for democracy than anything that has so far happened under the Scottish Parliament system, and I am profoundly grateful that Holyrood does not systematically misrepresent the balance of opinion among voters in this way.

The advance of the Greens – who increased their list vote by more then 50%, and tripled their number of MSPs from two to six, including the leading land reform expert and advocate Andy Wightman – provides the SNP with a potential pro-independence partner, at least in matters of confidence and supply, which can also feed genuinely radical and interesting ideas into the policy process. The Greens had one of the strongest manifestos in this year's campaign, genuinely confronting the long-term problems of transition to a low-carbon economy that other manifestos tend to avoid in a flurry of predictably bland, PowerPoint language. They are also the only party with a plan for developing a viable tax base for an independent Scotland, based on land, property and resources rather than the incomes of low and middle earners. It is good to think that these more radical and far-sighted ideas will have a greater chance of influencing public debate than seemed likely in the run-up to the election, when the polls were predicting another overall SNP majority.

In terms of reasons for concern, there was, in the aftermath of May 2016, huge media and establishment excitement over the return of Ruth Davidson's cuddly "Conservative-lite" Tories as Scotland's biggest opposition party. For voters interested in social justice and equality of opportunity, though, it is genuinely frightening to see Scottish pro-Union voters returning in numbers to a party with such a reactionary agenda in UK government.

For more than a generation, since the 1980s, middle-of-the-road, comfortably off Scots of a small 'c' conservative disposition have tended to support the Labour Party of John Smith, Donald Dewar and Gordon Brown as the strongest bulwark against any talk of Scottish independence, or indeed against any kind of destabilising change. Now, given Labour's confusion and collapse in Scotland over the past decade, some of them (around seven to eight per cent of the total electorate) seem to have turned back to the Conservatives, seeing them as the more robust and clear-headed defenders of the Union. It remains to be seen, though, whether this is serious support for Cameron, Osborne and their kind of Toryism, or something else – the birth of a new kind of moderate Scottish Toryism, increasingly detached from the ideological neoliberalism of the Westminster Tories, and pursuing a more practical type of business-friendly centre right politics.

Meanwhile, in the aftermath of the 2014 independence referendum, and now even more so with Brexit, Scottish politics seems increasingly divided along lines that are both constitutional and economic, with prosperous Scotland broadly continuing to back the Union, while those with less to lose have come to identify with independence, and the SNP, as their main source of hope for substantial political change. In the 2016 parliamentary election, the SNP continued to grow, and to take seats from unionist parties, in areas like North Lanarkshire, Glasgow, the urban south west of Scotland, and west Fife. But they began to see their share of the vote stabilising, and sometimes declining, in more prosperous areas, like Perthshire, the Borders, and parts of the north-east.

There is also an increasingly strong geographical dimension to the debate, with the SNP dominant in constituency seats across much of Scotland and down through the central belt, but unable to take either Orkney and Shetland in the far north, or the broad blue bulwark of Tory seats along the border in the south. This presents Scotland's new SNP government with the difficult challenge of trying to govern in the interests of the whole country, hold on to support in the party's traditional rural heartlands in Perthshire and the North-East, and expand into strongly anti-SNP areas in the northern isles and along the border – while not disappointing its hundreds of thousands of new voters and supporters in former Labour strongholds across ex-industrial central Scotland, including many of the nation's poor and dispossessed. It's a circle that may prove impossible to square, in which case we may already have witnessed "peak SNP". However, recent history suggests that it is never wise to underestimate the SNP's skill in political positioning, or the passion of its campaigning supporters.

While the collapse of Labour in Scotland may have been richly deserved, in terms of the party's recent political performance, it remains true that the eclipse of this once-mighty party-cum-movement leaves a gap in the politics of the left that no other force is yet remotely prepared to fill. For all its brave talk of anti-austerity, the SNP has no firm ideological tradition or cutting edge when it comes to opposing the economic policies of the right, and shows little sign of acquiring one, despite Nicola Sturgeon's strong rhetorical support for social democracy.

As the history of the 1990's campaign for a Scottish Parliament shows, there were times when the wider campaigning force of the trade union movement in areas like gender equality, anti-racism and democratic reform – including support for proportional representation – played a key role in pushing Scottish politics in a more progressive direction, during the years of Labour dominance.

With that deepest structural link between party politics and civic politics all but gone, it therefore looks as if this is the moment for Scottish civil society to stir itself again, and to start ensuring that Scotland does not slide backwards (indeed continues to progress) in all the areas of 21st century policy, democracy and representation that the new Scottish Parliament was once supposed to embody.

It is not entirely an accident, after all, that the decline of female representation in the Scottish Parliament (from a record 40% in 2002 to a stubborn 34.9% in the last two elections) has coincided with the collapse of Labour, the one major party that ever really tried to implement a rigorous gender balance policy. That statistic should act as a canary in the coal-mine of Scottish politics; reminding us that whoever is in power, only strong grassroots social movements, campaigning for social justice, for equal rights, for a sustainable future, and for a constant progressive redistribution of power in our society, can ensure that our elected politicians remain servants of the people, and not mere front-men and women for a global system that increasingly seems interested only in ensuring that the many are made to pay, for the folly of the few.

Chapter 2

A 'famous five' approach to change

Irvine Welsh

What needs to happen in Scotland over the next five years, in a changing political landscape? Quite straightforwardly, I'd like to see us do these things...

First, challenge the debt economy orthodoxy of neoliberalism
That is, offer a clear guide to the dire consequences of being tied to the UK's debtor economy, within a neoliberal, pro-austerity economic orthodoxy. And don't fall into the trap of believing that our toy-town, toothless parliament in Edinburgh can do anything but administer this misery as humanely as possible. All forecasts till 2050 indicate that low growth, financial instability and lack of economic dynamism is all but guaranteed in the British economy, with growth heading towards one per cent per annum.

A major failure of the Yes independence referendum campaign of 2014 was its failure to tackle the No camp on that long-term negative prognosis for the UK economy, and the Blairite-Tory neoliberal consensus that supported it. Alex Salmond decided against taking this anti-debt line, as he thought it would be negative to campaign in this manner. In some ways he is correct, but every year Scotland is in the union, its debt rises.

Every year is another one wasted, when it could be developing a stronger economy. Who ordained that we should be a debtor nation in this world order? Remember: Scotland has accrued deficits (the ones that give unionists such a hard-on) *through its membership of the union, and attendant failure to develop a dynamic economy*. This will continue to grow as long as we are in the union. Therefore, we should be asking of our central government (the ones that control our economic levers) now, as we ought to have asked then, exactly what do you plan to do about this?

Scotland has fewer than six million people and is rich in natural and human resources. It currently has an invisible presence internationally, other than a vague, chronically underutilised goodwill. We are running out of excuses not to thrive. Being tethered to a crumbling, financialised one-trick pony economy (which only does that trick in South East of England) isn't going to do that for us. Financialisation, privatisation and the outsourcing of production have severely weakened the UK as a whole, and marginalised our status in it.

Second, support people in England, Wales and Northern Ireland

The secession of Scotland from the UK is going to alter the rest of it. We should not only recognise that, but also embrace it from a perspective of opportunity, rather than threat. We should be making a common cause with radical forces in England, to look at how we can work together to break up the centralist, imperialist, elitist UK state. This shouldn't be based on a 'we're alright – that's England's business' mentality. I'm personally as pro-independence as I am anti-British imperialist, and not a Scottish (nor English) nationalist. I see as many possibilities in the decline of the UK for England as I do for Scotland. I believe in dissolving the antiquated, elitist chains of UK government and letting smaller, more localised democracies breathe. We have to resist the narrative of 'leaving them to face the entrenched Tory establishment' and encourage the one of 'inspirationally leading the way to get rid of the entrenched Tory establishment'.

The depressing picture of Nicola Sturgeon holding *The Sun* during the May 2016 election campaign (yes, I know, 'different paper, different editorial policy, Labour and the Tories brown-nosed Murdoch much more,' etcetera) was a crass insult to the people of Liverpool, especially coming out right at the time of the result of the Hillsborough inquiry. People in this city have been as shabbily treated by the UK establishment as any part of Scotland. Please SNP, no more of that bullshit, or you might soon find that the broad church you assembled after September 2014 will be getting considerably narrower.

There are many small independence or devolutionist advocacy parties in England (Mebyon Kernow in Cornwall, Yorkshire First, North East Party, Wessex Regionalists, and more) trying to gain traction for progressive, decentralist policies. Such groups should be supported by Scottish democrats just as much as Plaid Cymru in Wales. Yes, they might not be that significant in size, but neither was the SNP at one time.

Third, make a noise. Make a dirty, vulgar noise

Let's argue and squabble, as that's what democracy is about, but let's also try and keep a song in our hearts and a smile on our faces as we do it. Ignore all the windbag Tartan Tory piss about the 'left' – both outwith and within the SNP – shutting up. Thankfully, that's never going to happen. If it had, the SNP would still be a taxi-load of MPs from Angus and Perthshire, the Yes vote would have been 25%, not 45%, and a recent Strathclyde University study would not have found SNP supporters were to the left of Labour ones.

The SNP deserve their position of prominence within the Yes movement, but also deserve and need to be challenged by other pro-independence voices. Their membership quadrupled in size after the referendum, as they appropriated much of that loud, unruly and beautiful mess of idealists. These people shouldn't be asked to shut up. The party needs to display humility and remember that dominance, in this era of political volatility, can be taken away as quickly as it's bestowed.

Yes, the unionist parties are split, but only nominally, as Labour and the Conservatives, whatever they say, have effectively been one party in Scotland, all their firepower turned on the SNP and the Yes camp. This has been to Labour's detriment, and despite some voices for change mooting the resurrection of devolution and home rule, it's likely that the ostrich tendency will prevail and they will stay a Tory lite concern.

As long as they remain caught in that trap, Labour will stagnate and the Conservatives will ossify as the main naysayers and slavish puppets of their Westminster masters. This will continue to present opportunities for the independence movement. So we don't need one monolithic voice for everything on the Yes side. Therefore, we should mouth off. And we should seek to provoke, yes, but also inspire. 'Don't be an arse just for the sake of it', is a decent enough working mantra.

Fourth, don't hate on No voters, but challenge those who do
They made their choice, and they had their reasons. Engage, listen, and win hearts and minds. If every No voter was a dyed-in-the-wool, right-wing, unionist Tory, then No would have polled 22% in September 2014, and we wouldn't be having this discussion. That 22% of Tories doesn't speak for all the 'No's, and no matter how vocal they get, don't ever make the mistake of feeding their delusional conceit by acting as if they do. Shouting at, or denigrating people who don't agree with you –even if they happen to be the ones instigating this – isn't going win them round. Yes, this is a pious and self-righteous thing to say,

and believe me it goes very much against my own instincts: but we have to be better. We have to take the high road. We are the dreamers, the builders, the creators. They are the ones who won't let go, who are tied to the strings of elites that care nothing for them, and are driven by fear. Let that thought nourish you, yes, but keep it out of the discussion. We need to make the country work together. The shabby, declining UK isn't going to inspire. The inspiration has to be provided by the Yessers. And we won't do that with blaming, finger-pointing, victimhood-embracing and Bannockburn/Culloden fantasies.

How, then, do you inspire No voters to get with a project of change in tough times? By pointing out why those times are tough. By speaking the truth to power. I believe that there are still radical No voters who want to do that again, but who have simply lost sight of how to go about it. They've been locked into an outdated partisan war with the SNP/Yes for so long that they can't conceive of how it has shape-shifted to encompass so many of their own people and values. Some still believe that sniping at a government in a limited parliament with no strategic powers actually constitutes you doing this speaking the truth to power, rather than being misguided establishment mouthpieces. We need to convince such people that their energy is all in the wrong place and encourage them to lift their heads up.

One practical example is the elderly voters, who voted overwhelmingly for the status quo. Amongst other reasons, they believed their pensions would be safer. Their pensions are *not* safer with Cameron and union, any more than their NHS was, or their grandchildren's university education is. Let's engage with them and push that message.

Fifth, define, develop and promote radical social democracy
If there's one consensus that's developed around the SNP and the Yes movement, it's the idea of a civic polity based on a radical social democracy. We have to try to continue to define what this is, how it will help us to negotiate the decline of capitalism, and how it can assist us in tricky maneuvering along a just and pragmatic route to that scary but exciting place of no paid work or profit – the one that technology seems to be driving us towards. This anarchistic, conceptualist society is not just about the demise of capitalism; it's also about the end of its industrial bedfellow, traditional tax-and-spend socialism. Keynesianism failed in the '70s, and for reasons beyond the 'union excess, amplified by media hysteria, let the bad guys in' orthodox narrative. But fail it did.

So Jeremy Corbyn's socialism comes up short for the same reason as Osborne's capitalism. There won't be enough people in paid work to be the taxpayers who will fund the spending projects, just as neoliberalism's low wages and debt deflation destroys the number and power of consumers who buy goods and services. Simply moving from the myopia of 'privatise and cut' to 'nationalise and spend' is chasing fool's gold. That strategy ran into difficulty when capitalism was in its buoyant productive prime, and will wither quickly if deployed in its wheezy old age. We certainly need a fairer, progressive tax system, but that won't be anything like enough, as the wealth of the very rich isn't largely derived from taxable income.

Therefore, radical social democracy has to as far from insipid, neoliberal, brown-nosing Blairism as possible: it needs, as I have said, to be speaking the truth to power. That means looking at ways to prevent and reverse the one per cent's ongoing, middle-class hammering, asset-to-debt swapping project. It means wealth taxation and compulsory land purchase from absentee landlords. Because we need to redistribute wealth and property, not just income. To this end, it's a step forward that we have a bigger Green Party influence in this Scottish Parliament, and we particularly need people like Andy Wightman. Yes, a strong, united, disciplined party is all very well, but there will never be a shortage of people who will want to conform to party lines. If we don't have our share of mavericks, asking awkward questions, we stagnate and decline.

We need to be designing and developing models for the Scotland we want to see, and analyzing weakness as well as strengths. As I type this, I'm hoping that some University department or think tank is busy somewhere designing a Scottish currency and a Scottish central bank. The independence movement has come a long way through thought, intelligence, high principle and pragmatism. When the entrenched power of the state and media is lined up so resolutely up against you, to extent it was in the 2014 referendum, (and still is) you know that you are ruffling the right feathers. That's the road by which we'll continue to profit – not getting into shouting matches with the establishment's stooge apologists.

Chapter 3

Creating an ideas-rich environment for Scotland

Robin McAlpine

If we look at Scotland today with a cold, hard light, you would struggle to describe us as an ideas-rich environment. The legacy of the independence referendum has been changing that as activists become more interested in what is possible. Brexit poses massive new challenges. In this context what you might refer to as our 'collective thinking infrastructure' has not been particularly strong, and obviously that needs to change.

What do I mean by this? Well, let's start from the reasonable assumption that it is rarely governments or political parties that create the big ideas that define an era or the small detail which dictates success or failure. Reagan didn't invent Reaganomics – that was the 'Chicago School' of right wing economists. Thatcher didn't invent Thatcherism – that was right-wing think tanks like the Adam Smith Institute. And if Blair took 'third way' theory from Clinton, Clinton in turn took that from a range of well-funded centrist US think tanks.

So where, generally, do ideas come from? It is tempting to begin with academia where the blue-sky thinking is meant to be done. And it does – but a lot of the outputs of academia are generally not yet ready for practical use. The concepts and analysis they develop can be crucial, but they generally need to go through another stage of development before they have influence.

That is where public and semi-public institutions and think tanks come in. It is important not to see think tanks as primarily policy-focussed vehicles. Throughout the independence campaign any think tank that opposed Scottish independence was treated as if it had been set up by philanthropists whose only interest was in the betterment of society as a whole. In reality, think tanks were devised in the first half of the century by the public relations industry as a way to 'launder' bad ideas and make them look respectable.

Now it is very unfair to suggest that all today's think tanks are a PR exercise (as someone who runs one, I hope we're more than that). But think tanks should be thought of not as neutral seekers-after-truth but rather as campaigning organisations which come from one political direction or another. What it does mean is that unless there is a wide range of think tanks and unless they are properly funded, they risk being completely unbalanced and on occasion little more than blogs with pretensions. But a rich think tank environment is a good way to bridge the gap between academia and a more practically focussed consideration of public policy.

Another place where this takes place is in public and semi-public institutions. These might be public agencies tasked to deliver policy objectives which have their own policy function, membership-driven organisations campaigning for member interests (for example trade unions), supra-national institutions such as the World Bank or the European Commission – and of course the civil service or the direct public bureaucracies in other layers of government such as in local authorities.

These can be a mixed bag. Some are enormously risk-averse, seeing radical ideas as a threat to 'neutrality' and viewing change as something which is politically loaded. Some are simply undemocratic and wholly captured by ideology. A lot of them see themselves as institutions of management and delivery and shun the idea that they are about big ideas. Some are simply seen as vested interests. And all of them tend to be afflicted with all the usual problems of institutions and bureaucracies – slow to change, staffed with people who do well out of the status quo, keen to please paymasters and so on.

Then there is a campaigning and advocacy sector. This sector is mostly on the more liberal and left end of the scale (right wing and business interests tend to prefer buying direct influence...), but not wholly. So while there are lots of visible campaign groups on everything from the environment to racism to gender to poverty, there are also religiously focussed campaign groups and single-issue campaigns which sometimes tend in the other political direction. What is slightly strange is that campaigning groups are routinely written off as vested interests in a way that think tanks and business interests aren't. Their analysis and ideas often tend to be treated with more suspicion, in a 'they would say that, wouldn't they' kind of way.

A next layer you'd expect to find in an ideas-rich environment is a broad media sector. This does not just mean strong, daily newspapers with well-commissioned opinion and analysis sectors, it means specialist policy publications, investigative journalism, new media discussion sites and basically any other medium via which the ideas produced by others can be looked at, scrutinised, discussed and debated. But if you want this to function well, it requires balance, a readership and an audience. If every newspaper is owned by one wing of politics, if every journal is geared towards an internal readership and if no one is investing in investigation, this sector will not fulfil its job.

Finally, there are vested interests. In various ways, much of the above lies in the public domain. They are public discourses to which we can all be party (if we want). Beyond these is a large, very well funded and almost completely secret world of lobbying in all its forms. Sometimes lobbyists use think tanks to 'launder' their ideas (oil companies, big tobacco and those involved with pushing for GM crops are particularly bad for this) or use the media to press their concerns. Other times they just push government for policy and spending decisions directly. Mostly, they don't want public discussion of these ideas; they just want to cut deals directly and in private. It is possibly reasonable to argue that this line of 'idea generation' has a greater impact on final public policy than any of the others outside the civil service itself. And of course, the private lobby sector works closely with and on some occasions has actually placed itself inside the civil service.

The last paragraph begins 'finally'. It shouldn't. There ought to be some mechanism where ordinary citizens are given the access and power to discuss, debate and influence ideas. But other than in some small and mostly experimental instances (such as developments in participatory budgeting), they don't. Ideas are something that the elite do, not the wider public. (And this was what made the Scottish independence referendum such a breath of fresh air – ordinary people in their own communities really did get involved in a debate about ideas.)

So if this maps out the components of an ideas-rich political environment, what does it look like when it works? Put simply, there is breadth and depth, balance and transparency. Think tanks would come from many different political stances and have something like equal resources. Academia would be better funded for public policy and be a bit more orientated towards policy-makers (while being protected from increasing encroachment on their academic freedom from their managers). The media would be diverse, properly funded and properly read. Campaign groups would be listened to as much as big business and very little of this would be done in secret. The civil service and other public agencies would be able better to balance the need to take risks and the need to ensure some kind of policy continuity and stability. There would be much better mechanisms for public engagement in ideas. And politicians would have more incentives to make the best decision and not the safest one.

So much for the ideal – what do matters actually look like in Scotland? Well, not like that. Academia is fairly uneven in its relationships with government (and the regimes in Scottish universities are undemocratic and career structures discourage trouble-making and risk-taking). There are few think tanks and they're barely resourced (that Common Weal is the biggest is a constant source of surprise to me, given how little resource we've got). Also, they are not generally all that well integrated into decision-making processes, partly because none really have the resources to meet the demands that would place on them – but also because they're mostly all new.

The 'traditional' media seems like it is on its last legs. There are few policy journals about Scotland and fewer people who read them. The print media is disinvesting left, right and centre and its readership dwindles seemingly by the hour. Our 'national' broadcaster is seldom viewed in a particularly positive light when it comes to big thinking and covering national politics. And while there is a comparatively flourishing new media scene, it is barely funded.

Our public institutions are steeped in a low-risk mindset and are mostly utterly conventional and content to manage their own little fiefdoms. The civil service in particular is an uncomfortable amalgam of big thinking and administration. Because of the lack of alternative source of ideas it is often the civil service which is tasked with doing the blue-sky stuff (and I should add that there are many very good and very bright people in the Scottish civil service). But as they also have the task of implementing policies, and as success in implementing policies is generally measured as 'no-one noticed', there is an internal conflict of interests. There is a strong incentive to scale back big thinking to meet the 'safety first' imperative of implementation. So we often don't even know if there was a big idea in the first place.

We have a reasonable series of campaigning organisations in Scotland, but it is not as rich as it was. Though cooption as some big NGOs became contracting bodies for government services, because of the steps to limit the campaigning activities of charities by right-wing government in Westminster and because of the general scaling-up and corporatisation of the NGO sector, we have good, smaller campaigning groups in specific areas but not in others (for example, Scotland has never had a dedicated anti-PFI campaign and no real lobby for high quality social housing).

The combination of all this means that we have a comparatively empty ideas agenda – and this is a vacuum the lobbying sector is happy to fill. A lot of economic policy in Scotland in particular looks rather like a straight life from some of the corporate interests. It is important to be clear that Scotland does not have anything like the corporate capture that we see in Westminster – but then it has less of the balancing think tank and campaigning sector either.

When it comes to the ideas environment which surrounds the Scottish Parliament, it sometimes looks a bit better suited to a large regional authority than it does a national government. And it is perhaps because Scotland still seems to be caught somewhere in between these two notions (national and regional) that we haven't developed that fuller 'thinking infrastructure'.

And this really matters. Say what you like about the direction of travel in government in Westminster, but it is ambitious, radical, determined and detailed. It is a right-wing programme which has been developed by a wide range of right-wing thinkers dedicating serious resource over a sustained period of time to create that agenda, from the dismantling of a wholly-public NHS and the neutering of the BBC to the permanent protection of tax havens and the radical overhaul of the structure of state schooling. If there isn't an agenda in Scotland, we will drift. And drift is a very attractive attribute to the secret lobbyist who is happy to bring 'easy, non-risky' solutions to the table.

So what can we do to fix this in Scotland? Here are four specific suggestions. Two of these could be seen to benefit Common Weal directly so I will do no more than outline the ideas generally.

First, Scotland has no funding of any sort for alternative media. In fact, there isn't really any direct funding for media at all (though public sector advertising helps to keep some publications going). Scotland has a media which is in existential crisis. The overheads of print media in relation to their declining sales means sustaining them is a difficult problem to solve. But funding for new and on-line media (probably in the not-for-profit sector) is much easier and cheaper to support. We really do need to take media more seriously, recognise it as an important part of our democracy, accept that what we have is almost certainly not fulfilling that role – and dedicate a little money to it. The kinds of sums we're talking about here are negligible in the scheme of public budgets. Of course there are difficulties in being seen to be even-handed, but the imperative to support places where debate and discussion can take place is too strong to do nothing.

Second, even more difficult to balance is the question of funding campaigning and think tank work. Inevitably, public funding for campaigning and think tank work has been made controversial by Westminster and the right-wing media which constantly questions whether 'unpopular causes' should get 'your taxpayer's money'. But then what they really want is that only organisations which can get money from rich donors are able to participate in democracy. While there would be some political hurdles to overcome, recognising that a society without a non-governmental, independently minded civic sector which deals in ideas, thinking and analysis is not properly serving its democracy would help us to move forward. We need sustainable and reasonably funded think tanks of every political persuasion if we want a strong policy debate in Scotland. Some modest public support would help enormously.

But that's enough of what might look like special pleading. There are other important steps we can take. A third one is to democratise decision-making generally, opening up closed systems to public debate. Common Weal has written and published quite a bit on how to make participatory democracy work. Particularly relevant here is the way in which advice and consultation processes are carried out. At the moment the standard model is to create either a consultation managed by the people making the proposal (who will clearly have vested interests in certain outcomes) or to set up an enquiry of some description, generally made up of 'experts' in any given area.

These both have major problems associated. It is pretty universally recognised that consultation almost always takes place too late in the process or has too little impact on actual outcomes. They also tend to be passive processes, attracting only restatements of the already-established positions of organisations which are resourced to respond. There are much better ways to manage consultation. Taking responsibility for the act of consulting away from the body which is making the proposals would help. So would using much more supported practices which help many more people engage with an idea – and at the very earliest stage. Genuine public participation in ideas at an early stage is a realistic goal. It could very easily increase the quality of ideas being generated.

Even more importantly, the process of enquiry and advice should move from being one controlled by insiders (or 'experts' as they are generally referred to, in the way my cat is an expert on mice) and rather make it a more neutral space controlled by citizens. Rather than a number of people from very similar backgrounds with very similar views getting together and agreeing with each other in private, processes such as citizen's juries and deliberation polls open this process up. Of course expert views are crucial – but rather than controlling the process of developing thinking, they would simply be feeding in their views along side others who generally have less privileged access. If expert advice is persuasive enough, it will of course shape decisions. But it would enable ideas to be tested much more fully and completely, and would create a solid avenue via which alternative ideas can be fed in.

Fourthly and finally, for the purposes of this piece of reflection, we need to address the weaknesses in the 'blue sky' and analytical part of the process. The dual role of the civil service as thinker and doer is problematic – because as explained above, these two responsibilities can very easily be in conflict with each other. Unfortunately, the civil service is not devolved to Scotland so any substantial restructuring or redesign is not possible here. However, the civil service in Scotland does have extensive ability to second people to external organisations. This is an effective route to developing a better system

Scotland could establish a series of 'policy academies'. These would probably be set up by linking them to universities (though the governance would be entirely independent). Policy academies could cover any range of subjects wanted – a Economic Development Policy Academy, a Poverty, Equality and Social Justice Policy Academy, a Policy Academy for Towns, Cities and Housing, a Rural Policy Academy and so on.

Once they are established each would be staffed through a process of seconding civil servants, attaching practicing academics and by enabling other organisations to be located in and around the academies (with very great care taken to ensure equality of access and to avoid issues of 'capture'). Each academy would be governed in a transparent and democratic way, providing access not only to interest and expert groups but also using the best practices in participatory democracy to engage the wider public. There should be means and routes which would enable individuals or organisations to submit ideas which would be examined and where appropriate developed. Government would go to an academy as a first port of call when devising big new policy ideas. Parliamentary committees would ask academies to scrutinise and comment on government proposals. It would be expected that academies may well produce 'plural' outcomes – more than one opinion, more than one proposal, more than one piece of advice. In the end it is for elected politicians to decide. The role of academies is to think, not to dictate.

These four steps – funding media, funding think tanks and 'thinking NGOs', putting in place participatory democracy practices, and creating national policy academies – would for the first time give Scotland some serious 'thinking infrastructure'. It would make us a nation where producing big ideas was normal, engaging people with those ideas would be everyday, a citizen with a bright idea would have somewhere to go with it, proposals would be effectively scrutinised and vested interests would find their voices balanced by a wider range of other voices.

Scotland is in a fascinating, transitional period. It is being changed from a regional administrative centre of the British State to being an independent and independently-minded nation of its own (whether than nation has a state or not has yet to be finally decided). But in that transition it is sometimes trying to behave like a nation with the intellectual infrastructure of 'the provinces'. This is a recipe for bad thinking and for policy capture by vested interests. We can do better than this. We have all the ingredients necessary for a much better nation with a much richer ideas environment. It would require so little investment for the returns it would generate that I have come to believe this could be one of the most valuable developments we could see over the next few years.

I really do hope that a wider community begins to see just how important ideas are – and just how shallow is the pool from which we are currently fishing. Scotland has an amazing tradition of innovation. This would be the perfect time to rediscover that tradition and to engineer our public life as a place that thinks big thoughts. If we do, we'll all benefit.

Chapter 4

Scotland and Europe: renewing our vision

Alyn Smith[*]

For some time, most commentators have agreed (there's a dangerous phrase) that Scotland has been more pro-European and indeed more interested in international affairs than our southern neighbours. The fact that Scotland is the only nation in the United Kingdom to have voted overwhelmingly to stay in the EU on 23rd June 2016 puts that claim, with all the hesitations that may accompany it, in a clearer if unforgiving light.

My own view of how we face the Brexit challenge and Scotland's place in the world is shaped by 13 years in the European Parliament (with the latest two of them on the Foreign Affairs Committee) acting on our behalf. It was clear before June that Foreign Affairs, and EU matters in particular, remained one of the biggest fault lines of the devolved settlement and that people in Scotland wanted something different. That gulf is now a chasm.

With the post-May 2016 Scottish Parliament having bedded down within the national consciousness, and with Westminster looking increasingly distant, we in Scotland are turning more and more to Holyrood to articulate our view of world events and to represent us in discussions about the future. So the fault line will only grow, along with the need to change how we engage.

What follows are reflections that were originally put on paper before the outcome of the Brexit vote. Of course the EU referendum changes everything. But it is still important to get a sense of our direction as an internationalist nation based on where we have come from, not just in relation to the upheavals we will face over the next few years.

'Scotland in the World' is what got me into politics; that and the conviction that if we are serious about tackling the engrained poverty that holds us all back we need a better functioning democracy and

---

[*]   The situation with Scotland in Europe is changing on a continuous basis. Regular online updates are available from: http://www.alynsmith.eu

full powers at home to do it. Scotland independent will be a different sort of state, because small states do things differently. Better on multilateralism and international law, better on international development, keener on an ethical foreign policy – because we'll rely more on global co-operation to protect us, too. Shorn of the baggage and flummery of empire but still (lets be fair, because of it) with a globally recognised image other states would give their eye teeth for. We would be a voice for good, in the world's main language, straddling the Commonwealth, the EU and the English speaking world.

We had a referendum about independence two years ago, the people said No and we need to respect that. But that doesn't mean there isn't plenty we need to do, because the halfway house we have been part of won't hold much longer, and with the Brexit vote we are under even more pressure coming from different directions.

Our own referendum on independence was a master class in democracy and engagement, with various propositions put forward and tested, underpinned by an energising sense of possibility that other Scotlands (even short of independence) are possible. By contrast, the he UK decision on the EU was characterised by shrill personality driven poisonous puff, owing more to Trump-esque sensationalism than any democratic intellect. Hitherto serious and intelligent people were found earnestly repeating demonstrable nonsense like, "Now the EU wants to ban our kettles" (*Daily Express* front page, 12 May 2016). Even the Guardian joined the fun, fact checking, and thereby giving credence to, the boneheaded idea that traffic congestion is down to immigration (12 December 2014). The anti-EU campaign, wrongly but successfully, conflated the EU with immigration, and played a nasty sleekit game, appealing to the worst in human nature, relying on ignorance and fear to get their way. The consequence of all that is now plain to see.

But, to be involved in the democratic process is to be an eternal optimist, so I was hoping that we would see a repeat of the joyous phenomenon we saw in our referendum – that people would realise the gaps in their knowledge and take steps to inform themselves. The facts were there if anyone cared to look. I was of course struck by the difference in tone between the Scottish and UK campaigns. The UK Remain campaign was, quite deliberately, doing Project Fear 2, scaring the voters over the prospect of change, because they thought that worked in Scotland. Meanwhile, the Scottish campaigns (bear in mind all the Scottish parties were doing their own thing alongside the very decent non-party Scotland Stronger In Europe campaign) was much more focussed on highlighting the advantages we enjoy in the EU. We won the battle here, but at a UK level things turned out very differently, as many of us had been warning they might.

My sense was that most folk in Scotland, if they could be persuades that it matters to them, would turn out for Remain – as they did, by 62% to 38%, with all 32 council areas backing continued EU membership. Differential turnout was always going to be a decider, I believed. South of the border (where the vote was always going to be be won or lost, and where I hoped to see a wholehearted and enthusiastic endorsement of multilateralism and international co-operation) I thought people would reluctantly and grudgingly be swayed by the negativity. In the event Project Fear 2 neither won the vote nor the argument. Far from getting the Eurosceptic chip off Dear Old Blighty's shoulder once and for all, the outcome of the Tories' reckless gamble with our future was plain destruction.

The struggle now is about considering all possible options for Scotland to remain within the EU. That is a whole debate in itself. But step back for a moment. If we pulled it off, how would it work and how could we do Scottish international and EU stuff better, as a clear majority of Scots want?

The first thing we would need to do would be a bit of a psychological reboot – to get rid of the idea that Europe is 'somewhere else'. The second requirement would be to have a good rethink about what Foreign Affairs actually is in the modern world. (The third would have been to reassure the UK that there is plenty international work to go round and it is entirely legitimate and necessary for Scotland, within the Union, to do and say more on the world stage. That has now obviously shapeshifted.)

The root of the disconnect between the EU and domestic politics, leading ultimately to the Brexit vote in England, the 38% against in Scotland, and its massive consequences for us, is that the EU is, always, seen as not 'here'. We're not alone in this. Across the European continent this feeling exists to one degree or another and the fear has been that what Scotland and the UK have been enduring will be repeated in other states. The landscape looks a little different now, according to recent polling. But let's not forget. I could name you Belgian politicians who talk about "going to Europe" or you could watch the Danish TV *Borgen* episode, 'In Brussels, no-one can hear you scream'; or I could name you any number of MSPs or MPs (of all parties) who have asked ask me and my fellow MEPs how things are going "over in Europe".

The really important point that so many miss is that MEPs are domestic politicians, not diplomats or plenipotentiaries. We're doing domestic politics in a different, bigger, place. We are democratically elected to represent the interests of the people of Scotland in the formulation of technical (often dull, there, I admit it) legislation that touches on every aspect of your every day and 500 million other people too. While it will seldom make the front page, slowly but surely (and often behind the scenes) EU legislation protects and improves our environment in Scotland; guarantees our rights at work in Scotland; improves the efficiency of our cars, heating systems, vacuum cleaners and, yes, toasters in Scotland; regulates weights and measures and competition policy in Scotland, making the economy in Scotland more dynamic, creating more jobs in Scotland; and supports and regulates our farming, fishing and food in Scotland, making our food better and safer while ensuring we still produce food in Scotland, underpinning our rural economy in Scotland. I could go on.

But do you see my point? All this is not 'foreign affairs'. It is domestic politics. And that was and is the problem. The UK (and hence, Scotland) still views it formally as Foreign Affairs, viewing the EU through a prism and apparatus not much changed since the days of Empire, when the solution to a disagreement was to send a gunboat or some missionaries, or both. The UK Europe Minister, unbelievably, was not even a cabinet role before the EU referendum, yet EU measures cut across every single aspect of government. The Scottish government, while responsible for actually implementing most of it, has been arms length even to that process, so chary of taking anything but a strict literal interpretation of EU measures because nobody at home feels bought into or familiar with them.

In the Smith Commission Report, in paragraph 31, "The parties recognise that foreign affairs will remain a reserved matter". Then they go on to scope out new ways in which the views of the Scottish government can be taken into account by the UK in EU negotiations. This, even putting the politics aside, continues the fundamental mistake that just because the decisions are happening outwith the UK, they are somehow hermetically sealed off from domestic government. They certainly aren't in the way they impact upon the lives of the citizens we all serve, however. As we are discovering day-by-day as the Brexit fiasco unfolds.

In administrative terms, the civil servants have more or less made it work, and credit to them. "But it will not hold much longer, because in political terms it is and will remain a recipe for disaster," I wrote back in May 2016. For decades, UK ministers have been part of negotiations in Brussels which, when the results come to be implemented domestically, are often presented as foreign interference, not measures we voluntarily signed up for and helped formulate. The fact that MEPs have had a vote on each and every measure has been glossed over to boot, feeding a lack of legitimacy and a resentment among the people we serve that 'Brussels' is somehow dictating to us. That turned out to be exactly what too many people thought when the crunch came in June.

The Scottish government has been responsible for implementing all EU measures in devolved areas, and in devolved areas has total competence. It was always logical, then, that the Scottish government should be directly involved in their formulation, not as a junior part of an already junior UK delegation, but as a co-legislator. The failure to make this happen was always going to be hugely damaging.

In Finland, EU matters have been dealt with not by one minister, but all of them, through a Joint Ministerial Committee on EU Affairs, run by a Government EU Affairs Department based directly in the Office of the Prime Minister. This ensures not only that Finland has maximum heft in negotiations, but also that the eventual measures are smoothly and appropriately implemented into national law in the way that fits best. Denmark and Sweden, too, have some nifty ideas that we would have done well to emulate.

Thinking more generally about what Foreign Affairs actually is, I do not think the present definition fits the times we live in. The world is more complicated than simply one government talking to another. We're not currently independent so we have been represented by the UK Embassy network, but as a part of the UK, not in our own right. Go to any British Embassy or High Commission abroad, as I always try to do, to meet the (usually excellent) people there, and it is clear they're there to represent the UK, serve Brits abroad, and are looking for instruction from London. And indeed who can blame them? That is indeed their role.

But it fails to square the circle that the Scottish government is responsible for considerable competence at home, so it is entirely legitimate for the Scottish government to promote Scotland internationally as a place to visit, do business, trade with, or study in. The government is responsible for this at home so it is only logical to make more muscular efforts abroad. That is the direction the Scottish government took decisively in October 20016, with the announcement that it is setting up a new network of international trade envoys and establishing a permanent diplomatic hub in Berlin to demonstrate and benefit from the fact that the country is "open for business" in the wake of Brexit.

We can of course continue to use the UK network for consular services for the time being. We are still paying for it, after all. But Scotland is a distinct proposition from the UK, and promoting ourselves distinctly does not detract from the UK – indeed if we're more successful, then everyone benefits from that success. The Catalans have an impressive network, with seven overseas diplomatic missions supporting an active networks of 138 'Casals Catalan' designed to activate their considerable diaspora. In the recent past we have made some steps, with the 'Global Scot' initiative some years back and the positive but limited work done by Scottish Development International, VisitScotland, Highlands and Islands Enterprise and others. However, this is not a coherent 'Team Scotland' and the various operations of Scotland's trade, tourism, academic and government organisations need to be be knitted together into a dynamite proposition.

Just because it is economic development in a different place, does not make it Foreign Affairs either, and it is entirely economically necessary for us in Scotland to represent ourselves independently. This is also not independence, so need not cut against the current constitution, but in the current climate can point effectively to the kind of future we want.

Likewise, even when it comes to actual diplomacy, where there is a distinct Scottish interest in an issue and willingness to take it up, Scotland needs to see how it can lead. A clear example is the growing importance of the High North. Scotland is, as well as simply being closer, more directly impacted by the growing significance of developments in the Arctic region than Whitehall.

On trade, the Brexit consequences for us in Scotland are considerable. In terms of CETA and TTIP, it looks at the time of writing that both treaties are sunk because the democratically elected governments of the 28 member states, and indeed a big chunk of the elected MEPs, who will have the final say, are either unconvinced or actively hostile. But in the UK, in a discussion that will begin and end in a Palace on the banks of the Thames, the government could still sign us up to both and worse. Brexit Britain isn't going to be leading any ethical trade policy and we should all be concerned about that. A firm eye on social and environmental protection is therefore vital. We need agreements; I'm just unconvinced, like many others, about these ones.

There's another potential deal in the deep freeze with the Gulf Co-operation Council, the Arab Peninsula states, that the EU has on our behalf blocked over lack of progress on human rights. Conservative MPs are already salivating (and earning cracking consultancy fees into the bargain) at the prospect of a trade deal with the Sheiks, now that we don't need to worry, they believe, about all that 'human rights stuff' or what the rest Europe thinks of us.

So we are going to be living in interesting times in Scotland for many years to come. That was my thought earlier in year, when I was reflecting in terms of a narrow Remain win. But look around now. The latest iteration of Scottish democracy is barely in its teens. The Brexit challenge is massive. The need is to speak in the world much more loudly. And the evidence is that Scotland's voice is indeed being heard and responded to in these tumultuous times, as it needs to be.

Chapter 5

Not politics, but marketing: Scottish elections in the post-Blair world

Ian Dommett

For Philip Larkin, "Sexual intercourse began in 1963, between the end of the Chatterley ban, and the Beatles first LP". The death of Scottish Labour as a political force, I believe, can be similarly dated. It occurred between 23rd July and 27th August 2010. Scottish Labour, of course, did not realise it.

Sharp-eyed observers saw the election defeat of 2007 as being the end, but Labour dismissed that as a blip and carried on as if the planets would re-align and all would be well.

But why those two dates in 2010?

On 23rd July, Professor James Mitchell, then at University of Glasgow, published *Voting for a Scottish Government: The Scottish Parliament Election of 2007*. Here in one readable volume was an investigation into how the election had been fought and won by the SNP, the first time it had experienced widespread election success in its history. By undertaking a large-scale research exercise and then analysing the results it showed that the approach the party took to the election had been correct. But it also showed how simple and replicable that approach was, and how it was likely to set the template for future campaigns. It short, it summarised the new reality of politics in Scotland as having three key facets:

First, the electorate knows the difference between different elections: for Europe, for Westminster, for Holyrood and for local government.

Second, the electorate to a large extent knows that Holyrood is a 'comparative' parliament, not combative as at Westminster. Therefore it is all about 'better': how to make Scotland a better, healthier, wealthier, safer, smarter country.

Third, parties will be judged on trust: how trustworthy will they be to deliver what was best for Scotland?

25

Nothing here should have caused any discomfort for Scottish Labour. Indeed the SNP campaign had already commandeered the 2003-2007 Labour/Liberal Democrat administration's themes of Healthier Scotland, Smarter Scotland and so on, and used them throughout the 2007 election campaign.

On 31st July 2010 the SNP campaign team received the debrief of its own qualitative research into the likely themes of the following year's election, and the Scottish public's reaction to the recently elected Conservative/Liberal Democrat coalition at Westminster. The concluding expression was thus presented: "We all want Scotland to be even greater than it is. We can work together to achieve this."

A couple of weeks of political and communication thinking and you arrive at the final date, with this period culminating in the 27th August publication of the SNP campaign plan: 'Together we can make Scotland better'. Scottish Labour, meanwhile, was working on its strategy: A vote for Labour at Holyrood is the first step to removing the Conservatives at Westminster.

The SNP spent the following eight months refining and delivering their strategy. They won the election with Scotland's first ever majority Government. Labour lost the election, again.

As with most things in life, the answer to any puzzle or mystery is usually more obvious than you think. And it's often under your nose. Marketing campaigns work to simplify messages and then amplify them. New Labour knew this. So while one might understand Scottish Labour missing the Mitchell book about 2007, surely someone in Scottish Labour at some time must have read Philip Gould's book, *The Unfinished Revolution,* published in Autumn 1998? Someone? Anyone?

Or wondered about his motto: *Credo Populo* – I believe in the people?

Gould's book is a brilliant presentation of the formation and development of New Labour, culminating in the election victory of 1997. As an ex-advertising man, Gould fills it full of consumer (voter) insights: the need for "relentless reassurance" on union influence, the realisation that "a serious party that represents the ordinary person focuses on things that matter to people in their lives", the plan that "we would fight to convince the country we could be trusted", and the recognition that "people wanted smaller promises that they could believe in". They created and delivered the classic 'brand promise':

Promise: What Do I Promise To My Audience And Why?
+ **Personality:** This Is The Way We Go About What We Do +
Action: This Is How We Deliver On Our Promise =

Trusted brand

Gould believed, "[t]he most important thing a party can do in a campaign is listen to what the voters are saying". But once in power they soon dumped this idea. Deborah Mattinson, a long time colleague of Gould, described the voters' reaction to Labour post-'97 as "talking to a brick wall". Another nail in the Scottish Labour coffin has been to ignore his advice: "if our communications are professional, then it reassures people that we will be professional and competent ...". Everyone in the SNP campaign team read that bit.

If each election is about Representation of the People, then it must also be a reflection of the people. As much as politics, this is pure marketing logic. Gould knew it and Blair knew it and implemented it to overturn years of Conservative government. It remains even truer today, and more relevant to Scotland than anywhere else in the United Kingdom. Again there are three pillars:

1. Consumer insight, easily translated as voter insight

What do we know about the voters? What do they care about, talk about, believe, reject, love, fear, hope for, want and need – this is basic consumer behaviour psychology: simple to research, to evaluate and respond to. Particularly when most campaigns are more about promises than actions!

2. Audience data

The Scottish election system for Holyrood is complicated. Most voters don't understand it and most don't care enough to engage with it outwith election night. But the voting population remains quite static, electoral data exists on households and demographic tools such as MOSAIC can quite easily extrapolate data from a few constituencies to create a map for the whole country.

3. Product development and delivery

And from the first two, comes the third part – the delivery of a buyable (electable) product that answers the needs and desires of the target audience. It is my belief that at no point between 4 May 2007 and 4 May 2016 has the Scottish Labour Party presented any combination of people and policies that has come close to connecting with the Scottish population.

Scottish Labour lives in a 'left/right' world when it was clear to everyone else post-2014 that Scotland is primarily a 'Yes/No' country, and success in 2016 would be achieved by successfully pitching a party towards the best chance of benefitting from this voter split: getting a share of the potential Yes or No vote, aware that neither side would likely vote for a party across the divide.

The Holyrood 2016 election has been described as boring, but the result was anything but dull, and several campaigns built on the lessons of the post-1999 Holyrood elections and obvious marketing approaches. For Ruth Davidson (Conservative leader) and Willie Rennie (Liberal Democrat leader) it was endless photo calls in fun places to highlight their characters and possible appeal. Both moved from being List MSPs to Constituency success.

Working with the Scottish Green Party it was clear that their vote would come from Yes voters, with whom the Greens had openly campaigned. Research undertaken by Iain Black and Sara Marsden for Common Weal showed that many Yes activists, while even perhaps subsequently joining the SNP, shared views on issues such as fracking and land reform much closer to the Greens than the party they had joined. This enabled the Greens to adopt the campaign line 'A better Scotland needs a bolder Holyrood', and position themselves as the more radical, yet relevant, voice within the Yes electorate.

For the Greens there was a lack of media cut-through, with few impactful photo ops or headlines but a solid, professional and well-received campaign that delivered six MSPs, up from the two elected in 2011.

For Scottish Labour it was, with a couple of exceptions, an unmitigated but quite well sign-posted disaster. They decided to fight for a share of the 'No' vote that wasn't there, while simultaneously trying to grab a slice of the social justice mind-set that had long since shifted its allegiance to the SNP.

Before starting to work with the SNP in 2005 I had always seen myself as a Labour supporter. I voted for them in each election from 1987 to 2001, helping to elect Bernie Grant in Tottenham, but missing out on supporting Ron Brown in Leith as he was deselected before the 1992 election. However, Malcolm Chisholm was a worthy, if less flamboyant, replacement.

In 2011 Chisholm had won the seat for the fourth time by separating himself from the dying Edinburgh Labour campaign with a 'Vote Malcolm' approach that had delivered him to Holyrood with a majority of about 600. In 2016, Lesley Hinds unveiled one of the more bizarre Scottish Labour campaigns, with the same 'personal appeal' approach as Malcolm had used previously. She claimed to have 'sorted out the trams', seemingly unaware that the engaged voters of Leith connected her directly to this debacle (and in a constituency whose border almost directly touched the end of the shortened tram line!) and she highlighted her work with Edinburgh's schools against an intense media backdrop of the headline-grabbing PFI schools fiasco. To cap it all, she thought a photograph of her on the boards outside the polling stations would do the trick. She lost by 7,000 votes.

So is there any future for Scottish Labour? The answer lies in whether they are willing and able to create and deliver a new, credible brand promise. A promise based on an understanding of, respect for, and connection to, its audience, a complete tonal shift in its attitude of hostility and hatred towards the SNP and an overhaul of the presentation of the party. Maybe the first step is to go back to the result in 2007, read the Mitchell book and start again as if the last nine years had been just a horrible dream. Then work out how to be a trusted brand in a post-Referendum Scotland. Now that is a tough brief.

Chapter 6

Can Scotland become a Nordic country?

Alistair Davidson

Throughout the 2014 independence campaign, Nordic social democracy was used as a reference point, a political North Star guiding us to a better Scotland. There were meetings organised by the group Northern Horizons Edinburgh, and audiences for Scandinavian experts on everything from the welfare state to hutting. Scandinavian writers sent an open letter urging Scottish voters to ignore the No camp's campaign of fear. Newspapers even speculated that an independent Scotland might join the Nordic Council.

Where there has been criticism of Scotland's Nordic dream, it has focused on the high levels of tax in Nordic societies, and whether Scots would be prepared to pay so much. The tax take in Scandinavia is in the range of 40 per cent to 50 per cent of GDP, whereas the 2014 Scottish tax take was 36 per cent of GDP. The incoming SNP Government in May 2016 pledged not to raise the rate of income tax, although they moved towards a freeze the higher (40p) threshold, a gradual tax increase on the rich. Some SNP politicians argue that before raising taxes, Scotland has to raise wages. This is in fact an appropriately Nordic approach.

While taxation is a key part of the Nordic Model, the emphasis placed on it in Scottish debates is (ironically) peculiarly British. It is rarely noted that the UK's tax system is in fact more progressive than Nordic systems. Nordic tax systems have high rates of VAT, a regressive tax, and even workers below the median wage pay significant rates of income tax. This is politically acceptable because wages are much higher in Nordic countries than they are in Scotland. Addressing low wages, not raising taxes, is the first step towards a more Nordic country.

A disinterest in manipulating the labour market is just one way in which the spectre of 'Old Labour' still haunts Scotland. Old Labour's memory still limits what we describe as left and right wing. To be left wing is to favour raising tax, monolithic nationalised industries, uncompromisingly militant trade unions, and centralised bureaucracy. This leftism failed for good reasons, many of them internal.

Tax is a good thing, but not all taxes are good at all times. Public ownership is progressive, but the British left have at times wasted too much energy trying to protect failing industries that might have been better left to fade away. Fighting trade unions are essential, but undermining Labour governments in the 1970s proved to be a mistake. Centralisation may have its efficiencies, but we should remember that in the 1970s tenants were organising against councils for democratic control of their homes.

The SNP often seems more aware of the vital importance of actively shaping markets than the political left outside of the SNP. In a quiet, collaborative manner, the Scottish Government has set about promoting high-value, high-wage industries, reforming industrial relations, and steadily growing community ownership.

The aim of the Scottish Government's industrial reforms, designed by Jim Mather together with the trade unions and industry, are to foster "modern, co-operative industrial relations." To British ears this sounds worryingly like the "partnership" approach of the Thatcher and New Labour eras, in which defeated trade unions gave up their traditional adversarial role, arguably weakening their ability to defend conditions and wages. From a Scandinavian perspective, it doesn't have to be so – in Scandinavia, powerful unions and businesses, acting with enlightened self-interest, have been able at times to secure relative social peace without the unions abandoning their role as advocates of workers' interests.

Creating a Scottish model inspired by the Nordics will present challenges for us all. The SNP will have to accept that some conflict between employees and employers is inevitable, and that a high wage society requires employees to be empowered to win those conflicts. Scottish business will have to accept paying higher wages, in return for stability and a skilled workforce. Scottish trade unions will have to move away from the old, centralised vision of social democracy, and begin to think more like the Swedish Trade Union Confederation (ILO), which was every bit as interested in shaping markets as nationalising them.

Following the second world war, the Swedish Social Democratic Party (SAP) adopted an economic programme called the Rehn-Meidner Model, named after the ILO economists Gösta Rehn and Rudolf Meidner. A modified form of Keynesianism, it aimed to secure growth, full employment, and economic equality through powerful trade unions and government intervention.

The main plank of the Rehn-Meidner model was full employment. From the end of the second world war to the Reagan-Thatcher revolution, European governments saw guaranteeing near-full employment as one of their most fundamental duties. So much so that when UK unemployment rose above two per cent in 1972, Ted Heath's Conservative government launched a desperate (and doomed) "dash for growth."

During what has been characterised as 'the age of social democracy', it was widely agreed that government deficit spending could always create growth and employment, and that the resulting debts could be funded with the proceeds of economic growth. The consensus was undone by the 1970s oil shock, which created inflation without growth, and by President Nixon's dismantlement of the Bretton Woods system, an international agreement that controlled currency values and sought to eliminate trade imbalances. Without capital and currency controls, investors could move money out of countries whose politics they disagreed with.

There has been a concerted effort to make us forget that governments can create employment, and to make us accept massive, permanent unemployment. The Polish economist Michał Kalecki predicted these events as long ago as 1943:

> The maintenance of full employment would cause social and political changes ... the 'sack' would cease to play its role as a 'disciplinary' measure.

> Under a laissez-faire system the level of employment depends to a great extent on the so-called state of confidence ... This gives the capitalists a powerful indirect control over government policy: everything which may shake the state of confidence must be carefully avoided because it would cause an economic crisis.

> But once the government learns the trick of increasing employment by its own purchases, this powerful controlling device loses its effectiveness. Hence budget deficits necessary to carry out government intervention must be regarded as perilous. The social function of the doctrine of 'sound finance' is to make the level of employment dependent on the state of confidence." (Kalecki, 1943)

The government can create full employment, but it is not without challenges. The major economic problem with full employment is that workers can always find work, and so can demand wage increases from their employers. Knowing that inflation is three per cent this year, a worker will demand a four per cent pay rise. If this happens across the workforce, it will drive up costs and prices, next year inflation will be four per cent and workers will demand five per cent pay rises. Knowing this, economists often use "inflation" as a euphemism for "wages." It is much more politically palatable to talk about controlling inflation than it would be to talk about controlling wages. The Governor of the Bank of England, 'Steady' Eddie George, gave the game away in 1998 when he said that, "lost jobs in the North are an acceptable price to pay to curb inflation in the South."

The threat inflation posed to full employment policies caused Gösta Rehn himself to say that "socialists must hate inflation." The Rehn-Meidner model had two strategies for preventing inflation. Firstly, a small amount of unemployment was allowed to exist, with a generous welfare state to prevent destitution. Secondly, and most importantly, wage negotiations took place on a national basis between trade unions and employers. The same wage would be set for the same work across many different companies. In return for this powerful institutional position trade unions practised wage restraint, controlling inflation by deliberately limiting their wage demands.

As Rudolf Meidner later explained, "We rejected the idea that unions should be disciplined by unemployment. Our preference was for collective self-discipline imposed by the union's own wage policy" (Meidner, 1993)

One consequence was that less efficient companies, paying excess wages to their workers, would be forced out of business. At this point government training and re-employment schemes (active labour market policy) would kick in to prevent unemployment. Meanwhile, more efficient companies would earn excess profits, as trade unions curtailed their wage demands. The excess profits risked concentrating control of the economy into fewer and fewer hands.

Meidner's solution to the excess profit problem, opposed by Rehn, was a special tax on profits. This tax would be paid in shares, not cash, and the shares would be paid into "wage earner funds" controlled by the trade unions. His intention was to transition from a capitalist market with private ownership of large companies to a Socialist market, where workers had democratic control of their workplaces.

Although the leadership of the SAP had gradually moved away from Socialism, the dream of peacefully reforming towards a democratic economy was always central to the Swedish Model. Gunnar Adler-Karlsson compared the difference between capitalism and Sweden's reformist Socialism to the difference between absolute and constitutional monarchy: "Without dangerous and disruptive internal fights... After a few decades they (capitalists) will then remain, perhaps formally as kings, but in reality as naked symbols of a passed and inferior development state." (Adler-Karlsson, 1967).

Meidner and the ILO underestimated how controversial the wage earner funds would be. Swedish industrialists organised to stop them, importing techniques developed in New Zealand. They frightened Swedes with images of a Soviet-style planned economy, and exploited what Meidner would later accept was a mistake – that the funds were controlled by the trade unions, rather than the workers themselves. By the time the wage earner funds were finally implemented the policy had been diluted into worthlessness.

A modern, less controversial alternative to the Meidner Plan might be sovereign wealth funds. Scottish Government economic advisor Mariana Mazzucato is an advocate of these. Mazzucato notes that most basic research is conducted by governments, while profits are retained by private companies who commercialise the technology. Some governments have experimented with retaining a minority equity stake in businesses built on state-funded research and investments from state development banks. Managed by a sovereign wealth fund, just like Norway's famous oil fund, equity stakes ensure the state receives a fair return on investment, helping to fund the next round of research and economic growth.

If Scotland is to become a Nordic country, we will need strong trade unions, with the power to demand wage increases, but the wisdom to practice wage restraint. We will need something like the Meidner Plan or equity stakes to balance the excess profit problem. Deeply ingrained British habits and ways of thinking will need to be changed. Progressive politics will have to take a little of the emphasis off tax-and-spend and centralised nationalisations, and take much more interest in market manipulation and management. A national consensus will have to be built across the centre-left parties, progressively minded businesses, and the trade union movement.

Chapter 7

What can we learn from the referendum debate about Scotland and the EU?

David Gow

Generally speaking, Scots are more European than the English or Welsh. (The 32 counties of Ireland are a separate story). The historical ties between Scotland and Europe go deeper; they embrace literary and intellectual links as well as political, economic and military relations. This is not just the Scottish Enlightenment redux.

Polling in the run-up to the 23rd June 2016 referendum on the UK's EU membership confirmed this. In May, Scotland was trending towards 'Remain' (*Daily Record* poll, 9th May) by up to between two-thirds and three-quarters. The overtly 'Leave' party, UKIP, won just around two per cent support in the May 2016 Holyrood elections. (Though it won seats in the Welsh Assembly, it is a predominantly English nationalist party).

In May 2016 I wrote: "Depending on differential turnout – and that's a big caveat given the declines since 2014 and 2015 – Scottish voters could deliver a healthy Remain majority even if the English and Welsh vote narrowly for Leave. Is that likely? Or, more critically, desirable? Isn't it in the interests of the ruling SNP (but not its stated wish of course) for the EU referendum to be lost, even though Scotland votes Remain? Would that not amount to the 'material change' oft quoted by First Minister Nicola Sturgeon as the trigger for a second referendum on Scottish independence? With Cameron gone, Bojo and Osbo, maybe Theresa May too, could slug it out for the Conservative leadership. Then, while Westminster gets bogged down in protracted and difficult Brexit talks with a sullenly unyielding EU-27 and the Conservative civil war intensifies, the Scottish Government could begin preparing for a second independence referendum. Garner support from the shriveled ScotLab ranks, even a few ScotTory Europhiles, for independence and think of applying for EU membership from, say 2021."

Well, we now know what has happened. The UK voted Leave by

52% to 48%. Scotland voted Remain. Theresa May did indeed run for the Conservative leadership and has become PM. As for Scotland and the Scottish Government, we are still not sure about what kind of outcome there will be, or if and when a second independence referendum might come.

So how did things look back after the Scottish Parliamentary elections, in the run-up to the EU referendum, and what can we learn from the debate that took place on Scotland and the EU?

Here is how I saw things then:

Mid-May polling showed the UK split down the middle on Brexit, with Leave maybe marginally ahead but all within the margin of error (plenty of that around recently). What's more, SNP fears that it might lose its absolute majority in Holyrood on 5th May 2016 proved well founded, as the party lost support in parts of rural/small town Scotland (as well as finally sweeping Labour out of central belt cities). There may be a small pro-independence majority among MSPs (69-60 on paper) but there isn't one in the country at large. Or not yet. The 55-45 majority for the Union of September 2014 appears largely stable.

But, says (among others) Alex Salmond, "a groundswell of anger loud enough to trigger a second independence referendum" would erupt if Scotland votes Remain and rUK Leave (at European Policy Centre, 9th May 2016). Nicola Sturgeon has talked of a "democratic outrage" if Scots are "taken out of Europe against our will." Tony Blair has stated bluntly (but what does he know?): "If the UK votes to leave Europe Scotland will vote to leave the UK."

All we know is that Sturgeon wants "clear evidence" that Scottish voters want a second referendum that will deliver independence. But that is never defined. Is it, as many joke, Prof John Curtice consistently finding 60 per cent support? Even that level of support may not be enough. There is no guarantee that independence can be won and, with that, none that EU membership would eventually ensue as the SNP leadership (and others) would wish to see. Whatever the outcome of the 23rd June plebiscite, the EU in its current shape may not survive (Eurozone tensions, central European resistance, Greece, not least the Le Pen threat). And, here at home, the arguments on the economy and sovereignty don't stack up.

This is not the place to revisit the legalistic arguments of two years ago over whether indeed Scotland would be allowed to apply for and join the EU. Jim Sillars, a prominent Leave campaigner, asked (*CommonSpace*, 9th May 2016) why Scotland should shun Brussels given its response last time: 'get to the back of the queue'. But Barrosso has gone after his ten barren years as European Commission president – and so has Herman Van Rompuy as European Council president. There is always the renewed threat of a Belgian (*sic*) or Spanish veto but, politically, it makes no sense to turn away Scotland – and keep Romania in.

However, the price demanded could act as a deterrent (see Nicola McEwen, *Britain's Decision,* Hunter Foundation 2016, page 125). One reason why people in Scotland voted against independence two years ago was the currency issue, as Alex Salmond himself has admitted. This will have to be dealt with far more convincingly and properly prepared in contingency planning over the next few years. Membership will certainly come with the expectation or stipulation that Scotland joins the euro. The hard opt-out given to the UK and Denmark will not be available; nor is the soft one stretched out by Sweden. Newcomers have to join. (Of course, the Eurozone could have disintegrated by then but that seems more like wishful thinking by Brexiteers than likelihood).

Unless Scotland asks for and is given some form of associate membership, membership will come with the fiscal straitjacket of the 6-Pack, European Semester and so on. This is more commonly known as "austerity politics" as dissected by Basta!* and countless others. If, as is more than likely, an independent Scotland were struggling – at least initially – with a budget deficit and higher bond yields to finance it and government debt, then this could prove intolerable politically. And economically illiterate as well as self-defeating (though Ireland's recovery is a dramatic illustration of the leeway still available to national governments). That's why the battle against austerity is pan-European and must succeed in lifting the curse of the *Bundesbank* and *Bundesfinanzministerium* under Schäuble.

That's why, too, the next round of negotiations on the EU Budget for the period 2020-2025 has to produce an even greater shift away from, say, agriculture spending towards research, innovation, job-creation and social policy. As Salmond put it to the European Policy Centre think tank: "We want a Europe that prioritises growth and recovery, a Europe which reclaims the concept of a social contract…" Scotland's current share pro rata, according to Professor David Bell, amounts to £64 a head compared to the £106 for Norway (non-member). Would it go higher with independence and no share of the UK's rebate any more?

---

* http://www.socialistsanddemocrats.eu/newsroom/basta-our-alternative-vision

Sillars believes Brexit would hand back control of agriculture and fisheries ("decimated"), but this is a two-edged sword, as Professor Drew Scott has pointed out. Even prior to independence Holyrood would gain more powers over non-reserved matters when these are repatriated as a whole back to the UK. But the CAP is worth around £4 billion to Scottish farmers through guaranteed payments in the current budget period, 2014-2020. Would the Scottish Government have to pick this bill up in its entirety? Equally, would it have to subsidise the fishing industry? We need a full cost-benefit analysis ("impact assessment") of these issues over the next few years, too.

Enhanced sovereignty, in other words, could come at a cost. But, as with independence, would that not be worth it because it comes with greater democracy? Sillars and his Leave colleagues such as Tom Harris, ex-Labour MP, are unconvinced. They trot out the old canards about the Commission being "an unelected elite" with even greater powers when, in recent years, it has been the European Council (or summit) that has taken on more powers. As, indeed, has the elected European Parliament under the co-decision mechanism.

Absolute sovereignty is, obviously, a chimera in the modern world, as Chatham House and others have pointed out.* Pooled sovereignty is the order of the day and an independent Scotland would be willing to share its, even if newly won, within the EU. What we required in the run-up to 23rd June 2016, and what is needed in the months, probably years, beyond is a mature, full-hearted analysis of and debate about such issues as spreading subsidiarity and reshaping and rebooting democratic control of the EU's institutions (particularly the council of ministers). This should dovetail with a discussion at the same level of earnest intensity about the institutional settlement of the UK.

"Membership of the EU means a greener, fairer, healthier and wealthier Scotland and UK – that's surely something we can all get behind," is how Angus Robertson, leader of the SNP group of MPs, put it in the Commons on 11th May 2016. Whether Scotland remains a member as part of the UK or in its own right its political class across the parties should be working to make that stick – for years to come.

---

* https://www.chathamhouse.org/publication/britain-eu-and-sovereignty-myth

Chapter 8

Towards a Scottish foreign policy

Adam Ramsay

Ultimately, the case for Scottish independence lies in foreign policy. Everything else could be devolved without leaving the UK: tax rates, energy policy, social security, and rights at work. But once Holyrood has the power to ratify international treaties, once Scotland has its own seats in the chambers of the UN and the Council of Ministers, once we can choose not to send the Black Watch into Westminster's wars, that is when the threshold has been crossed.

For me, this is the simplest reason that I would prefer independence to devo-max or federalism. As I said to people repeatedly throughout the Scottish referendum campaign, I can see the case for a nationalised rail company being part owned and co-managed by the governments of Scotland and England together. I can understand why archipelagic pooling of university research funding makes sense. But why on earth is foreign policy the one thing you'd want to leave to a neurotic post-imperial Whitehall, fumbling to find its role in the world?

Because Scotland voted No, we don't have formal foreign policy powers. But, particularly as our parliament becomes more powerful, there is more and more we can do beyond our borders. After all, soft power is more important than ever.

Acting in this way seems key for three reasons. First, and most importantly, there is no reason to believe that we cannot have a positive impact on the world. Second, with Westminster running around trashing things in our name, it feels like we have some responsibility for trying to clean up the mess. And, third, it's through a demonstration of how things can be better that the case for independence is best made.

Of course, some things already happen. For more than a decade, Scotland has had its own international development programme; originally based in Malawi and now expanded to a number of projects across the Global South. When the EU, ECB and IMF crushed Greece, Nicola Sturgeon wrote eloquently in protest ('Let me tell you about referendums – threats won't help', *Guardian,* 30th June 2015), using the platform given to her by the Scottish electorate to argue against the brutal treatment of our neighbour. When presidential candidate Donald Trump's status as a 'global Scot' was revoked, headlines reverberated in the United States. There is, though, more that can be done, particularly if the SNP is willing to strain some more at the bit of the British state.

Some of what could be done is perhaps symbolic, though it's important not to ignore the power of symbolism in the drama of international politics. For example, 70 per cent of countries recognise Palestine as a state, but the UK does not, despite Westminster having voted in favour of doing so. Scotland opting to recognise Palestine would have no legal standing in the world, but it would contribute to the building of political pressure.

Perhaps Holyrood should pass such a vote, and Nicola Sturgeon should visit the West Bank and open a Scottish Embassy in East Jerusalem, Ramallah or Gaza City (we may be forced to call it 'office of the representative of the Scottish government' or some such). Just one representative there could do important work co-ordinating cultural exchanges, supporting the many groups from Scottish civil society who regularly make trips there, and helping monitor human rights abuses, though official consular duties would of course remain with the British Consulate General in Jerusalem. And perhaps we should do similar for Kurdistan and Western Sahara.

But some things are firmer.

For example, as John Finnie MSP has pointed out, there is an important question about the role of Scotland's justice system in prosecuting cases against torturers across the world. Torture anywhere in the world is a crime in Scots law under the terms of the Criminal Justice Act 1988; the law that meant Augusto Pinochet was arrested in the UK for torture carried out in Chile.

There is, in other words, a crime in Scots law, which we know is taking place. Perhaps the Scottish government ought to resource a specialist police unit to investigate specific cases of torture, and seek prosecutions against those who committed them. While defendants such as Donald Rumsfeld and Dick Cheney may refuse to come here to be cross-examined, and whilst the US may refuse to extradite them, a Western country making it clear that such figures will, if they land on our soil, find themselves in the dock, would be a major step for global justice.

And some such prosecutions are more directly linked to Scotland. In

2014, Lord Advocate Frank Mulholland ordered the Scottish police to investigate allegations around extraordinary rendition torture flights used Scottish airports. There seems to as yet have been no conclusion to such investigations. While politicians shouldn't interfere with police operations, there is no reason for the Scottish government not to be clear that it will continue to ask questions about this case until a resolution is found: Scotland's police cannot be allowed to sweep such questions under the carpet.

Scotland's judicial system could also play an important role in a very different way in the world. Jubilee Scotland, the campaign for debt justice, has long pointed out that there is a real need for a country or countries to act as arbiters of what is and isn't unjust debt. As the organisation put it:

> There is no global system for dealing with unjust or unpayable debt. And where debt cancellation has happened in the past, it has come with damaging conditions which which often leads to an even worse economic situation. For many years, campaigners have been calling for a fair and transparent system for handling sovereign debt. In coordination with academics, activists and legal experts Jubilee Scotland has created a framework for sovereign debt workout right here under Scots Law.*

Impoverished countries often find that their debts are used as levers to prize their markets open to deeper plunder from Western corporations. Scotland, with a legal system which is relatively trusted internationally, could well act as one of a number of hubs for arbitration, building up the appropriate legal and financial expertise.

These are just a couple of brief examples. There are many more: the Scottish Human Rights Commission has called for the incorporating of international human into Scots law. This seems a good idea.

In 2008, the National Museum of Scotland returned to Australia the remains of Aboriginal people which it had kept for more than 100 years. Perhaps it's time for a full review of artefacts in Scottish public collections, considering whether some ought to be returned from where they were plundered by imperial adventurers. And perhaps such a move could form a part of a process of national education about the violence of our imperial past.

Maybe, even, we should consider whether our first minister should apologise for some of the historic crimes in which Scotland was as complicit as the rest of the UK. While British leaders have often

---

* http://www.jubileescotland.org.uk/resource/scotland-as-a-seat-of-debt-arbitration/

avoided such formal acknowledgements of guilt in our country's actions overseas, perhaps we can begin to move on from our violent past if the Scottish government shows the way.

Scotland has clearly had a foreign policy since the parliament was reconvened in 1999. Largely, it has sought to co-operate with the UK where it has any powers, whilst our political leaders have shown how different they are through their statements on things over which they have no real power, like Trident.

A more feisty approach to the international arena might lead to quarrels with the UK government about jurisdiction and stepping over constitutional boundaries. But it's by pushing at these boundaries that the case for them to be abolished will be made, and, in the meantime, the thought of our sole representative on the world stage being a Westminster Conservative is horrifying – let alone Boris Johnson, appointed as Foreign Secretary on 13th July 2016.

With leading International Relations experts at St Andrews and Edinburgh universities and an increasingly confident politics of our own, it's time for us to develop a coherent national foreign policy, bringing together both government and civil society. After all, 45 per cent of us voted to join the world.

Chapter 9

A new politics for Scotland?

Maggie Chapman

The next five years in Scottish politics could be the most momentus yet since devolution, with Brexit and tensions in the United Kingdom adding a huge dose of unpredictability and uncertainty to a mix which will likely feature more changes in the 2017 local council elections and the floating question of another independence referendum.

Following the Holyrood elections in May 29016, the SNP is clearly now the hegemonic power in Scotland, having won the last three Holyrood elections by more than Labour ever managed to achieve. But governing by minority administration at a time when new powers are coming to Holyrood from Westminster means that opportunities for the unexpected abound.

In theory, the SNP will not struggle to do what they want: for most of their manifesto they will have support from at least one other party in parliament. But holding it together, trading in turn for backing from left and right, will prove tricky to negotiate and to justify to their own voters and members.

Notwithstanding the rise to power of Theresa May and the new economic focus in the light of the EU referendum, Scotland is still facing an onslaught of austerity from Westminster: deep cuts to Holyrood's budget, potential decimation of public services, and increasing inequality. The ideologically driven agenda of the Conservatives is going to prove difficult for the SNP to explain: why they are cutting public spending rather than using the new powers they will have over income tax to raise more revenue? So, will the SNP simply gradually buckle under the pressure, or will the hegemonic party use it's position to deepen democracy, to change the structures of power to improve people's lives, to change our politics and create a better Scotland?

The Scottish Greens are in an interesting position in all of this. As of the last elections, the Greens had roughly the same number of members as the SNP had in 2003. There is real opportunity for us (I am currently co-convener of the Scottish Greens) to use this, to build the party, to grow from this base to become the official opposition in the next parliamentary term. But I am not interested in opposition just for the sake of it. We fought the 2016 election campaign with the message to make Holyrood bolder. And that boldness – as my hopes for the party in the next term – has a purpose. I am interested in policies that enable us to fight austerity, to create jobs, to tackle inequality. I want the group of six Greens in Holyrood to use the next five years to push our radical and transformative agenda, to put people before profit, communities before corporations, and to give people hope.

It is important to understand how Scotland got to the position we are now in: a hegemonic, centrist SNP government with the Greens being the only voices for the pro-independence left in Holyrood. History operates like tectonic plates: it creeps along at an almost indiscernible speed, then suddenly it changes radically in an earthquake. Politics is different to geology though: we can shape our politics. As we in Scotland have been discovering in recent years, we do not have to accept the future dealt to us by those who controlled the past.

The independence referendum of 2014 changed everything. It was the earthquake (albeit one that happened over a few months) that has changed the political landscape for good. And we have the opportunity to build something very special out of this new political landscape – a new politics for Scotland.

What might this new politics look like? I think there are three key aspects to it, all of which overlap and intersect: policies, people and power. Arguably, these are the building blocks of any politics, but perhaps the ways in which they might be understood, used and negotiated in Scotland could result in a very different, more equal, happier country.

First, our new politics needs to understand that policies matter, and that they must be rooted in something meaningful. One of the comments I heard most often during the 2016 election campaign was that the campaign was boring: we all knew who was going to win. It struck me as quite sad that we could not turn this around and really engage with the issues that face people every day: unaffordable rents, fuel poverty, cuts to local services and jobs, and so on. Greens were the only party talking seriously about austerity, about how the hegemonic economic system serves the few at the expense of the many.

It is perhaps unsurprising that it was boring: the messages of the two largest parties were not about policies: the SNP's mantra was 'Nicola Sturgeon' and the Conservative's refrain was 'Ruth Davidson'. Not much about policies. Not much about a vision for a better Scotland, it seemed to some of us. Neither of those messages communicated any substance. Neither of them conveyed much beyond personality and style. Both were electorally successful, however, and we need to interrogate how and why that was the case.

When politics has become detached and removed from people's lives, when power seems distant and unassailable for the vast majority, it is perhaps no wonder that we individualise our political messages, creating not an engaging and stimulating landscape for debate, but a rather territorial and constrained turf war.

So, we need to redefine what we mean by politics. In many ways, the IndyRef debate started this process: people talked about how politics affected their everyday, in bus shelters, in supermarkets, at the school gate. People felt like they were a part of something, that they had a legitimate voice in the constitutional debate, that they mattered. And we need to recapture this.

I have always believed in movement politics. My roots in Southern Africa taught me the value of social movements, and how they can deliver radical change. It is one of the reasons I was so involved in the Radical Independence Campaign (RIC): it was about people, about people where they were, about communities. And this movement politics is foundational for the Scottish Greens too: we are a movement party.

So we need to reconnect with people. We need to focus work in communities across Scotland, to better understand where people are, but also to let them shape the politics that should be there to serve them. And to do this, we need a radically different approach to power.

We must reinvigorate our democracy: it must become more inclusive, more local. Green politics is rooted in an understanding that all issues are connected and that unless we flatten the pyramids of power in our society, we'll never win our battles for social justice or for the planet. So there are structural changes that we need to make to our political institutions: we must give local authorities more power, we must devolve power into communities, and we must learn how to support and value citizen engagement in daily democracy.

But it is not just a structural fix: culture and behaviour must change too. Political parties need to re-learn how to talk to people in meaningful ways, not simply through glib, one-directional media releases and television debates. We must start to live the kind of democracy we want to see: by being in and from communities, by working side by side with people, by sharing the struggles of citizens across the country.

We are, I would contend, some way down that route, though we must keep pressing on. Our messages need to resonate ever more with the lives of ordinary people. We need to continually be relevant to changing realities, and to never be afraid of afraid of standing with the downtrodden, no matter how controversial it is. In the 2014 European elections, for example, I insisted Greens put migrants rights front and centre, and we were rewarded for our principled stand with our biggest-ever national vote share. We also laid the foundations for a compassionate and dignified response to the humanitarian crisis sweeping across Europe from the Middle East.

We must work with our young people to give them a stake in creating their futures. Scotland's youth and student movements have done much to shape the nature of some of the debates we had during the election campaign: living rent was a central pillar of my arguments as Green social justice spokesperson, drawing on the excellent work of the Living Rent Campaign.

We need to work closely with Scotland's trade unions. The party which traditionally claimed to represent them, Labour, is falling apart, and now faces collapse into a pit of contradictions. As a long term Educational Institute of Scotland (EIS) organiser, I firmly believe we need to invest in building stronger solidarity with workers, and, to quote former Green Party of England and Wales leader Natalie Bennett, "ask not what the trade unions can do for us, ask what we can do for the trade unions".

We need to embrace the opportunities that remove power from debating chambers and hand it over to communities. Other countries around the world have been doing this for decades, and we can learn from them. For example, the participatory budgeting scheme I launched when a councillor in Edinburgh, £eithDecides, has involved many thousands of Leithers in agreeing together how their public money is spent.

We need to make sure we communicate meaningful ideas and deliver transformative policies; empty platitudes and abstract slogans about change are not enough for those for whom politics is more than a game. I was the first politician in Scotland to demand a Living Wage for public sector employees, and thousands of my constituents directly benefited when it was introduced.

And we need to look beyond the next election day: democracy must be so much more than simply putting crosses or numbers in a box on a ballot paper. We need a plan that goes way beyond 2021; a plan created by the people of Scotland for generations to come.

I want Greens to lead this work across Scotland. We have the policies designed to deal with exactly the economic, social and environmental changes which are happening around us. We now need to bring people into a revived democracy to deliver a better Scotland, and to enable us to engage in the struggle for Europe and the prospects of another vote on independence.

Chapter 10

Choices facing Labour in Scotland

Bill Gilby

In 2017 it will be 40 years since I joined the Labour Party – or the Party joined me, as I will explain below. Eight years of hyper-activism which changed my life for the better ended when my NUPE (then UNISON) job took me to London for 29 years. Retired, and home since 2014, I find myself lured back into local political activism. It's that experience that informs my thinking for this article.

I always try to look forward while searching for lessons; looking back, not harking back to the past – a legacy of studying my Fife community's history as a postgraduate. If that approach offends any academic, journalistic, or bubble-istic sensibilities, then so be it. I have read so much 'opinion' masquerading as analysis over the years, much of which didn't stand the test of time, that I'm tempted to conclude that the only reliable electoral facts are the results – in our case an election with a turnout of just under 56 per cent, where the party which has dominated Scottish politics in recent years secured the votes of 26% of those eligible to vote, and my party came a long way behind with 13 per cent. That's not good news for progressive people of whatever party if we're looking for a fundamental change in our society.

Back in 1977 I went into a Labour Party meeting in Bo'ness, West Lothian, concerned about the performance of Jim Callaghan's Labour Government and the rise of Scottish nationalism. I came out as the new secretary of a long unused branch. I finally got my membership card a few months later – to my earlier concerns were added the failure to recruit members and the aversion to campaigning between elections. The list has got longer over the years. There's something about being part of a broad church, anti-establishment (the real one) party that doesn't lend itself to a smooth transition to lasting social progress in your own lifetime.

Anyway, we started recruiting and campaigning, I even became the CLP secretary, aged 24, and in 1979 we faced the challenge of the SNP's Billy Wolfe, who had been steadily whittling down Tam Dalyell's majority. The SNP controlled the district councils, the party was split down the middle over the first devolution referendum, Tam was public enemy number one in much of the media, and someone called Alex Salmond seemed to be running the local SNP campaign. Result? The largest Labour majority in Scotland – 20,000. Lesson? Polls and trends can be bucked, organised local people can make a difference, just as they did later in London when our local MP, Clive Efford, consistently saw off the Tories in one of their target seats.

By the 1980s I was on the Labour Scottish Executive, involved in rolling out a rudimentary target seat strategy that by 1997 saw Conservative parliamentary representation reduced to zero. When we tried to adopt a similar approach to membership recruitment we were politely (well impolitely, actually) told it was none of our business and that the staff were employed by the NEC, not the Scottish Executive. Hence began an interest in, if not a federal party, then at least a party where members and staff could work in partnership towards common objectives! Electoral politics are central to any political party's *raison d'être*, but if the party is run largely in the immediate interests of MPs, councillors and candidates, as opposed to the wider membership (especially those who've not had the chance to join!) there will be a reckoning. And so it has transpired. For a more recent example witness the undue time, energy and resources devoted to the regional list ballots – a system seemingly designed for the candidates rather than the members, and bizarrely excluding new members who had voted in the UK leadership elections.

At least three lessons from my 'exile' south of the border also inform my current thinking. The first stems from direct involvement in the process that saw Cohse, NUPE, and Nalgo merge to form the public services union, UNISON. We were all trades unionists but from three different cultures, so we had to build alliances, compromise, exhibit trust, take risks, retain the best of the old and contemplate new untested methods to build the consensus for the common good that made UNISON possible. The second was that we could construct political fund arrangements that gave members the choice of continuing to affiliate to Labour, contributing to a general political fund, doing both or neither. Thirdly having put all that time, energy, and resources into building this new union, the rulebook requires a two-thirds majority, not just a simple majority, to bring about any fundamental change.

Retired and returning to Scotland in the midst of the independence referendum campaign, my previous frequent visits north didn't prepare me for what was to come – a sense of (sometimes bitter) division among Scots, not on traditional political lines but on the Yes/No question. I felt a little less comfortable with symbols of Scottish identity (and me having recently having been the secretary of the London Tartan Army!). I remember looking at a train timetable thinking they must've built a new station between Kinghorn and Kirkcaldy – until I realised it was the Gaelic translation of the latter.

Conventional politics seemed to have been suspended. But in the run-up to the 2015 General Election I was quite excited by the prospect of a Labour/SNP alliance, shaking Labour out of its tribalism and putting the SNP on the spot. It was not to be. And what we have now, despite two very separate institutions, is the strange phenomenon of a second Conservative government in Westminster, and the Scottish Government in Holyrood as the official (Scottish) opposition.

So, where now for Labour in Scotland, after the 2016 Holyrood elections, the EU referendum result (I was a solid Remainer) and the re-election of Jeremy Corbyn to the UK Labour leadership? Firstly, no doubt to the consternation of the pundits and other dreamers, there is no quick fix for an organisation whose job it is to challenge the status quo and the current economic order. We need to learn from others, we need our own version of this:

"In 2005, SNP strategists identified five key priorities: 'communications, governance, message, organisation and resource.' Detailed policy or ideology were not among them, but in presentational terms a new, relentlessly positive campaigning machine was about to be born." That is David Torrance, writing on 21st May 2015, on 'The Reinvention of the SNP'.[*]

We need a version of this that does not involve ditching the ideology or policy-making. We should be the Scottish part of a federal party, punching our weight financially and organisationally, with mutual support for and from our comrades in England and Wales.

We need to learn how to deal with multi-party politics – after all, Labour introduced the electoral system for the Scottish Parliament and reformed local government voting, but it was our opponents who adapted best.

Labour has had three waves of new members – around the referendum, the General Election, and the UK leadership election. But most of them found their way to us, we didn't find them. We need to go out and actively recruit amongst our supporters to extend our reach in

---

[*] http://www.theguardian.com/politics/2015/may/21/how-alex-salmond-nicola-sturgeon-pulled-off-political-triumph-lifetime

our communities. We need to engage with those communities between elections, listening, learning and campaigning and our policy making needs to be rooted there. That is where we challenge what UNISON's Dave Watson calls the "Scandamerica myth that we can have social justice without cost." We can't allow the tax rise to be the headline, when the real news is what you get in return.

We need to build alliances across parties, something which may be easier for members locally than for our professional politicians. Stop and think how much common ground there is among Green, Labour and SNP progressives – fracking and Trident spring to mind for me, locally. There will be other issues. The Conservative government in the UK is with us for at least another four years, but they can be knocked off their preferred course – witness the challenges against Trade Union Bill, disability benefit cuts, child refugees, academies. Not outright defeat, but change. People at the sharp end can't afford to wait for an "independent Scotland" or the "next Labour Government".

But you can only build these local cross party alliances if you can reassure your own tribalists, and get something back from your potential partners. The crisis in Scottish local government funding would be a good place to start. Any seasoned political operator knows "how to lie with statistics". So we point to the UK Tory government cuts to Holyrood's budget (10 per cent over five years), not just being passed on to local government, but being passed on with a bonus charge resulting in a 24 per cent cut.

The SNP government dispute this and say they're fighting austerity, but won't use the parliament's powers to ameliorate things. Local government workers and the recipients of their services are about to find out which version is correct, unless we all unite to pressurise the SNP Government into a change of course. The services we've lost since 2010, and those we may be about to lose are presumably those which would be part of the fabric of a social democratic, independent Scotland, but reconstructing what's been needlessly demolished takes time, so why allow it – unless that's a part of your strategy? Hopefully not.

Looking down on the electoral map of Scotland is a depressing sight for a Labour member like me. But from another vantage point looking around at the untapped potential of the 10,576 supporters who stuck with us in Edinburgh Northern and Leith gives us hope and yet another challenge. We're rebuilding. We want everyone to have the opportunity to make the life they want for themselves. We want the places we live to be healthy and prosperous. And we want the kind of politics where decisions are made together with the people those decisions affect.

Chapter 11

Where next for socialists in Scotland?

Connor Beaton

The failure of socialists, this time mostly under the RISE banner, to win representation in the Scottish Parliament for a third consecutive election is a painful one for all committed to that tradition as a distinct, organised force.

It was particularly painful for me and three talented, dedicated socialist candidates narrowly to trail the National Front in the North East Scotland region, as part of a tight scramble between fringe parties to avoid last place.

Despite a 2014 independence referendum campaign that led to an unprecedented level of political engagement, Scotland's socialist movement was unable to channel the awakening of people in working class communities two years prior into electoral support for a coherent radical programme of left-wing reforms and a second independence referendum.

Then there's the Brexit vote. As Cat Boyd observed in The National (28th June 2016), whatever you make of the EU issue, and the xenophobic Leave campaign, "a justified roar of rage from working-class communities must not be dismissed as simple ignorance."

So where did it all go wrong? Members of the Scottish Socialist Party (SSP) were left dazed after the 2014 referendum, when around 3,000 people applied to join – part of a mass demonstration of solidarity and resistance across Scotland in the wake of the narrow No vote.

Poor administration and divided opinions on whether or not the SSP should stand in the 2015 Westminster election after the SNP's rejection of a Yes Alliance caused some damage to the party's growth and momentum, but not nearly as much as the SSP's subsequent poor showing in the four constituencies where it did stand candidates.

The election result rocked activists' confidence in the party's ability to win popular support for its radical message. When a proposal to explore the creation of a new left-wing electoral alliance was put to the SSP conference only weeks after many new members' first experience of outright electoral humiliation, it was grasped with both hands – we had nothing to lose.

The outcome was RISE (Respect, Independence, Socialism and Environmentalism). A year later (after countless meetings, conferences, and press releases) we put RISE – Scotland's Left Alliance to voters and the reaction was disappointingly familiar.

The number of votes cast for RISE in 2016 in the Scottish Parliament constituencies of Glasgow Pollok (185) and Glasgow Shettleston (213) closely resembles the number of votes won by the SSP in constituencies like Glasgow South West (176) and Glasgow East (224) in 2015.

The idea, instinctively seductive to many newcomers to the movement, that the left could benefit substantially in electoral terms from cosmetic tweaks – a rebranding exercise or a professionalised media operation – was thoroughly discredited by the result last May.

Though dogged with minor errors, including a typo-riddled manifesto and the absence of its emblem from the ballot paper, RISE's election campaign was remarkably well managed. A series of well-edited, powerful videos made an impact through social media, and a deeply moving election broadcast, perfectly channelling the spirit of Scotland in Summer 2014, became an instant point of conversation during street campaigning and conversations.

The RISE campaign mobilised more activists across Scotland than any recent left-wing bid for parliamentary representation. But an army of canvassers in Glasgow, modelling their tactics on those of the referendum's Radical Independence Campaign (RIC), struggled to return one per cent of the vote, even with a prominent, credible and likeable candidate in Cat Boyd.

A detailed post-mortem of the RISE election campaign could undoubtedly fill an entire book of its own. It was to my great disappointment that the SSP's 2015 campaign was never afforded a serious degree of post-election scrutiny, and the same mistake cannot and should not be made again.

As well as highlighting what worked and what did not during RISE's election campaign itself, a thorough analysis should also take factors involved in the alliance's genesis into account.

RISE was conceived as a post-referendum marriage of the Scottish Socialist Party and significant elements of the Radical Independence Campaign, uniting the socialist party that sat on Yes Scotland's advisory board with people from the grassroots organisation that played many of us would argue, a huge role in shifting Labour's traditional heartlands towards the Yes vote.

The combination of two organisations with a different political character led in part to competing internal dynamics within RISE, with some parts more closely resembling a political party while others resembled the broad movement politics of RIC.

Some RIC members were keen to stress that it was not formally involved in RISE, but the central involvement of RIC's founding members in Glasgow guaranteed a sense of continuity between the groups.

Early successes of RISE included its ability effectively to mobilise women and young people through RISE Women and the RISE Youth Network, which operate on a semi-autonomous basis and welcome non-members to their meetings. They have thrived through their focus on protest and direct action rather than traditional electoral work.

Elsewhere, RISE struggled to put together functioning structures for internal democracy and intra-party communication, leading to unanswerable questions about democratic accountability and decision-making processes.

The rush to agree terms of affiliation of the SSP to RISE ahead of the election resulted in a deeply unsustainable relationship between the two organisations, which must be revisited if the affiliation is to continue.

RISE has no elected leadership, and the open-ended question of its long-term future after the 2016 election will be answered very differently depending on which of its local groups, affiliate organisations or former candidates you ask.

The Scottish Socialist Party's annual conference, meeting for the third consecutive year in the immediate aftermath of referendum or election defeat, spent hours tackling that question.

Where consensus undoubtedly exists is on the next five years as ripe political territory for Scotland's socialists, with the territory now facing the upheaval of Brexit and further threats to the living standards of working communities.

Assaults on working class people from the Conservatives in Westminster are bound to continue, while the SNP's return to minority government creates a realistic prospect of securing concessions from the Scottish Government through left-wing pressure on backbench and opposition MSPs.

Socialists will find it easier to define themselves in relation to the Scottish Conservative opposition than the Scottish Labour one, which often sought to wrap itself in socialist clothes.

Many SSP and former RIC activists, in finding common cause during RISE's short and spirited election campaign, have built friendships and a spirit of camaraderie that will come in useful as we work together to build united campaigns in future.

The Scottish Socialist Party, which struggled to identify its own organisational purpose during the RISE campaign, could stand to benefit greatly if it can inherit a fraction of the energy and enthusiasm with which RISE activists tackled the election campaign.

The SSP has already overcome the reluctance prevalent in parts of the left to take a clear position on the coming referendum on European Union (EU) membership, planting itself firmly on the Remain side, and breaking ranks with left critics burned by the treatment of Greece's Syriza government.

Few imagined that a socialist campaign in the EU referendum would have a great impact on the outcome, or play a particularly large role in developing the party's forces. But it was one of a series of opportunities for socialists to distinguish themselves from the mainstream parties.

The EU referendum also created a particular opportunity through which to develop closer links with left parties and movements across Europe, from which Scottish socialists stand to gain a good deal – sharing in a wealth of experience from our more successful counterparts in Germany, France, Spain and Greece.

The long march to the next round of Westminster and Scottish Parliament elections is no bad thing. With a sharp decline in participation between the 85 per cent who voted in Scotland's referendum to the 56 per cent in the 2016 election, signs of voter fatigue are starting to set in, particularly in the working class communities on which we relied in the referendum.

The next four or five years give Scottish socialists the time we need to identify our faults, tighten our organisational failures, and cut our teeth in community struggle. Labour's dramatic electoral collapse against the Greens' failure to win the record number of MSPs they predicted shows that there remains a space in the Scottish political landscape for a working class, socialist alternative.

RISE injected enthusiasm and fresh thinking into the Scottish Parliament election. We now have a responsibility to find the best way to channel more grassroots energy in practical, sustainable ways.

Chapter 12

Out with the 'new' and in with the 'bold'

Emily St Denny

Talk of 'new politics' in Scotland first emerged during the campaign for the Scottish Parliament in the mid to late 1990s. According to proponents of home rule, 'new Scottish politics' would offer a welcome departure from 'old' Westminster's discord and divisiveness. Advocates of home rule welcomed 'new Scottish politics' as the potential dividend of new institutions, new policy processes, and a new more inclusive political culture.

The heart of Scottish devolution – its new parliament – had been imagined as a forum for constructive deliberation. Its head – the Scottish executive – would incarnate principles of civic consultation and wide-reaching democratic participation. Further, the proportional electoral system used to elect Members of the Scottish Parliament (MSPs) was supposed to preclude parliamentary majorities and normalise a politics of negotiation and coalition building.

By and large, expectations of new Scottish politics have never fully been met. Nevertheless, the politicisation of Scotland's citizens generated by the 2014 referendum debate, and the devolution settlement it yielded, means that the new parliament now has the opportunity to leave behind the timid legacy of 'new' Scottish politics and craft a 'bold' form of participatory democracy with which to grapple with hard policy questions in a transformative yet accountable manner.

Two eras of Scottish politics

The extent to which devolution has allowed Scotland to develop a truly distinctive mode of politics is contested. The institution of a Scottish parliament has repatriated debate and negotiation on devolved policy issues. This has allowed the adoption of a number of distinctive policies, such as free prescriptions and the abolition of university tuition fees, north of the border.

That being said, policy divergence between Scotland and the rest of the UK tends to be inflated in political narrative. Our differences – and we do have a few – are not nearly as spectacular as we often like to boast. For instance, Scotland's current moratorium on hydraulic fracturing ('fracking') contrasts with the UK Government's enthusiastic courting of energy firms, but a moratorium remains a far cry from an out-right ban.

Another 'distinctive' aspect of Scottish politics concerns the Scottish government's relatively consistent involvement of partners in discussing and designing policies, including local authorities, third sector actors, unions and professional bodies. Here too, however, the impact of new institutions on politics in Scotland has tended to be overstated. Scottish party politics in particular remain a fraught and often acrimonious competition for attention and electoral support in a saturated political environment. Cooperation, when it happens, tends to emanate from a perceived mutual advantage and, less frequently, from the pursuit of a specific shared goal.

In the seventeen years since the foundation of the Scottish Parliament, we therefore have yet to see a wholly new political culture emerge in Scotland. A second age of devolved Scottish politics, however, was recently heralded. The Scottish independence referendum and the debate that preceded it generated exceptional democratic participation. The debate was largely characterised by a tone of civic state-building made possible by the uncharacteristically inclusive and grassroots campaign strategies deployed, to a greater or lesser extent, by both Yes Scotland and Better Together.

These wide-reaching and participatory campaigns generated an unprecedented level of public engagement over the question of Scotland's future, including from those who have historically been underrepresented in UK politics, such as women, young people, and black and ethnic minority groups.

The consequences of the 2014 referendum have been profound. It has directly led to Scotland obtaining new devolved powers as part of the Smith Commission settlement. Indirectly, it contributed to the SNP's resounding win in the 2015 UK elections (taking 56 of Scotland's 59 seats in Westminster), and provided the precedent for allowing 16 and 17 year olds to vote in Scottish elections. Perhaps most importantly, however, the referendum debate constituted an invaluable process of social learning for those taking part.

Social learning refers to the acquisition of new knowledge and skills through direct observation and participation in a social context. In this sense, the referendum empowered many of the people living and working in Scotland to take part in politics, and widened what people understood as politics from narrow party competition to broader conversations about social justice and sovereignty. It gave people an opportunity to develop their confidence and skills not only to understand and discuss complex issues that directly affect their lives, but also to navigate increasingly complex electoral politics from the local to the national level.

This newly energised citizenry may yet succeed in generating truly new politics in Scotland, where new institutions, new policy processes, and attempts at a new political culture have so far fallen short. The post-EU referendum context provides fresh challenges here.

At its core, capitalising on our people's energy and engagement will require rethinking the way we enact participatory and representative democracy from here on out. This means acknowledging the legacies, challenges, and opportunities facing the Scottish parliament today, as well as how we engage with, and empower, our local communities.

In this way, while it may have been elected more than a year and a half after the referendum, the new Scottish parliament still stands at the juncture between the timid 'new' Scottish politics of the 2000s and the 'bold' politics generated by the referendum debate. Like the outgoing Parliament, it faces a number of 'wicked', pervasive, and resistant policy challenges.

There are 29,000 more people under 30 living in poverty in Scotland today than there were in 2002/2003; people born in Glasgow can still expect not to live as long as those born in Edinburgh; the number of people using food banks in Scotland increased 398 per cent between 2012 and 2014; and cities like Glasgow regularly breach safety levels for air pollution. Unlike its predecessor, however, this Parliament can make the most of the new powers it recently acquired through the Scotland Act 2016 to address these challenges, including a new Scottish Rate of Income Tax, and powers on welfare matters.

Thus, the 'new' Scottish politics of the 2000s may have failed to generate miracle solutions with which to address the issues facing Scotland and its people, but the new Parliament certainly has the opportunity to inaugurate a 'bold' and transformative politics in Scotland.

Towards a politics of empowerment

The electorate's appetite for doing politics differently has been repeatedly communicated in the last two years. During this period, Scots and many of those who live and work in Scotland have been to the polls three times: in the 2014 referendum campaign, the 2015 General Election, and most recently the 2016 Scottish Parliament elections. In Scotland, these campaigns have all shared a particular focus on issues of sovereignty, social justice, and the quality of democratic representation.

These campaigns have demonstrated that constitutional politics continue to drive debates north of the border. Subsequently, the make-up of the new parliament reveals three political trends that will need to be taken into account in future political debates. First, the resurgence of the Scottish Conservative Party challenges the popular belief that Scotland is more left wing than the rest of the UK. This is important because recognising the Scottish electorate for what it is – complex and diverse – will allow us to have more meaningful discussions about what we want Scotland's future to be.

The vast majority of Scotland's people will agree in principle that they would prefer to live in a fair, healthy, and prosperous society. This is no guarantee, however, that we all agree on what 'fair', 'healthy' and 'prosperous' mean. Yet discussing these matters openly and rigorously is necessary for informing and securing the legitimacy of future decisions, such as the upcoming referendum on the UK's membership of the EU.

Moreover, in Scotland, these questions are closely entwined with constitutional issues. This is the second trend made manifest by the recent Holyrood election: it is clear that the Scottish electorate is still strongly polarised on the issue of independence. This will likely have implications for the way in which the Parliament will choose to use its new powers.

Depending on where you stand, the Scotland Act 2016 grants rather too few or too many powers to Holyrood. In either case, you have a stake in Holyrood using its new powers well. This will require a measured and careful discussion that we cannot allow to be overshadowed by ongoing constitutional debates. This means carving out a space for continued deliberation over Scotland's constitutional future that does not impede the use of the Parliament's new powers to implement progressive policies.

The third trend revealed by the latest Holyrood election in May 2016 concerns the Scottish electorate's apparent appetite for a politics of scrutiny and accountability. The SNP fared well in an electoral system supposed to preclude majority or comfortable minority government. Nevertheless, the election of Green and Conservative MSPs suggests a desire to see the Scottish Government put through its paces rather than allowed *carte blanche.*

Rather than an obstacle, the SNP and its supporters ought to embrace the democratic value of opposition politics. We have a tendency to associate opposition, with the unproductive adversarialism demonstrated in the Commons. Yet opposition can be transformative. We ought to (re)learn to embrace a constructive form of 'agonistic' politics.

Agonism refers to a potentially positive form of political conflict that can only take place when arenas are created in which people's differences can be truly and meaningfully expressed and taken into account. Thus, opposition is not inherently incompatible with progress, rather it can be a welcome ingredient to deliberative democracy.

Politically, we need to better recognise and reward the capacity of the people living and working in Scotland to participate in discussing and deciding on policies and services that improve their lives. This will require two particular efforts. First, we must absolutely cease to conflate consultation and empowerment. Allowing people to have their say in the policy process is the bare minimum required to label a process as 'participatory', and we can and ought to do more. Too often still, it remains unclear to those feeding into the policy process how their ideas and opinions helped shape the outcomes of decisions.

The Smith Commission consultation process offers a recent and striking example of another missed opportunity to go beyond consultation and truly engage with the full breadth of experience available in Scottish society. Therefore, and secondly, we must strive to create the forums in which people's voices can be better heard, the institutional channels through which their ideas and concerns will be listened to and acted upon, and the means of fairly generating the resources required to implement the services people need.

Practically speaking, part of this transformation will require devolving more powers to instances closer to people, local authorities in particular. More generally, however it will also entail using the Scottish parliament to drive a democratic revolution. By encouraging the development and use of radical democratic methods, such as citizen juries and participatory budgeting, Holyrood can nurture and reward Scotland's vibrant and politically engaged population.

The policies and services developed this way promise to yield more effective outcomes in a more sustainable manner. Now more than ever, Holyrood has the opportunity to build on the democratic and participatory legacy of the referendum campaign, and truly become the 'People's Parliament'.

Conclusion: truly participatory politics

When thinking of what 'new' Scottish politics might look like in the future, we therefore need all the lessons from the past, as well as a good understanding of the challenges and opportunities that face the people, parties, and institutions in Scotland today. Frustrated expectations of 'new Scottish politics' during the 2000s have taught not to take our distinctiveness for granted. But that was then, and this is now, and now is the time to make good on the democratic and participatory legacy of the referendum campaign in order to craft a truly bold and distinctive politics – a politics that welcomes and rewards participation, that likes a good challenge from the opposition, and that recognises and nurtures' people's capacity to make sense of their world and contribute to making it fairer, healthier, and more sustainable.

Policies and Perspectives

Chapter 13

Key choices facing higher education in Scotland

Doug Chalmers

The passing of the Higher Education Governance Scotland act in the dying days of the last Holyrood government indicated a major achievement for the ruling SNP administration and indeed other supporters of democratising higher education, in the shape of the Labour Party and the Scottish Greens. This was the passing into legislation of the majority of the recommendations of the Von Prondzynski report into the failings of university governance, highlighted on the report's original publication in 2012.

The implications of the act should not be underestimated – some of the more publicised aspects being the necessity for chairs of university courts (essentially the bodies that legally oversee the running of universities) to now be elected by both staff and students, with the powers of existing rectors safeguarded, and agreement that campus trade unions would have as a right, two seats on court in addition to existing staff and student representatives.

Also of key importance, however, was another feature of the act that changed the composition of university senates. A university senate is normally the body tasked with the 'academic leadership' of universities – a power ceded to them by courts – of which they are usually legally a subcommittee.

Over the past decades, growing managerialism in many universities has tended to mean a downplaying of the voice of staff on such bodies, with a preponderance of senior management or university policy managers changing the culture from one of live academic debate amongst equals, to one where a minority of staff may be faced with a *fait accompli* from management, in terms of academic direction.

The changes brought about in the new legislation mean that senates will now have to consist of a majority of members elected by staff – something which will hopefully begin to move senates towards being proper, deliberative, academic bodies.

There is still 'unfinished business' remaining around the issue of democratising governance however, which the UCU will be continuing to campaign for in the next period. A key aspect of this is moving towards gender equality on university bodies – one of the unfulfilled aspects of the original Von Prondzynski report on governance and which still needs progressed.

While the higher education debate in Scotland has been dominated over the last couple of years by questions of governance, the resolution, or partial resolution of this question means the issue of how to fund the sector – and indeed the further education sector is likely to move centre stage once again.

While this article was being written, university unions were once more in dispute with management over the issue of pay. Having lost approximately 15 per cent of salary in real terms over the last five years, and at a time of growing workload pressure, staff are rightly comparing their situation unfavorably with the growing largesse being consumed by university principals and senior management.

With university principals now earning quite astronomical wages (their average salary is now £272,000 – twice the salary claimed by Scotland's First Minister, and dwarfing the salary of the chief constable of Police Scotland who earns only £210,000) university unions have been forced to embark on industrial action seeking to recoup some of these losses.

The other two prongs of current industrial action are for an ending of the gender pay gap – still a shocking feature of higher education, with women academics paid on average £5,700 less than their male counterparts – and an end to staff on precarious or casualised contracts. In relation to the latter, figures in 2013 found that universities and colleges were more than twice as likely as other workplaces to use zero hours contracts.

In the view of the UCU there are sufficient funds to solve the gender pay gap, provide permanent jobs and pay staff decent wages in tertiary education. Figures obtained by the union indicate a current surplus of over £1.6 billion in the UK sector. Yet, too often, decisions are taken that privilege new buildings over staff, forgetting that without fairly paid and well-motivated staff, Scotland will not be able to maintain its rankings in world university leagues.

From a wider and less immediate perspective perhaps, over the next five years or so, a key principle that needs upheld is that of university education in Scotland remaining free at the point of access, and students not having to pay tuition fees. Access to higher education should remain dependent on your ability to learn and not on your parents' income. In contrast to the situation in England and elsewhere in the British Isles, we are fortunate in Scotland, in that only the Conservative are actively campaigning for tuition fees to be re-imposed on our university students.

Having said that, and for reasons unconnected with the no-fees regime, Scotland to our shame still has a poor record on widening access. This raises the issue of the need for proper funding of student support, and for the safeguarding and expansion of available bursaries. We know that higher education benefits the students who attend university, but it is also hugely beneficial to society in general and to our businesses, who gain from the increased knowledge, innovation and access to the skilled graduates our universities produce.

That is why UCU believes that higher education should be funded through progressive taxation. We also welcome the current debate on the principles and purposes of Scotland's new tax powers, limited thought they may be at present.

Behind much of the financial pressure on universities elsewhere in the UK, but which have an unfortunate knock-on effect in Scotland and in the other devolved nations, is the ideological divide between those who wish to marketise and monetise universities, and those who wish to maintain and develop the concept of the 'public' university.

The UK government's Green Paper earlier this year (which applies to higher education in England; in Scotland it is devolved) and which is ironically misnamed *Fulfilling our Potential: Teaching Excellence, Social Mobility and Student Choice*, is currently about to become a White Paper, before being put through the Westminster parliament. It is a clear example of the wish to monetise and marketise higher education even further, through removing the barriers to private firms being given university status.

Indications are that it will be a major step towards 'for-profit' education in England, with the Pearson conglomerate perhaps set to be the first FTSE company to apply to become a university. We currently have no 'for-profit' providers in Scotland. Current Scottish policy is that a university education is a four-year process (and thus more expensive for private providers to contemplate) and that all universities should undertake both teaching *and* research. But trends south of the border are a portent of increasing pressures towards education marketisation in the UK overall.

Of course, the Green Paper was never really about fulfilling potential. Rather, it was and is about increasing competition within higher education to allow universities in England to lift fees even higher than the obscene levels that they occupy at the moment. If the measures are successful, it seems certain that the current fee cap of £9,000 will be removed, making it more lucrative for private firms which wish to enter the sector.

The way this will be enabled will involve re-defining universities so that they no longer have to cater for the present normal existing range of subjects, or carry out research as well as teaching. Neither will these new 'for-profit' providers have to offer library facilities, given parallel moves by the government to make research provided by traditional universities available through a system of on-line 'open access' to all.

This will, in all likelihood, lead to a new type of 'university' which in reality does not deserve the name, and which will essentially be a stripped-down version of what we have all grown up to expect in higher education. The probability is that it will concentrate only on a single teaching function delivered on a 'for-profit' basis by private providers.

To do this profitably will likely mean it is on-line based, with its only local provision being tutorials taught by staff on teaching only contracts, or perhaps hourly paid.

One direct way of how this may impact Scotland is through the increasingly insidious use of league tables or university rankings. Another key aspect of the Green Paper/ White Paper in England is the proposal for a 'Teaching Excellence Framework' (TEF), which will seek to rank all universities by their 'teaching quality'. Universities gaining a higher ranking will thus be able to charge higher fees to aspiring students (and will be thus more profitable for private providers).

The widespread adoption of this preposterous approach – *how can you rank the teaching on a postgraduate astrophysics course taught to small classes, against for instance a mass first year undergraduate lecture on media studies, or specialised practical based courses in nursing?* – would lead to students believing that unless the ranking of their university was as high as others the quality would be less. In reality of course universities cannot be compared in this manner. Universities cannot be understood as 'teaching factories' with raw students in one end and cultured graduates out the other.

This approach totally debases the concept of education in the tertiary sector, but its widespread adoption would lead to pressure for a similar system in Scotland, to enable universities here to be compared to universities South of the border and thus ensure students were attracted.

It would also increase the pressure for a two-tier university system, where some universities would be expected to concentrate on teaching, and others on research. This is a sterile division which would undermine much of what is excellent within Scotland's universities.

To conclude: there is a lot that remains excellent within Scottish higher education, both in terms of where it stands in the world, and also what it provides to its students. Our present Scottish government, and indeed the majority of parties in Holyrood, still seem committed to the university as a public good, benefiting society as a whole, and with a key role in developing Scotland's economy and society. The negative changes to the higher education system in England are creating pressures on our own system, however, which do need to be resisted. Failure to do so will result in repeating the mistakes that are increasingly fracturing English higher education and through this the future of our young people south of the border.

Chapter 14

A challenging landscape for the Scottish media

Paul Holleran

A major measure of any functioning democracy is the state of its media. Anyone looking closely at the newspaper and broadcasting industry in Scotland today would be rightly concerned about the current position of the fourth estate, in particular. That is where I want to focus my attention in this article.*

Despite the efforts of the Scottish Newspaper Society to talk up the industry and minimise the facts about the downward spiral of sales and advertising revenues, we continue to see job cuts impacting journalism across the country.

There are fewer than half the number of journalists in newsrooms of the Scottish indigenous broadsheets compared to ten years ago, while daily tabloids have also suffered from budgets being slashed. At this time, not long after the Scottish parliamentary elections, many local newspaper offices around Scotland are the focus of disputes and industrial action ballots as members fight for better staffing levels and to protect hard won terms and conditions.

Amazingly, as redundancies are decimating journalist posts, Newsquest Media Group are trying to cut sick pay entitlement and impose an extra two-and-half hours a week on work schedules, while reducing holiday entitlements, too. The Johnston Press experiment known as 'Newsroom of the Future' has cut dozens of jobs and union members are refusing to accept the newly established staffing levels as being unsustainable. Among other things, this is for the reasons of their health and safety, because of the increased stress of dealing with newly set workloads for each individual. The other stress factor for journalists is the negative impact on the local identity of the titles because of the use of much more generic feature copy employed across many titles to help compensate for lost jobs.

The refusal of companies like Newsquest to absorb falling

---

* Initiatives like CommonSpace, Bella Caledonia and others are a significant part of the media mix in Scotland now. My focus here, however, is on newspapers and broadcasting, which remain important within the overall ecology, despite changes.

profits without slashing budgets is leading to the demise of great Scottish papers such as The Herald and its sister titles. Hopefully the management regime at Newsquest in Scotland will be successful in growing advertising and circulation revenues as they did in running Clyde & Forth Publishing in recent years. However, their London bosses appear keener to follow in the footsteps of their US parent company Gannett, and cut jobs rather than pursue growth to meet budgets.

Let us be blunt, the positivity being pushed by the SNS and employers is correct, in that the papers are still very profitable for their owners. But the reality is that they are not pulling in as much money as they used to.

This is perhaps the crux of the matter. How much money do papers have to make to encourage publishers to keep them alive? At a public meeting a couple of years ago in Glasgow, organised by the National Union of Journalists (NUJ) and the Co-operative movement, the importance of press ownership was discussed. Paul Wood, managing director at The West Highland Free Press, told the captive audience that his company set a minimum target of one per cent profit per annum. Their view was that their title was a community asset, a cornerstone of their local democracy, and not just about coin.

The NUJ Scottish Executive Council will be placing this issue firmly on its agenda for the next few years, with a view to exploring different models for press ownership and development in this country. We have recently engaged with Robert McChesney, an American professor who specialises in the history and political economy of communication and the role the media plays in democratic and advanced capitalist societies. Further discussion is planned with this founder of Free Press, a US media reform organisation, and supporter of community owned media.

A real enigma facing the industry, which is also having a major impact on staff, is the demand not only to fill the pages of the print copies but the online editions of each title as well. The inability of most publishers to establish an alternative and comparable revenue line by this route is a tragedy, which is further undermining the industry. Insufficient video journalism online and a lack of innovative ideas to attract advertisers and more readers has plagued print media. There has been much effort in this area, but not enough smart thinking. The additional workload is obviously another obstacle facing journalists trying to produce the best product every day and week, with a diminishing pool of resources.

It is clear that the numbers of journalists in each newsroom cannot be reduced any further without causing very serious damage to the substance of the titles and the health of staff. The very existence of some local newspapers is at risk and steps need to be taken at government level to put in place mechanisms to protect all titles from closure.

It remains to be seen if there is anything resembling a considerable impact for print media through the recent announcement in the Westminster White Paper on BBC Charter Renewal. Certainly there could be opportunities for young people taking on modern apprenticeships in partnership between local papers and BBC stations.

However, staff working at BBC Scotland are more interested in how much extra resource will be provided as part of the licence fee agreement. Varying messages have emanated from senior executives in relation to extra money being diverted to the nations and regions. Remarkably, the management team at BBC Scotland's Pacific Quay in Glasgow showed great ambition in their proposals submitted to Lord Hall and his acolytes in London, before these were apparently kicked into the long grass.

The NUJ had also submitted similar proposals, with employer and union putting forward arguments for an expanded news service across Scotland, including a new radio station to supplement Radio Scotland. The injection of money into increased operating budgets would lead to growth in news and current affairs, but also increased drama and music from Scottish writers and artistes. The boost to Scottish culture and entertainments industries would be invaluable on many fronts, enhancing our economy and reputation with a "made in Scotland" stamp on the new productions.

However, following another pathetic licence fee settlement negotiated between Westminster and BBC senior people, we were told "the nations and regions will be getting nothing extra". Fortunately the Scottish government, backed ably by their SNP colleagues at Westminster, and in partnership with Welsh and Northern Irish politicians, lobbied ferociously for a better deal. In October 2016 an amendment to the new draft agreement for the next BBC charter was tabled, with a call to "deliver maximum devolution of broadcasting" for Scotland

As ever, the question on the other side of the rhetoric concerns how much will actually be delivered. An expansion of journalistic jobs across BBC Scotland and a possible 'Scottish Six', providing a new perspective on news and current affairs, would be a great boost at a time when everything else appears to be going in a downward spiral. Although the amount of investment is not going to be be anywhere need what was on the shopping list it will be a shot in the arm for a beleaguered industry. Broadcasting in Scotland should continue to be in a reasonably healthy condition, particularly if STV plough on with their steady growth, developing further with stability and innovation the keywords.

Training and providing the correct skills for journalists is an essential issue for the future of the media industry. Projects such as the Modern Apprenticeship in Digital Journalism operated by the NUJ, backed by Skills Development Scotland and supported by many employers, is proving a success. The extension of this by building links with local schools will go among way to providing the right kind of 'fresh blood' with the relevant skills for a changing industry.

Employers need to realise that partnership is essential. Imposing change just to save money isn't smart. Reducing resources and demanding more from those who remain isn't sustainable. Both the NUJ and the STUC have now called for a major reviews conference on the future of the media in Scotland, and we hope that this will be backed by the Scottish government, following encouragement from the SNP's National Council on the newspaper sector particularly.

There is still a lot of quality in the inherited Scottish media. But it is continually being undermined, thereby reducing the ability to generate revenue. Of course substantial amounts of those profits need to be reinvested in a qualitative fashion. Our country needs a renewal of properly funded media across all platforms in keeping with the needs of a modern, democratic nation.

Chapter 15

A new approach to refugees and asylum seekers

Khuloud Alsaba

The Universal Declaration of Human Rights is clear. People have a right to asylum. In the face of war, subjugation, oppression and persecution, it is the right of those who are suffering to leave for a safer place, where they can live free from without oppression.

This was agreed after the Second World War in 1948, as part of a global consensus on peaceful international relations. That consensus did not last long. It came under pressure from the aftermath of the war, the Cold War, the collapse of the Soviet Union and the transition to democracy and market economies in the Eastern European countries. The new millennium started with an environment of massive aggression, as the so-called 'war on terror' started to draw a new map for the Middle East.

The United Kingdom was, unfortunately, part of the military aggression in Afghanistan and Iraq. In addition, The British government has helped sustain many of the dictatorships in the developing world. The ten tax havens under British jurisdiction are still facilitating the illicit movement of arms and the theft of billions of pounds, draining countries of resources which could dramatically improve the lives of their citizens. This is spelled out in Health Poverty Action's 'Open Letter on Migration'.[*]

A development process in reverse process has been sustained by international powerful corporates and government to maintain profit through the illusion of a 'trickle down economics mode – one exploited both within and between countries. The Arab uprising a few years ago started as a result of the long and internationally supported life span of dictatorships in the region. While some Arab countries are going through shaky transitions, others have descended into conflict and chaos. This has been sponsored and fuelled by the governments of the United States, the United Kingdom and France. These countries seized upon the uncertainty rising as a result of demands for political change

---

[*] https://www.healthpovertyaction.org

in the Middle East and North Africa (MENA) region – delegating other regional powers, like Saudi Arabia and Turkey, to 'manage' conflicts like those in Syria, Bahrain, and Yemen.

All this has caused further polarisation among local warring parties, and aggravated identity conflict fuelled by the geopolitical interests of the international powers. It is both past and ongoing conflicts of this kind that have created and are still creating what is now dubbed 'the refugees crisis' in Europe. The strongest governments and corporates in the continent remain the main sponsors of the conflicts across the MENA region and the rest of the developing world.

In the largest international population movement since the Second World War, Medicins Sans Frontiers (MSF) estimates that 60 million people have been displaced across the globe due to violence, poverty, and oppression.* To put the scale of this crisis in context, we must understand that those crossing the Mediterranean are fleeing conflicts in Afghanistan, Syria, Iraq, and Libya, among others. They are people fleeing for their lives. In 2015, 3,239 of those trying to escape to safety died in the sea, according to UNHCR data. This massive movement is another face of political and economic globalisation that is rarely contextualised and examined as such. In 2016, 183,000 people made it to Europe, risking their own and their loved ones lives across the Mediterranean.

The year 2015 was the deadliest for the conflict in Afghanistan to date. Civil unrest and chaos in Iraq also continues, with enormous human cost. Yet the country remains safe enough for international corporates to maintain oil flowing to the rest of the world. Meanwhile, the Syrian conflict alone has caused the largest population displacement this century – over 10 million people, which is 45% of the country's population, have been displaced and uprooted More than six million of these people are still in Syria, while over a million are in neighbouring Lebanon, comprising almost a third of the population there. Around three million Syrians fled to Turkey, where the European Union chose to make a deal with the government to block the flow of asylum seekers to Europe. This has been described by MSF as an "inhuman deal".†

People fleeing violence have little if any 'choice' to make about where they go. It is simply not possible for many to survive in a conflict zone. It is also impossible to stay in a country where you do not legally exist as a human being, where you are not allowed to work, where

---

* http://www.msf.org.uk/european-refugee-crisis

† http://scpr-syria.org/publications/policy-reports/confronting-fragmentation/

your children are not allowed to go to school, and where you are not able to access critically needed health care. These are not choices; or at least they are impossible choices.

What of our response in Europe, in the UK and in Scotland? On the other hand, European governments have an array of choices to make in response to people dying in the Mediterranean in attempt to reach to safety. On the other, no British, French or German person died in the Mediterranean trying to make it to their vacation spots in North Africa. This situation is morally and politically wrong. What makes watching people fleeing from war, while doing little or nothing, acceptable? Is it their differential identity: their nationality, their race, their religion or their gender?

It is plainly wrong to make economic justifications – buttressed with unpleasant predictability in the light of the Brexit vote – to build walls to exclude desperate people, and to turn our heads the other way. It is also unacceptable to make cultural differences the basis for fear and hatred, manufacturing myths about 'the other' so as to turn her or him into a threat. The language coming out of Theresa May's Government has been extremely depressing. The world is facing a human catastrophe and human beings should stand together in facing it. People in Syria, Lebanon, Jordan and Turkey are receiving refugees within host communities that have few resources and poor infrastructure, but are showing human solidarity and compassion nonetheless.

Scotland (within the limits of its powers), the UK, Europe, and the rest of the world can and should make better choices. Better than contracting out to other governments to operate as a police and border control point for refugees. Better than building walls. And way better than watching people drawn in the Mediterranean. Choices should not be made based on a one-sided calculation of the resources absorbed, by corrupt institutions, or on the basis of fear-mongering and illusions of difference and superiority. Choices in times of crisis should be made on a moral basis – the morality that leads us from moments of despair toward peace, enlightenment and human solidarity.

Safe passages should be guaranteed for those fleeing violence. Countries in Europe have a lot to offer and share. As I see it, Scotland has a flourishing society with a reputation reaching out for those under crisis. People need to be taken in to safety, with due regard to different kinds of vulnerability. It is not acceptable to focus on women as victims of gender-based violence and refuse to take in young men who are escaping recruitment to fight. Scotland can set an example here. In doing so it will benefit from having new and resilient people within its population.

But safe passages are not the only requirement in facing this humanitarian crisis. The long-term solution should be focus on ending war and conflict. This can only be achieved through serious disinvestment from the arms trade, through clear and transparent trade and corporate regulation, through investment in peacebuilding, and through political support for civil society in the affected countries. Scotland can press the UK and the EU towards more accountability for governments and corporations currently investing in conflict zones and in the economy of violence.

The Scottish government can also work toward improving the quality, accountability, and fairness of humanitarian aid. The failure of the humanitarian aid system is continuously maintaining the status quo, and mistrust between the supposed beneficiaries and funders. In some instances it is even acting as a catalyst in the fuelling of violence. Aid should be designed in a participatory and transparent way, and should be moved from a technocratic to a human development paradigm.

Scotland does not have stand-alone solutions to these huge problems, but it can play a part in being a welcoming society and in arguing for international action in a genuinely progressive way. The recent openness to refugees, while it leaves a lot more to be done, is pointing in the right direction.

Chapter 16

Is the time right for urban land reform?

Lee Bunce, Sara Marsden, Niamh Webster and Hamish Allan[*]

One of the most striking features of Scottish politics since the onset of devolution in 1999 has been the revival of land Reform as a political issue. From the Abolition of Feudal Tenure Act of 2000 to the Land Reform Act passed earlier this year the lifetime of the Scottish Parliament has witnessed genuine progress in a previously neglected aspect of public life. But at the same time it is clear that land reform in Scotland has come to mean rural land reform – be that reforms to allow community buyouts of land such as that seen in the Isle of Eigg, or provisions to provide greater security for Scotland's tenant farmers.

But Scotland's urban centres face land challenges of their own. With a housing shortage and rapidly rising rents it is fast becoming clear that Scotland faces a housing crisis, and furthermore a crisis linked firmly to issues of land. Could this be the next step in Scotland's land reform journey?

Consider, for example, the Lorne Street Community in Leith, which attracted headlines late in 2015. The case involves more than 200 residents facing eviction from more than 80 flats on Leith's Lorne Street after their landlord, a charity called The Agnes Hunter Trust, announced its intention to cash in on its assets. That 200 people, some of whom had lived in their home for several decades, could be so vulnerable to the whims of their landlord provoked a lively campaign by residents and supporters, with some decrying it as a modern day clearance.

Quite apart from the obvious distress caused to residents, it is not at all clear why they should be expected to leave their homes (such an outcome would be unthinkable elsewhere in Europe), or where they

* The authors are all involved in Common Weal Edinburgh North and Leith
Facebook: https://www.facebook.com/CommonWealENL/
Twitter: @CW_ENL
Web: http://commonweal-enl.org/

are expected to go. As one resident remarked in an interview with the *Edinburgh Evening News:* "Even if we were able and could afford to move out easily, all of the flats are unfurnished and there simply aren't any unfurnished flats in Edinburgh to deal with the huge scale of this upheaval." At the time of writing the influx of support for residents had pushed the Agnes Hunter Trust to agree to a 'moratorium' on eviction notices until early July 2016, giving residents time to attempt to set up a housing cooperative to buy out their homes.

The case of the Lorne Street Community represents a particularly egregious instance of wider societal trends. Across the UK as a whole we have witnessed rises in rents vastly outpace rises in wages, and research by the Resolution Foundation think-tank has suggested housing costs have risen faster in Scotland than anywhere else outside of London.

There are a number of reasons for this. Partly it is the result of the increased availability of mortgages, meaning more credit is chasing borrowers. Partly it is a result of financial speculation. And partly it is a result of inequality, as a large portion of the extra living space created in recent decades has found its way into the hands of the richest members of our society. There may also be a demographic element, with more single-person households among both young and old than ever before. It is also related to the value and availability of land.

Not far from Lorne Street lie swathes of derelict land on the Granton waterfront. Here land valued at £40 million in 2006 was sold for just £2.6 million in 2012 to a company registered in a British Virgin Islands tax haven. The large loss in value was a consequence of the 2008 financial crash. Once part of a grand plan redevelopment scheme, the land now sits tied up in the hands of obscure owners who avoid tax as they wait for the value of the land to appreciate.

The relevance of the Granton waterfront development becomes clear when we start to think about solutions, which are not in short supply. To protect those living in rented accommodation one option would be a stronger system of rent controls and tenant rights that would offer tenants greater security in the private rental sector. Such systems exist in many other countries, most notably Germany, and the idea has now gained the support of many SNP members.

But moving beyond rent controls, it is clear that more homes must be built, including socially rented homes. Indeed, all the major political parties, other than the Conservatives, made proposals along these lines in their 2016 Holyrood manifestos. The action-based think tank

Common Weal has proposed a National Housing Company as a means of doing this, which would fund the building of a new generation of social housing by borrowing against future rents. But all of this is contingent on the cost and availability of land.

How then can we bring derelict land such as the Granton waterfront into productive use? One option, proposed by Andy Wightman MSP, is that where land has been allocated for housing and the owner fails to develop it, the local council would be able to purchase the land at its original value. More generally however, a land value tax (LVT) would help bring derelict land into use. Although the precise details of LVT can vary, the basic idea is that taxation is paid on the value of land, and not on any developments that might exist on top of it. Land would be valued regularly with the tax taken being a percentage of that value. This discourages speculation in land and encourages productive use, since any gain in land value will be offset by tax. LVT has other benefits too. The revenues raised could allow for the scrapping of the outdated and unfair council tax, as well as capturing unearned wealth due to rises in land value. An example might be the rise in house values for homeowners along the Edinburgh tramlines, courtesy of massive public spending.

These ideas are not especially new or radical. Indeed many of them have been considered and rejected by previous SNP governments. As already mentioned, rent controls and secure tenancies exist already elsewhere in Europe, and the previous SNP government itself introduced some limited rent control mechanisms as part of its Private Tenancies Bill. Land Value Taxation has a long and distinguished history, and has been backed by economists as far back as Adam Smith. More recently it was strongly recommended for consideration to the Scottish Government by the Land Reform Review Group in 2014, while a Scottish Green Party amendment to the Land Reform Bill that would have brought derelict land into taxation was rejected just this year. So why should this parliament be any different?

The major story of May's Scottish Parliament election results was the loss of an overall majority for the SNP. As a minority administration the government must seek support from other parties to pass legislation and arguably the enlarged group of Scottish Green Party MSPs seems like the most likely avenue. The Scottish Green Party made housing and land reform priority issues in their Holyrood 2016 campaign, and their MSPs now include land reform campaigner Andy Wightman, a man whose name has become synonymous with land reform in Scotland.

But why assume the SNP will look for support from the Greens? Might they not just as easily look for support from elsewhere, and might they perhaps avoid land reform issues altogether?

There are reasons for optimism. For one, there exists considerable external pressure on the Scottish Government for greater action on urban land reform and housing issues. The sheer scale of the problem has made it impossible to ignore, giving rise to groups and campaigns like Living Rent. More established groups like Common Weal have also taken on the cause, launching in 2015 the 'Our Land' campaign with Women for Independence, journalist and land reform activist Lesley Riddoch and Andy Wightman. The momentum around these issues appears to be accelerating.

Equally there exists considerable internal pressure on the SNP administration from SNP party members. At its autumn conference in October 2015, SNP members made clear their desire for more radical action on land reform while the Land Reform Bill was still making its passage through parliament. It is likely that this pressure will persist.

All of these factors combined might just make change a possibility, and Scotland's land reform journey might just take a bold step forward.

Chapter 17

A right to health for the people of Scotland

Anuj Kapilashrami, Sara Marsden and Tony Robertson*

It is fundamentally unjust that systematic inequalities in Scotland today mean that some people live healthier, longer lives than many others. This is not just a concern for those most unfairly impacted: while declining deaths from alcohol, heart disease, most cancers and respiratory disease are encouraging, Scotland's population as a whole remains, in European terms, comparatively sick.

This can only change if there is a fundamental transformation in how we view health and how we understand its underlying causes. It is not about individual lifestyle choices; it is about structural change. We need our government in Scotland to commit to establishing a right to health for all. As a first step we need to foster a debate about exactly what a 'right to health' entails and then work together to address underlying social, economic, political and commercial determinants of health to address real change in the nation's health. A peoples' movement with a committed government can do just that. And it can make Scotland healthier.

Our question here is whether the outcome of the recent Scottish Parliamentary elections moves us toward a healthier Scotland? Another successful election performance from the back in May SNP left them clear winners, although without an overall majority how they work with other parties in parliament remains crucial. The SNP manifesto is therefore a good marker for judging the trajectory of policy.

The SNP is rightly proud of its tenacity in resisting the drift to a privately run NHS seen in other parts of the UK, and its 2016 manifesto made clear this continuing commitment. A publicly owned

* This chapter was written on behalf of the People's Health Movement steering group. See also: Kapilashrami A, Smith KE, Fustukian S et al. (2015). Social movements and public health advocacy in action: the UK people's health movement. *Journal of Public Health*, fdv085. Also *Scottish People's Health Manifesto 2016*, People's Health Movement (Scotland): https://twitter.com/PHMScotland/status/709771879578542081

and run NHS is essential to the health of the nation and access to it, an individual right. But for the health of the population overall, this is a sticking plaster.

While improving staffing in health facilities and reducing waiting lists to tackle ill-health is important, addressing the upstream determinants (e.g. food insecurity, inequalities, poverty) of ill-health is equally, if not more, significant in the long run. For instance, if a water supply becomes contaminated causing an outbreak of disease, an immediate health services response is of course essential, but an urgent priority is also to prevent continuing contamination, and also to understand and reduce the risk of a repeat incident.

There are not such 'quick' fixes to Scotland's ills, but we must not ignore the upstream determinants. Investment in a publicly owned NHS delivering quality healthcare is essential building block, but for prevention of ill health we know we need to go beyond this, and beyond asking people to make lifestyle choices which are supposedly better for their health. Without addressing upstream issues, we are not going to make the radical difference needed to reduce the burdens of ill health and the unfairness of its distribution. Peoples' health is affected by a complex interplay between numerous political, social, economic, environmental, commercial, as well as behavioural, factors. Not only that, they change over time.

One of the biggest current threats to health is the austerity plan of the UK government, something that the Scottish Government has tried (and hopefully will continue to try) to mitigate against. But the reality is that they have limited influence over direct policy changes. Studies have shown that austerity can have wide-ranging health consequences, particularly for the most vulnerable members of society, including, but not limited to, food poverty and benefit sanctions; psychological wellbeing and suicide; disability assessments and mental health; child health, and mental health.

This problem goes beyond the UK though, with Europe suffering from similar austerity policies. These changes, largely based on ideology rather than evidence, cause ill-health and the damage they do is not evenly distributed across the population, with the extent of damage depending on how that complex interplay of social, economic, commercial and environmental factors plays out.

Furthermore, changes in global political economy, brought about by developments in trade and economic policies, and international politics of warfare has significant impact on health. For example, another potentially looming threat – now thankfully looking as if it is hitting the buffers – is the Transatlantic Trade and Investment Partnership (TTIP) agreement prioritising the interests of companies ahead of public health, so likely constraining government action in the fight against (for instance) alcohol and tobacco-related ill health, and in maintaining standards of workplace health and labour standards. Precarious employment is endemic, our ageing population will have different needs, stigma is increasingly attached to welfare reliance, and corporate-led solutions or partnerships are now normal.

These are just a few of the complex factors at work that may negatively impact on the population's health, as well as increasing health inequalities. The unequal impact on health can be seen in various groups, particularly those most vulnerable and socially excluded. Health inequalities are found across many measures, not just those defined by indices of deprivation. For example young people have been more impacted by the austerity agenda through rising unemployment, and refugees, asylum seekers and undocumented migrants have relatively limited access to health and other services. One piece of research showed that people reporting as being from a mixed ethnic group and of African or Chinese origin were at higher risk of mental health detention, particularly long-term detention, compared to those from a white Scottish background.

It is in this context that the People's Health Movement (PHM) Manifesto came about. It was conceived as a way to spark debate, discussion and action to mitigate and ultimately prevent the harm caused by these threats. And it has sparked debate! The PHM Manifesto was developed and agreed upon from the involvement of, and dialogue between, hundreds of individuals, organisations and community groups from across the country. Its current iteration – this is a process – makes 20 demands (of everyone in our society, not just politicians) set around six key themes. They include health and care services, but go far beyond this including, for example, tackling poverty and inequalities; ensuring health is a core component in all policies; and putting democratic debate and accountability higher up on the agenda.

While there are synergies, it is striking how health is reduced largely to health service provision in the narrative on health in the SNP manifesto. Even where population health is explicitly addressed, its dominant focus is individual lifestyle choices and disease specific programmes (e.g. the provision of insulin pumps for diabetes).

The unfairness in health inequalities needs to be more explicitly acknowledged, as do the measures that will prevent them, in addition to those for treating ill-health as equitably as possible. Although there are building blocks for a healthier Scotland in non-health areas in the SNP manifesto, the narrative on health needs attention. Policies need to consistently acknowledge this with people and communities more meaningfully engaged to identify and address key priorities. And the more they do this, the more communities are enabled and empowered to help identify solutions, or at least make policies more directly speak to priorities. We have seen this develop amongst those engaged with the PHM Manifesto process.

Without explicit reference to health, the SNP manifesto does resonate in places with the PHM Manifesto. For instance, the SNP is committed to tackling poverty and inequalities, including setting up a Poverty and Inequality Commission to advise Ministers, and monitoring across all government portfolios. Poverty and inequalities are key determinants of health and health inequalities so should be included in this new body's remit, but not just as an after-thought.

The lack of changes proposed for the Scottish tax system are also disappointing, given the strong links between income inequality and health inequality and taxation policies being one of the key potential policy tools available to most governments. The SNP manifesto also lays out a plan for investing in children and young people's well being and education, and for ensuring community participation in key decision-making. It is also committed to protecting and promoting human rights, and a key provision here is the commitment to involving civil society in a process to identify which rights should be enshrined in law. The PHM's participatory process has identified that a right to health, along with health equality across any axis of vulnerability/ social location (e.g. ethnicity, disability), should be firmly on this agenda.

Perhaps the most concerning element of the SNP platform has been the very limited discussion of corporate power. Commercial determinants are powerful determinants of health and well-being, through many routes. Directly this can occur via their marketing strategies promoting unhealthy food and drink, the quest for profit above all else (rather than any 'good' for society) and through health and environmental impacts of production, safety, health and employment protection standards in the workplace. More indirectly, corporate lobbying at all levels in government and the EU contributes to the maintenance and strengthening of these increasingly exploitative and unhealthy dynamics.

On many issues it is clear that the SNP will need to continue to gain agreement from MSPs from other parties in order to govern effectively. As has been commented elsewhere, the election voting patterns seem to have revolved around Scotland's big constitutional question, and as the only other pro-independence party represented in parliament, the Green Party would seem natural partners here. Going on party manifestos, it seems likely that the overarching narrative of the unfairness of health inequalities and their structural causes would likely be strengthened if the SNP were to work predominantly with the Greens. They make explicit their position that health inequalities are unacceptable and also begin to acknowledge the structural causes. As well as helping develop a more holistic and incisive narrative, the Greens may be able to build on the SNP's limited proposals to challenge corporate power in their proposals for food sustainability plan and a new alcohol and obesity strategy.

Scottish Labour seem less likely partners if this were to depend only on the constitutional question, but the previous minority SNP government worked across party boundaries and the Labour manifesto has something in common with the SNP in its commitment to poverty alleviation and addressing inequalities in general, as well as supporting child development. However, despite acknowledging the link between ill-health and inequalities, and indeed austerity, the health narrative is dominated by health service discussion and some discussion of lifestyle choices particularly around physical activity. There is no explicit commitment to addressing commercial determinants of health, and very little policy addressing this, limited to a mention of the sugar tax.

No party is strong on addressing the structural determinants of health, including the Liberal Democrats and the Conservatives. And although there is some broad agreement on the need to tackle inequalities and poverty, as well as the need to support early years learning and development, the very dominant narrative of health is the NHS and health and social services more generally. So, if the SNP work issue-by-issue with different parties on different issues, the narrative of health determinants beyond health services is unlikely to develop coherence, and any challenge to corporate power would be particularly vulnerable to collaboration with parties less willing to regulate industry and tackle the social determinants of health.

How do we make the right to health a reality? Alongside tackling the wider determinants and encouraging a less superficial narrative on health, we need to focus our attention how policies and manifestos are developed, implemented and evaluated, including removing unfair power dynamics that prevent the real engagement and participation of communities. It seems the People's Health Movement and its allies has work to do.

Chapter 18

This restless house: where next for gender justice in Scotland?

Lesley Orr

A few weeks before the 2016 Scottish Election, on International Women's Day (IWD) Scottish Women's Aid (SWA) held its annual conference at Easter Road stadium. The theme was social justice – a fitting way to celebrate forty years of a feminist movement with the tagline 'changing attitudes, changing lives'. SWA not only provides vital services, refuge and advocacy in support of women, children and young people affected by domestic abuse, but has led the way in driving significant legal and social change in Scotland. Surrounded by pictures of Hibernian's 'Famous Five' from an era when men were men and women were supposed to know their place, First Minister Nicola Sturgeon congratulated SWA on its fortieth anniversary and highlighted its achievements at the forefront of a wider movement which, from the 1970s, rocked the complacent patriarchal status quo and claimed women's rights to live in freedom from fear, violence and the stultifying constraints of inequality in every aspect of their lives.

The mood was celebratory, as Women's Aid workers, activists and their allies from public and academic sectors, recalled that there had indeed been notable progress – particularly since devolution – in analysing, naming and developing a strategic approach to violence against women in all its manifestations, recognised as a cause and consequence of wider gender injustice. Sturgeon used the occasion to announce funding for supporting survivors of domestic abuse into employment. Women experiencing violence (and the men who perpetrate it) have always understood the connection between income disparity and power. When asked which interventions would be most effective and helpful, they list childcare, housing, income support, and education and skills above refuges. Economic inequality restricts choices, reduces access to justice, and makes it impossible simply 'to leave', whether the space being left is an exploitative workplace or one controlled by a coercive and abusive partner. But these resources for human flourishing are vital for *everyone* and are central to the project of gender justice.

The First Minister made her IWD 'Pledge for Parity' that day, stating, "I am determined that Scotland leads the way on gender equality." More than once she has said that this is her top priority: women's rights are human rights, and global evidence is clear that gender equality leads to better decisions, fairer policies, more participation, prosperity and peace for everyone in a society. With a 50/50 Cabinet, the symbolism and rhetoric all heading towards 'the tipping point on gender equality' she predicted in a speech at the Women 50:50 Conference in Edinburgh last year. Sturgeon say she wants to inspire girls to believe that the sky's the limit.

Campaigners for gender justice might be forgiven, in the current political landscape in Scotland, for thinking that it's hard to see the sky beyond the dirty glass ceiling. Aspirations and mechanisms to bring parity of representation in the Scottish Parliament have stalled at 35% behind Ruth Davidson's tank full of Conservative men, the sad demise of the last Lib Dem woman, and the perplexing failure of the Greens' well intentioned strategy to balance their list candidates. So we still haven't got beyond the 40% critical mass, and over-representation of men remains the norm rather than an outdated aberration in Scottish political life. And it's much worse in local councils.

The Women 50:50 campaign, highlighted elsewhere in this book, has galvanised wide cross-party support for equal access to power, decision-making and participation across political and public life. There is substantial evidence (most recently from the Republic of Ireland) that quota mechanisms are a vital key to accelerating parity and raising the profile of social justice issues more broadly. Unfortunately, the Scotland Bill failed to incorporate devolution of power to set gender quotas at all levels of politics, though there is commitment to do so for public boards.

But gender equality is not just a numbers game, and the new minority government will have to co-operate with other parties in developing policy and passing legislation. Both Labour and the Greens made significant manifesto pledges on gender equality issues, and there is considerable scope for the Parliament – in partnership with women's organisations, stakeholders and activists, and feminist academics – to be bold in tackling enormous challenges. This constitutes the 'velvet triangle' identified in research for the Fairer Caring Nations project by the Centre on Constitutional Change as one of the key features of policy development in countries with good records on gender equality – and it works effectively when based on interdependence and trust.

Professor Kirstein Rummery writes that during the 2011 majority SNP government: "Whilst funding to support the third sector continued, and good relationships between networks were developed and supported (for example between the Equalities and Budgetary Advisory Group and the Scottish Women's Budget Group), the power shifted. Academics and activists no longer felt as though they were key partners in the policy process, but that their role had been downgraded to be more advisory/consultative rather than participatory".[*]

Angela O'Hagan, convener of the Scottish Women's Budget Group, has noted that the civic and academic sides of that triangle are dynamic and extremely engaged in developing alternative proposals for long term, coherent and sustainable programming which mainstreams gender analysis and budgeting across all areas – tax and fiscal policy, welfare and social care, employment, transport, housing, justice and representation. Yet despite extensive consultations, briefings and responses from the women's sector, neither the Smith Commission nor the Scotland Act showed much interest in departing from an approach to political economy which masquerades as neutral, but is stubbornly androcentric. For a truly just and sustainable future, feminist voices must be heard and promoted beyond feminist spaces, and participatory gender budgeting analysis (GBA) is a pivotal demand.

This approach takes account of public spending decisions at all levels as they impact differentially on women and men (and on particular groups of women and men). Resource allocation frequently leads to unintended and unfair consequences. GBA highlights gender biases (rooted in unexamined perspectives and assumptions) within processes which are assumed to be gender neutral. It is an effective tool for strengthening equality of outcomes across all departments. To build on post-devolution progress in this direction, the Equality Budget Statement processes must be extended into a full gender analysis of the Scottish Budget.

For in spite of the rhetoric, and notwithstanding important progress, Scotland remains a nation where seemingly intractable gender injustice has profound impacts on the safety, opportunity and space for action of girls and women in all aspects of their daily lives. The wider context of global neo-liberalism, UK Government austerity measures and so-called welfare reform has sharply accentuated the

---

[*] CCC blog, 9th May 2016, *Backwards for gender equality in the new Scottish Parliament? Or a new Scottish velvet triangle?*

feminisation of poverty. The current relentless attack on hard won rights and benefits means a grotesque transfer of resources out of the hands of women – who are disproportionately affected by poverty, low pay, precarious employment, disabilities, discrimination and abuse. Between 2010 and 2014, 85% of the £26 billion worth of cuts came from women's incomes. The intersections of gender with ethnicity, age, legal and refugee status, rural location and so on compound the pernicious impacts in particular ways. A strategic approach to mitigate welfare reform is urgently needed to redress these inequalities.

Scotland has a deep well of knowledge and experience to draw upon for developing solutions to these challenges. Women are at the heart of politics as if people mattered – in protests, grassroots efforts to meet needs and respond to crises, in local campaigns, trade unions and civil society. Thinking globally and acting locally, women's and feminist organisations use participatory processes for listening and learning from the experts in their own lives; the diverse voices and stories which for far too long have been silenced or ignored.

Engender, Scotland's feminist organisation, gave excellent leadership in the run up to the 2016 Election and produced a Gender Matters Manifesto, setting out twenty achievable goals for the current Parliamentary term, within the scope of Holyrood powers:

> All of the issues that we raise and calls that we make in this manifesto are from an intersectional and inclusive perspective. This means ensuring equal access to change for women from all backgrounds and for women who face multiple discrimination...
> We are calling for diverse groups of women to be involved in designing and delivering the steps to progressive change that we set out, as one key route towards achieving these core aims of gender equality and empowerment for women.*

The Manifesto calls for a Gender Equality Bill to create a framework of 'gender governance' for coherent and strategic action across all devolved policy areas. It would enshrine political commitment at the highest levels, with ministerial accountability and mechanisms for compliance. Engender has mapped parties' manifesto commitments onto their own call for action, across key themes: politics and power, fair economy, care, social security, employment and the labour market, education and training, media and culture, violence against women and women's rights. Engender members and partners intend to hold their representatives to account and expect meaningful action.

---

* *Gender Matters Manifesto: Twenty for 2016,* p4.

Since the 2014 referendum, Women for Independence (WfI) has emerged as a significant non-aligned membership movement combining local activism and national campaigning. Before the May election, WfI conducted a major Listening Exercise involving hundreds of women in cities, towns and rural areas asking, "What do women want from the Scottish Parliament?" All the groups identified similar issues and priorities. WfIs want long term and more adventurous approaches to the care and wellbeing of older people; they are looking for enhanced flexibility and options in childcare; more power, participation and budgeting in and for the communities where people actually live. They challenge public sector authorities to take gender impact assessment seriously, because they know from harsh experience why it matters. Radical land reform, responsive health services and the politics of food are vital and connected issues for women who want good quality, affordable and locally produced food for their families, and space for their children to play in. WfI Justice Watch continues its high profile campaign on proposals for a progressive justice system which protects the rights of women and children rather than punishing them for the poverty, abuse and ill-health they suffer.

There is growing anger that women who mostly carry the double burden of labour – paid work and unpaid care – are also bearing the double blows of austerity. Funding for the public and third sector services they need is being cut to the bone, and that means mostly women's jobs too. It's time women counted – their huge unpaid contribution to 'productive' economy remains invisible in GDP and standard measures of national 'progress'. They are four times as likely to give up employment for multiple caring responsibilities, and to be in low paid, low status and part-time work. This has major impacts on their health, education, career progression and pensions.

Forty years on, SWA is still calling for long-term political commitment and resources to secure access to legal services, justice, safe homes and safe contact for women and children experiencing domestic abuse. The welfare and rights of refugee and asylum seeking women are particularly precarious. And the manifold mundane sexist violations and constraints of everyday life from cradle to grave are so pervasive as to be accepted as normal. These are cancers eating away at the health of our body politic and obstructing any facile claims of equality achieved.

The mainstreaming of gender, of using laws, policies, services, and budgets to distribute power and resources more equitably between women and men, is essential if we are to dismantle the conducive contexts for violence against women. Introducing a citizens' basic income, recasting social security as lifetime investment in wellbeing, and providing universal childcare would help to reframe care, less as a 'women's issue', but as core to economic development and sustainability. Quotas to create critical mass in industrial sectors, reframing traditional gendering of education and skills, and revaluation of 'women's work' in care, cleaning, catering, and administration would dismantle the horizontal gendered segregation that besets the Scottish labour market. Reconfiguring working patterns would provide increased flexibility and enable a fundamental recalibration of the balance between labour, leisure and life for women and men alike.

As the 2016 Holyrood election unfolded, the National Theatre of Scotland and Citizens Theatre were presenting a powerful reimagining of the Greek tragedy *Oresteia*. In *This Restless House,* a family and nation suffers the ruinous destructive consequences of violence and power abused Zinnie Harris subverts the patriarchal triumph

Gender equality is the heartbeat of justice. It must be strengthened to nourish and revitalise the commonweal, enshrined as foundational to our values and practices. The stewardship of Scotland's household (*oikoumene*) for fair sharing, sustenance and space to flourish is a noble and serious responsibility, and we have a right to expect nothing less from our Parliament.

Chapter 19

Enabling the participation of disabled people in politics

Jamie Szymkowiak and others[*]

I am very pleased and honoured to be elected to the Scottish Parliament but disappointed that so few other disabled people were elected. I think in the next five years all political parties need to see what can be done to encourage more disabled people to stand and get elected. If I can help in that process I will.[†]

On 5th May 2016 Scotland cast its votes, electing a fresh selection of yellow, blue, red, green and orange politicians to our parliament. Since then much ink has been spilled about the state of the parties, who is up and who is down. Less attention has been paid to who the 129 rosette-clad individuals are and what experience they bring.

A healthy democracy demands a parliament that reflects all those it seeks to serve. Disability can affect any one of us, in any number of ways, at any time. In Scotland, one in five of us are disabled. While our new parliament may not be devoid of disabled members, it is unfortunately far from representative. So far we know of only one MSP that has defined themselves as disabled, and another who has openly spoken about having a significant impairment. This may prove to be an underestimate if, in time, others choose to share their own experience. Even so, it is clear we have a long way to go – a representative Parliament would have 23 disabled members.

Scotland's vibrant and vocal disability movement will continue to lobby for change, but nothing compares to having individuals with first-hand experience of the barriers that disable us in the room when decisions are made and policy written.

More disabled people in politics means more who understand our lives and the challenges we face. That in turn means policies that work for everyone – and ultimately a fairer Scotland where we can all reach our potential.

---

[*] Written by: Gordon Aikman, Sarah Anderson, Hannah Bettsworth, Pam Duncan-Glancy, Ryan McMullan, Lorna Murchison, Nicola Ross, Jamie Szymkowiak and Jamie Walker.

[†] Jeremy Balfour MSP, Scottish Conservative Party, Lothian Region.

This chapter puts forward a series of positive, proactive measures from the One in Five campaign, which if implemented as a package, we believe will result in more disabled people being elected to office in 2021. We hope these proposals are something that all political parties can not only agree on, but can work together to deliver. Until we have a parliament that reflects all Scots, we have a job to do.

Political parties and accessibility

We call on Scotland's political parties to reaffirm their commitment to holding their meetings in accessible venues. This is just as important for regular local meetings as it is for launches and conferences. Asking the needs of your members is the only way to ensuring the venue is accessible as considerations beyond the obvious lifts and ramps may be necessary.

We ask Scotland's political parties to be more inclusive by embracing new technologies which offer the ability to live stream events and important meetings. Transport can be inaccessible or too costly, personal assistants might not always be available and crowded or busy spaces can be intimidating or uncomfortable for some. We recognise that in some rural locations, an accessible venue may prove difficult to source. In all of these circumstances, increasing the use of live streaming and other forms of "telepresence" can be a cost effective way of being more inclusive to all members.

The 2016 Scottish Parliament elections witnessed the production of a far greater range of accessible manifestos than ever before. We encourage Scotland's political parties to ensure future documents are produced earlier in the election campaign period thus allowing disabled people the time required to fully analyse their contents, including postal voters.

Accessible materials should not be limited to election manifestos and we would like to see the progress made in this area extended to other party and government documents.

Facing down exclusion with positive inclusion

People who have learning disabilities too often face lifelong exclusion and lack of opportunity to be part of their community, through work, transport, access or welfare. But their voices are too often not heard by those who represent them. That needs to change and ensuring people who have learning disabilities are empowered to participate in the democratic process as active citizens is a significant part of that change.

Timely, accessible, easy read information from political parties and government will make a real difference to people who have learning disabilities who are keen to exercise their democratic right and hold their elected representatives to account post-election.

Political parties must think about how they are engaging with potential voters, including those who have learning disabilities. Sometimes it is about thinking differently, but the solution you find works better for everyone." Kayleigh Thorpe, Campaigns and Policy Manager, ENABLE Scotland.

We should not limit accessibility to written formats. Communication through British Sign Language (BSL) interpreters and the use of hearing loops and subtitles will make politics accessible to more people.

We encourage Scotland's political parties to spot and harvest the talent of their disabled members through the creation or reestablishment of disabled members groups. If developed properly, these groups can contribute to policy creation and will provide a platform for disabled members to gain confidence, leading to increased considerations given to standing for elected office.

As a minimum requirement, we call on each of Scotland's main political parties to create a position on their National Executive Committee (or equivalent lead managerial body) for a Disability Officer. This will demonstrate to all members that the party leadership is taking positive steps to include disabled members within their party structures. Disabled people face different barriers to other underrepresented groups; it is our view that an Equalities Officer is not sufficient. In Parliament, we would encourage each party to appoint a Disability Spokesperson.

Where possible, we would like to see this filter down to local levels where each constituency party or branch has their own Disability Officer. Consideration should also be given to clearly defining organisational tasks and responsibilities yet ensuring they remain flexible enough to empower individual member ability.

We recognise that being an elected representative can present unique challenges and, of course, the same can be said for political activism in its entirety. Public speaking, tele-canvassing, speaking to a stranger on the doorstep or entering an on-line debate can be stressful and tiring. We encourage Scotland's political parties to look at appointing a Mental Health Representative who can champion mental health and help ensure the wellbeing of their party membership. Where possible, we would like to see each constituency party or local branch appoint their own mental health representative. In Parliament, we would encourage each party to appoint a Mental Health Spokesperson.

Everyone is Scotland can play their part in reducing the stigma associated to mental ill health. We invite Scotland's media, politicians, political parties and their members to use positive language when discussing mental health and disability in general.

To record our progress, we need more information on how we are doing now. We encourage Scotland's political parties to track their number of self-identifying disabled elected representatives including councillors, MSPs, MPs and MEPs. Parties may want to consider internal equality monitoring forms to ensure their party meets their member's accessibility requirements.

Elected office requirements

Given that one in five of the people they represent are disabled, it is imperative that 100% of MSPs attend Disability Equality Training (Inclusion Scotland is offering specifically tailored training for MSPs). Local authorities should consider similar training for their councillors.

We call on Scotland's Parliament and local authorities to consider including gym membership as part of their overall remuneration. It is our view that there is a link between mental health and physical activity. Physical activity allows people to become fitter which can enable people to better deal with issues such as anxiety and depression.

We call on Scotland's Parliament to provide their Members with the support of a Welfare Officer. This Welfare Officer would not be a member of any party and would provide support and non-political guidance confidentially, without the Member fearing internal party reputation damage. This should be available to both MSPs and parliamentary assistants. We believe having the support of such an individual will go some way to reducing the stigma associated with disability and mental ill health in politics. Parliament may wish to consider annual appointments for all its Members. Local authorities should consider similar support for their councillors.

Internships and Apprenticeships specifically created for disabled people should be established in every Scottish Government department, NHS Board and Local Authority. These should be supported through the expert advice on ensuring accessibility and inclusive practice, and peer support for the disabled interns during placement. – Phyl Meyer, Employability and Civic Participation Manager, Inclusion Scotland.

From declaration to implementation

We live in a Scotland where our aspirations for a better world are not just distant dreams of the disempowered; they are shared by many, from the streets to the benches of our Parliament. Nearly every day we hear public figures declaring that inequality must be addressed and human rights protected. That gives us hope. But hope is not quite enough. The 1 million disabled people in Scotland also need action. It's time to move from declaration to implementation.

If one in five of our MSPs or local councillors were disabled people, not only would there be pressure for action, we'd know more about what that action should be.

Initiatives such as the £200,000 Democratic Participation Fund and the Access to Politics Project, suggested by disabled people and set up in recent months are huge steps along our path to that better world. But if we are to see more disabled people returned to Parliament in 2021 or indeed in Councils in 2017, we also need to take the steps we have outlined above. The good news is, we know they will work, we know they are part of the solution to a more representative Parliament and an equal society. How do we know that? Because disabled people themselves have come up with these solutions. What we have set out above is not a random list of suggestions, but a set of concrete actions that lived experience and a bit of political know-how have developed.

Disabled people are innovative by design. We have to be. Just to get from A to B can require a lot of 'work arounds'. Supporting us to have our say in our country isn't just the right thing to do, it's bloomin' sensible! Our innovation should not be lost. To create a truly equal, prosperous and flourishing Scotland we have to harness the talents we all have and the experience we all bring.

We at One in Five are a group of disabled people who have come together with the common aim of making our politics more representative. Through our collective and disabled people led approach we have achieved so much more than we ever could have alone. That's why we believe in and embody, through our aims, the disabled people's mantra; 'nothing about us without us'. And we ask you the reader to do the same.

This is everyone's job. We need our political parties, Parliament and their people to work together and act now. Let's work our socks off so that when we wake up the morning after the 2021 election we switch on our televisions to a sea of disabled talent. We can be the nation that does it. We can lead the way.

Chapter 20

Fear, loathing and gentrifying paradise: regenerating arts and culture

Neil Cooper

On 27th April 2016, eight days before the last Scottish Parliament Election, I went along to a 'cultural hustings' which had been organised by the Scottish Artists Union at Out of the Blue in Edinburgh. The Scottish Artists Union is a visual artists lobbying body set up like other trade unions such as Equity and the Musicians Union to protect the employment rights of its members, particularly where issues of professional fees are concerned.

Out of the Blue is a community-based arts trust based in an old army drill hall in Leith. It is a mixture of studios, exhibition and meeting spaces and offices for small arts organisations. There is a café there too, and there's sometimes music as well, though nothing too late or too loud, because it's in a residential area. A promenade production of the stage adaptation of Irvine Welsh's novel, *Trainspotting*, was on there too, which was produced by a young unfunded theatre company called In-Yer-Face Theatre.

Out of the Blue originally began in 1994 as a shop-front gallery space in Blackfriars Street, just off the High Street, which later moved down the road to an old bus depot on New Street, where an initiative that connected artists studios to a music and club venue became better known as the Bongo Club. When City of Edinburgh Council decided to sell the New Street site to developers, the Bongo and Out of the Blue were forced to find new homes. While the Bongo moved into the University of Edinburgh's old Moray House student union, Out of the Blue took over the old army drill hall where it is now based, and where the Cultural Hustings took place.

The Bongo, meanwhile, was eventually forced to move again after the University of Edinburgh decided to convert the old Moray House site into offices. The Bongo moved into a space beneath Central Library which had been christened the Underbelly after Edinburgh-based site-specific theatre company Grid Iron produced a promenade show about food and sex called *Gargantua* there in 1998. Despite naming the venue, Grid Iron are not connected with Underbelly Productions, the London-based arts production company who take over the space in August during the Edinburgh Festival Fringe, when the Bongo Cub temporarily moves out.

Meanwhile on New Street, the old bus depot that housed the original Bongo Club and Out of the Blue was flattened by developers to build something called Caltongate. A wave of public protest did nothing to prevent the development, while assorted financial crashes conspired to leave a gap site in New Street for more than a decade.

When new developers came on board and the project now branded as New Waverley picked up the pieces, further public protest was again ignored, both by City of Edinburgh Council's Planning Department, and by the developers themselves. Somewhere along the way, a salve to culture was given by way of granting the Hidden Door pop-up festival access to house the 2014 festival in the old arches that had lain derelict and unoccupied on Market Street for years prior to development.

This is typical of developments brought before CEC's Planning Committee, which usually come armed with unspecified arts provision seemingly thrown in at random, and which mysteriously disappear off the plans when the development becomes bricks and mortar. Take a look at the most recent home for Hidden Door, who in 2015 and 2016 took over a former CEC owned lighting store on King Stables Road, which was flogged off to developers with plans for a hotel, residential property and, yes, an unspecified arts building. In the meantime, Hidden Door have been given grace (or more likely had to hire) to run a temporary arts village hosting a programme which in 2016 goes under the name of Electric City.

In a newspaper interview in April 2015, the convenor of CEC's Planning Committee described the site of the New Street Caltongate/New Waverley development's former use as 'a bus station'. He made no mention of its decade long tenure as the Bongo Club. Whether ideologically calculated or blissful ignorance, the statement was telling of a civic ignorance about Edinburgh's year-round arts landscape which seems to prevail across all departments, where a lack of anything resembling vision is nakedly transparent.

When I was writing this, a bunch of what are described as artisan retail outlets opened up in the now cleaned-up arches. It was being housed under the collective name of The Arches. Which, given that the Glasgow arts venue and club also called The Arches was forced to close down in 2015 after Police Scotland recommended that Glasgow Licensing Board revoke the late license that brought in the venue's main revenue stream, is accidentally but deeply ironic.

But at the 'cultural hustings' at Out of the Blue, it's unlikely that any of the six candidates on a panel hosted by Jim Tough were aware of much if any of this. This is understandable, because unless you live on Leith's doorstep and are keeping an eye on this kind of stuff, these things tend to get wiped out of history along with the bricks and mortar that made it. Jim Tough might know some of it. He's Executive Director of the Saltire Society, and used to be Combined Arts Director and then later Chief Executive at the Scottish Arts Council, Scotland's arts funding body that was given a glossy makeover and transformed into Creative Scotland.

As dysfunctional as the SAC could be sometimes, Jim Tough was one of the better things about it. Prior to working at the SAC, he established WHALE (Wester Hailes Arts for Leisure and Education), and probably knows more about arts access and all the other things discussed at the Cultural Hustings than anyone else in the room combined, party reps included.

The 'cultural hustings' featured representatives from six parties: Conservative, Labour, Liberal Democrat, SNP, Green and Rise. Tough read out a message from the local UKIP candidate regarding their thoughts on culture, which advocated the positive aspects of a night in the pub. No arguments there. Each representative then introduced himself or herself by outlining their own policies on arts and culture, before they took four pre-arranged questions from SAU members.

These introductions focused on access, cultural strategy, the state of Creative Scotland, the importance of art in people's everyday lives, the potential for arts funding increases, and notions of aspects of the arts being ring-fenced off for an elite. In response, the four questions raised issues of whether public galleries which charge admission fees are elitist, the fact that most artists lived below the poverty line, the creation of trusts to run public art spaces, and thoughts of furthering Scotland's links with Europe.

I'm sure reader could work out for themselves which party talked about what, and what their respective responses were to the four questions, although the full evening has been storified by the SAU on Twitter, complete with on-the-spot caricatures by cartoonist Terry Anderson.

Given the time restraints, no further questions could be taken from the floor. While this was a shame, given the format it was understandable, although it meant that things never really let rip beyond respective party lines.

There were two questions I wanted to ask at the hustings. While it may be unfair to the party reps to ask those questions here, now they've no right to reply, I'll ask them anyway, with a few thoughts of my own thrown in for still slightly unfair measure.

The two questions I would have asked the six political party representatives at the Cultural Hustings hosted by the Scottish Artists Union at Out of the Blue in Edinburgh on April 27th are:

- What are your views on the Agent of Change principle?

- How do you intend to prevent property developers using grass-roots arts and culture as a short cut to gentrification?

These are really two aspects of the same question, and relate to my opening comments as much as to what follows.

It's important that an event like the SAU's 'cultural hustings' was held in Out of the Blue, which is a pillar of how arts and culture develops from a community-based grassroots. It was significant too that we were in Leith, an area which both the political and financial establishment are starting to realise is, was, and always has been, a place where art and culture thrives.

This can be seen in events such as the annual Leith Late festival, which each year hosts an array of arts happenings in bars, shops and church halls in the neighbourhood. LeithLate's 2016 programme over a late June weekend was based around Out of the Blue, and among other things not only hosted a debate on the gentrification of the area, but produced a Leith bank note for distribution.

There have been significant independent art spaces in Leith such as Rhubaba, situated in an old warehouse on Arthur Street, and the Embassy, in a room beneath a yoga centre off Broughton Street. There is new music venue, Leith Depot, housed in what until recently was regarded as the worst pub in the city, and grassroots drama in the Village Pub Theatre.

The Biscuit Factory is a magnificently dilapidated space that houses exhibitions, events and club nights, and which in the morning smells like the early days of the Arches (Glasgow version). There is also the ongoing rebirth of Leith Theatre, a long neglected venue that once housed international theatre during Edinburgh International Festival as well as touring main-stage bands.

All of these are within walking distance of Out of the Blue. There is Leith Dockers Club, immortalised on film in the Dean Cavanagh and Irvine Welsh scripted TV movie, Wedding Belles. And there is Pilrig Church, where DIY music promoters Tracer Trails used to run an annual mini festival called Retreat!, and where spoken-word night Neu! Reekie! holds its annual Burns Supper.

This is all great, but also within a stone's throw from here are four supermarkets owned by multinational companies, and which exist a few blocks from each other, pricing local businesses out to the extent that at least one corner shop has closed this year, unable to compete. After being brutalised once in the 1960s, Leith Street is undergoing a second wave of renewal by way of a hotel development. Those behind its design rather fancifully style it as 'The Ribbon', though it is better and more accurately known locally as 'The Turd.'

Expensive student flats and hotels are being built on every patch of land going, not just in Leith, but across the city, like those in Tollcross where seminal music venues the Tap O'Laurieston and the Cas Rock used to be. The community in Lorne Street, meanwhile, is being forcibly evicted by a charity who are about to flog what used to be homes but is now mere real restate off to the highest bidder. Edinburgh Football Club social club, up by the Playhouse, where post-punk venue the Nite Club used to be, is about to be converted into flats. This is the case even though it exists above long-standing club bar, Planet, and even though CEC's Environmental Health department expressed reservations to CEC's Planning Committee, who granted the move, that there might be issues with noise, vibrations and odour from below.

All of which, in one magnificent messy boulevard of broken dreams, sums up, not just Edinburgh's Jekyll and Hyde relationship with art, whereby the city's artistic institutions and high-profile festivals up town act as a cover for the far more interesting things that feed them from the shadows of Leith and elsewhere. It also shows how the naked greed of property developers, hoteliers and supermarket chains will use all that great grassroots artistic activity that exists on our own doorstep as a shortcut to gentrification.

All of this is a very, very local issue. I know this because the current (October 2016) Culture Secretary, Fiona Hyslop, quite correctly told me so on social media. This was after I asked her in 2014 if anything could be done about the fact that the site of the Picture House, the former cinema turned music venue before it was sold off to Watfordbased pub chain, JD Wetherspoon, was being converted into a 900 capacity superpub.

Planning permission was granted by City of Edinburgh Council's Planning Committee Development Management sub-committee on a six-to-four vote. This was despite a petition from more than 13,000 local constituents objecting to the move, and despite four members of the fifteen-strong committee being absent, while one abstained. At time of writing this, what was once the Picture House, the Caley Palais and legendary arts venue Cafe Graffiti has been boarded up, with no visible signs of work, since December 2013.

But, given Ms Hyslop's response to my tweet, when does local cease to be 'local' and become something of national import? This is another question I would have liked to have asked the panel at the hustings, because on the rare occasion that CEC Planning Committee do make a sensible decision and adhere to local democracy, it suddenly becomes a national issue.

This has happened twice in Edinburgh recently. The first was when developers were granted permission on appeal to bulldoze away a restaurant in the Canonmills district so they could build flats. This was despite a high profile public campaign against the project which resulted in the developers proposals being unanimously rejected by CEC. An appeal by the developer saw the decision overturned by the Scottish Government.

The second and still ongoing incident concerns the long-running saga of the old Royal High School, in which developers and hoteliers proposal to convert the shamefully neglected building into an upmarket hotel was again rejected by CEC planning officials. A counter proposal by St Mary's Music School to take it over as their new premises that would include a 300-seat concert hall, has also been lobbied. Those behind the long-standing hotel bid have since appealed the decision against them, with a decision coming, again, not from local officials, but from the Scottish Government.

Both incidents are key to how local democracy and local arts and culture can be undermined by wealthy developers who can afford to hire expensive lawyers to take on both a cash-strapped local authority and grassroots initiatives, neither of whom have the financial resources to fight back.

Now that the Scottish Government has set a precedent of over-ruling local decisions and making them national in such a high profile and undemocratic manner, maybe they should go further. How about looking at the nationally imposed laws on public entertainment licenses, which in 2012 saw the absurd situation of a community group in the Highlands and Islands almost forced to pay a three figure sum to host an Easter egg and spoon race and bonnet competition? This happened because a particular local authority interpreted it as something that was okay because the Scottish Government legislation as written seemed to suggest that.

All of which, in various ways, is related to the Agent of Change principle, which, if implemented, could be the single biggest protector of grassroots arts and culture across Scotland in a way that demonstrates the seemingly contrary relationship between the local and the national in a positive, progressive light.

The Agent of Change principle is an initiative already implemented in Australia that is designed to protect small clubs and music venues in a way that puts them on an equal footing with developers. As it stands, if a developer puts up flats next to an existing venue, and the new residents complain about any noise from a venue which may have existed for several decades, the venue managers are presumed to be the bad guys, and the onus is on them to implement what might well be expensive sound-proofing on top of the regular sound-proofing they already have in place. In extreme cases, licenses can be threatened and venues closed.

The Agent of Change, on the other hand, says that, if a venue is an area first, then it is the developer's responsibility to provide sound-proofing, while, conversely, if a new venue opens close to residential property, then it is quite rightly the venue's responsibility to provide sound-proofing. Again, this is protecting the local from big business, whichever side of the fence that business may be on.

At the Out of the Blue hustings, only the Conservative representative on the panel mentioned Agent of Change, although apparently a few days earlier at another hustings that took place at the Wide Days music industry conference it understandably became something of a feature.

There are other things a progressive government should look to. As some of the candidates at the hustings advocated, a universal basic income should be introduced, not just for artists, but for everyone. This not only prevents the stigma of poverty, but opens up possibilities for those beyond a class who can already afford the breathing space to explore artistic endeavours of their own if they so choose to.

That will require a major cultural shift, and with that shift, there needs to be an end to top down thinking and a recognition that cultural strategies, cultural quarters and the managerialist invention of the creative industries are social engineering by any other name. While issues of access, inclusion and diversity in the arts are vital, attempting to define what art people should make or see is at best patronising, both to artists and audiences.

Cultural strategies were not responsible for the work of Robert Burns, Walter Scott, Irvine Welsh, J K Rowling or Ian Rankin. Nor can any cultural strategy take the credit for the work of Rebel Inc, Neu! Reekie!, Rally & Broad and the flourishing new wave of spoken-word nights that proliferate in Edinburgh and beyond. Nor were Bill Forsyth, Lynne Ramsay and Andrea Arnold part of any cultural strategy.

Edwin Morgan, Liz Lochhead and now Jackie Kay may have all been worthy Makars, but they were and remain artists of their own making first and foremost. As do Alasdair Gray, James Kelman, Janice Galloway and a new generation of fiction writers who followed in their wake. Rachel Maclean may be representing Scotland in the Venice Bienale, and Young Fathers may be playing the Edinburgh International Festival, but they became they artists they are out of something that has bugger all to do with cultural strategies. Artists make art, plain and simple. Bureaucrats strategise and categorise them at their peril.

Cultural strategies can't even take credit for the Glasgow Miracle, a superstitiously loaded rabbit's foot of a phrase which would rather put faith in some unspecified invisible force than the unique set of social, political, cultural and geographical circumstances that made all the Glasgow-based artists that cultural strategies have never been responsible for so world-beatingly successful.

No one told Jim Haynes, Richard Demarco and all the others to found the Traverse Theatre. Alan Horne didn't start up Postcard Records from his West Princes Street wardrobe because it ticked all the right boxes. And Bob Last and Hilary Morrison didn't create Fast Product records in their flat next to Edinburgh College of Art because they made up the quotas. Yet all of these went on to change the world.

As did as well Andy Arnold when he set up the Arches in a dilapidated railway viaduct beneath Glasgow Central Station. To be fair regarding the latter, if Glasgow hadn't been European City of Culture in 1990, it might never have happened, even though the Arches had never been part of any official plans.

Glasgow 1990 also gave rise to Tramway, the former Old Transport Museum in which Peter Brook housed his epic staging of *The*

Mahabharata in 1988, and which became a permanent venue two years later. In Tramway's early years, major international theatre-makers, including Brook, Quebecois maestro Robert Lepage and New York avant-gardists The Wooster Group seemed to play there every other week.

This was a key influence on the generation of Scotland's theatre-makers who followed in the wake of such ambitious programming, were exposed to such work where previously they could only hear about such legends second-hand, and who are now producing internationally renowned work of their own. Getting home grown work abroad is crucial, but a two-way traffic needs to be retained. Artists don't create in a vacuum, and exposure to work from cultures and traditions from elsewhere is as crucial as developing a tradition and a canon of one's own.

None of this was helped by the sad closure in 2015 of the Arches, a shameful example of social engineering of the worst possible kind, which tarnishes Glasgow as a city, and which undermines everything that 1990 was supposed to be about. Over its almost twenty-five year existence, The Arches grew to become one of the world's greatest venues for young performers to develop their performance-based work.

As a club venue, the Arches also played host to the most democratic, inclusive and participatory art form of all. Its closure is a damning indictment of an ideology-led decision which decrees that forms of culture seen by some as a threat will be shut down, no questions asked. And if Police Scotland and Glasgow Licensing Board want to clampdown on drug taking in public spaces, try any bar in any city centre anywhere. Most of the drugs are on tap.

Something similar to what happened with the Arches demise occurred when Glasgow's city fathers banned punk gigs in the 1970s, and when the Criminal Justice Act in the 1990s attempted to outlaw club culture. All any of those incidents succeeded in doing was to politicise those involved in those scenes and help make them savvier to institutional interference.

The notion of cultural quarters, meanwhile, is a dishonest and dead-eyed phrase designed to make property developers rich. Cultural quarters are short-term pursuits that gentrify areas once pumping with messy freeform energy before those developers rip the heart out of them even as they remain happy to trade on those areas' gloriously unlegislated pasts. See New York, London and beyond.

As for the Creative Industries, as the phrase itself points to, the idea of putting two seemingly contrary words together and forcing them to mean something looks clever, but think about it for a minute and it isn't really. Yet there is a generation of arts bureaucrats out there who went on expensive management training courses and came out believing they were leaders who are evangelical about such guff.

Listen to any arts bureaucrat giving evidence at Holyrood about, say, the ongoing inability to support a film industry which has been trying to get backing for a permanent film studio to be built for decades now, and while individual words might sound impressive, strung together in such a way they are rendered as meaningless as the word 'Creative' itself has become.

It's like 'Centres of Excellence' and 'Emerging Artist.' They mean well, these big, buzzy, soundbitey phrases that are there, initially at least, to try and justify flagship arts buildings with a sweep of triumphalism in the former, or to empower those taking baby steps as artists in the latter. In the end, however, these phrases become as reductive as the ideologies they sprang from.

And so to Creative Scotland, which almost imploded in 2012 following an artists revolt in response to what appeared to be an organisation more interested in itself rather than the artists and organisations it was there to serve. The language used was the sort of managerialist twaddle outlined above, while those in charge appeared to believe they were curators or producers rather than the administrators they were. The pictures of the CS team at the Cannes Film Festival as artists earning below the minimum wage struggled to fill in incomprehensible funding application forms back home didn't help much either.

Creative Scotland has really tried since the organisation's then CEO and deputy were ushered out of Waverleygate, the former post office where arty types used to cash their dole cheques in what was regarded by many as an Arts Council grant by stealth, but which has now been converted into a hot-desking state-of-art office block. CS brought in a new CEO and seemed to have brought the artistic community back onside when a palace coup had been brewing. They said they'd changed the language they used, brought in apparently simpler application forms and introduced an open funding stream alongside regularly funded organisations. Which sounded great until you read the CEO's blog, which used the word 'journey' in a way defined by the title of Tony Blair's autobiography.

On top of this, barely a day seemed to go by throughout 2013 and much of 2014 when I didn't stumble on an unprompted conversation with artists or else receive unsolicited emails and phone calls from artists or those working in established arts organisations who were tearing their hair out trying to wade through one of the new forms. No one knew who was making decisions. Artists were being turned down for applications with standard letters, and only when those artists appealed did they sometimes discover that the funding stream they'd been advised to go through wasn't relevant to them. And every time I sat down to write an email explaining to CS' head of communications why I thought nothing had changed at CS, something else happened to confirm it.

Discovering that the high profile management training company which the same CS head of communications assured me had never been used by CS had in fact been funded to the tune of £15,000 in the same funding round that DIY music festival, Music is the Music Thing, had been knocked back for the same amount, however, bothers me still. But at least no one was telling anyone what art they should be making anymore, even if the language still resembled that used in BBC based mockumentary sitcom, W1A.

Don't get me wrong. Creative Scotland has a lot of fine people working for the organisation who are dedicated to the cause more than the likes of me have probably given them credit for in the past, and CS quite rightly supports or has supported many of the artists, projects and organisations mentioned here. I know of at least one member of CS staff who I regard as a visionary. Unfortunately they are not in charge of the organisation. Nor, I suspect, would they want to be. But until those who are in charge are more open about who is making funding decisions and why, suspicions that they are operating with the same top-down managerialist philosophy as the old regime will remain.

CS recently announced a list of forty-three 'independent Peer Reviewers.' Drawn from an open call, these forty-three artists and arts professionals have been appointed by CS to 'help in the work to deliver an Artistic and Creative Review Framework' established to 'create an open dialogue with Regularly Funded Organisations (RFOs) regarding the artistic and creative quality of their work.' At first glance, beyond the lingering managerialist tone, this looks like a good move, akin to the SAC's old panels of assessors drawn from the arts community. And they are all fine names, the new CS 43, who come armed with serious knowledge about their respective specialisms, and who collectively might even know as much as Jim Tough.

What perhaps isn't clear is how much influence they will have, and how readily their advice may be ignored as faceless mandarins make their own decisions beyond what may well be little more than a 43 person wall of pseudo-democracy ring-fencing a closed room of unaccountability beyond. And if publicly funded artists need to be accountable, so do publicly funded arts bureaucrats.

I fully appreciate that the 3% funding cut that the Scottish Government has imposed on Creative Scotland when the arts budget should really be doubled makes it difficult to operate effectively. But then, CS cutting regularly funded organisations' annual budgets – however difficult that decision may have been for whoever made it – isn't a good look either.

But beyond funding bodies, if arts and culture are to become central to people's lives, and not seen as the play-things of the rich, as more enlightened politicians say is the case, they need to experience it from an early age.

At a conference on the Declaration of Human Rights act in Glasgow earlier this year, I was invited to sit on the panel looking at Article 27 of the Declaration, The Right to Participate in Cultural Life. While this gets to the nub of issues of access and diversity, it was acknowledged from the off that 'Cultural Life' is such a broad term that it can't really be pinned down as one particular thing, and that's fine.

I found myself talking about the Pavilion, Glasgow's great popular theatre, which, unfunded and largely unsung, packs in the sorts of working class audiences that most subsidised theatres would kill for. It is in the Pavilion, which styles itself as 'Scotland's National Theatre of Variety', and other venues like it, where something akin to a hidden audience take part in a form of culture that isn't written about in the broadsheets, but which counts just as much.

It is a culture that comes from spit and sawdust social clubs and cabaret that existed long before the pub chains moved in, and which still exist, just about. Once upon a time such places were as key to providing a central base for a local community as church halls were. They are the sorts of spaces too – the Leith Dockers Clubs and the Pilrig Churches – that a younger generation of performers and audiences are returning to beyond the purpose-built but often soulless centres of excellence mentioned earlier.

At the Declaration conference, I also found myself talking about

Biffa Bacon, who is one of my favourite characters in adult comic, Viz. Biffa Bacon is a potty-mouthed pastiche of Bully Beef, who terrorised less physically endowed and more bookish looking kids in the pages of DC Thomson's comic, The Dandy, where his main adversary, Chips, invariably outsmarted his dim-witted nemesis.

This is where education comes into play at its most broad. If one library is closed, if one school can no longer afford theatre trips or music tuition, if one school can no longer bring visiting writers into enlighten students, all because of local authority cuts which have been implemented by Holyrood, the Scottish Government will have failed themselves, the country's artistic community, and, crucially, future generations of Scottish citizens.

Beyond all this, I would urge everyone involved in supporting arts and culture in Scotland to do one thing. Get out more. Failing that, at least try and widen your cultural frame of reference. 7:84's production of John McGrath's *The Cheviot, The Stag and the Black, Black Oil* was a theatrical landmark when it first appeared in 1973, and it remains important, as Dundee Rep's latest revival (the Scottish tour ended on 22nd October 2016) has shown.

But quite a lot has happened since then, both in theatre and in other art forms. John Byrne's The Slab Boys, the National Theatre of Scotland's productions of Black Watch and Our Ladies of Perpetual Succour, and less obvious but equally thrilling work like This Restless House, Zinnie Harris' epic reimagining of Aeschylus' Oresteia, seen recently at the Citizens Theatre in Glasgow.

Contrary to popular belief, the working classes can cope with difficult work as well as the stuff that goes on at the Pavilion. The Citizens is a prime example of this. Back in the 1960s and 1970s, the Gorbals-based theatre was taking Goethe, Schiller and Noel Coward to the masses in a way that has continued under the theatre's current regime.

All of that is as vital and as important as anything 7:84 did, but go and see Mary Poppins as well next time it comes round. It may not be produced in Scotland, but it is the best piece of touring commercial theatre you're ever likely to see, and anyone who claims to be or has aspirations to be radical in art or life can learn tons from it. And stop saying opera is elitist. It's not. Those ridiculously circular arguments about what constitutes high or low art were put out to grass a long time ago, and reviving them is a step back into the dark ages.

Opera is for everyone. Remember Pavarotti and Nessum Dorma

at the 1990 World Cup? Tickets are probably cheaper than a football match too. Oh, and art for art's sake is just fine, thanks. Not all the time, because different artists have different concerns at different points in time depending what is or isn't going on in the world, and a one size fits all approach just won't work. And that's okay too, because no art or artist in any field comes fully formed, and for every work of international genius that defines a moment, it's usually taken years of unsung experiment to get there. It's a bit like Alasdair Gray's much vaunted early days of a better nation, really. Nobody really knows what they're doing until they get there.

These are some indicators as to how arts and culture needs to be developed, nurtured and preserved. Because unless the Scottish Government start saying no to property tycoons and starts protecting the grassroots local culture from those who would price it out of existence, then that culture will be strangled at birth. So let's not gentrify the roughshod paradise that exists in Leith and other places where culture thrives of it's own volition. The early days of a better nation are already here. Why bulldoze them away?

Chapter 21

Childcare reform and the case for a major cultural shift

Vonny Moyes[*]

In all of my adult life, almost nothing has been as difficult as returning to full-time work. It has been the single most challenging issue in a decade of parenting.

Like most little girls in the '80s, I grew up fully believing the myth we inherited from third-wave feminism: the world was ours, and we could have it all. I could pick a career, get married, pop out my 2.4 children, and as long as I paired it with some shoulder pads, a briefcase and a hunger to achieve, success was guaranteed. There foundations had been laid by our mothers and grandmothers: there was no longer any need to choose between vocation and procreation.

So I stuck in at school. I worked hard. I studied. I carved out a career path and did the things that were expected of me. Then, as many women do, I did get married. I had a family, and then, in opposition to my well-made plan, I also got divorced. And soon the bills outstepped my income. So I had to go back to full time work.

I was lucky. I'd spent years freelancing around my family, and I had the skills to offer, so I found my Goldilocks job quickly. It was enough to set us on the right path. I wouldn't have to count beans. I could be the mother who did it all.

I made it through a lengthy, excruciating recruitment process. The whole time knowing that the right childcare was the keystone in the plan – without it, it was meaningless. It was around this point that I found myself in unchartered territory without a map. I had to find care for four children that fit my hours. I had to find the money to pay two childminders weekly until my first wage came through. I had to beg for leniency from my new employer. There were so many obstacles before I'd even set foot in the door.

I sought advice from support groups, but there were none. The Job Centre was no help, even when I itemised my costs and asked

---

* Related: 'The high price of getting fit is a barrier to women', The National: http://www.thenational.scot/comment/vonny-moyes-the-high-price-of-getting-fit-is-a-barrier-to-women.22829

for a bridging loan. If I wanted a life beyond my own four walls, and beyond the definition imposed by parenthood, I had to become the cartographer of and the navigator through my own childcare crisis. I had to bootstrap my way out of motherhood and into the work. No one could show me the way.

The most soul crushing moment was the realisation that after application, interviews, exams and selection, I may have to turn down the job offer. The only way I could take it was to initially split my children up, borrow money, and add 60 minutes onto either end of my commute for the first few months. I lost count of the times I considered if it was worth it. What was worse: feeling like a failure or total emotional burnout?

This is just my experience, and is by no means universal. But canvassing my peers, many of whom are also parents now, I see versions of the same story playing out in each home. Facebook posts about jobs turned down. Friends whose entire wages are negated by fees. Childcare is crippling families. No one can offer any solace; just their own horror stories of trying to have children, and be something other than a parent as well.

Of course it's simplistic to consider it a women's issue – but when childcare becomes the deal-breaker, it's often mothers who have the biggest sacrifice to make. Careers given up. Careers not started. Opportunities passed up because of the split priorities. Breaks taken when their male colleagues are leaning in and reaping the rewards. Women cede their dreams, their aspirations, their earning potential and even their dignity to bridge the gaps in the system. They tell their own little girls the same Cinderella story, that they can be whatever they want, knowing full well their example counters it. We are the generation of mothers who cannot lead by example.

A working childcare system is an indicator species – it's the marker of a healthy society. Surveying the childcare landscape in Scotland, the conclusions drawn are of anything but. Inflexible, costly, geographically unequal provision demonstrates a culture that isn't serious about women's prospects. Equality is lauded at every turn, when the most fundamental barrier to women's full participation in work, study and improving their own prospects is unavailable or unsuitable.

On paper at least, the new Scottish government seems committed to overhauling Scotland's childcare offer, going so far as to state their wish this to be the best place for children to grow up. But what about mothers? Generations of women have leaned out of their potential because they've been forced to play second fiddle to their biology, and the inherited disparate division of home and emotional labour that comes in tandem with motherhood. No doubling of free childcare hours will be enough to fix that.

Delivering these plans is an ambitious task – one that I'm not sure is realistic. Though I hope that the SNP understand the weight of this ambition; if they fail to put childcare reform front and centre, they fail to repair the systematic erosion of women's worth. The price of the delivery is far higher than becoming just another empty political promise.

At the October 2016 SNP conference the party leader and First Minister, Nicola Sturgeon, announced that the government she leads will embark on what she called a "childcare revolution". This means parents choosing the non-school childcare provider of their choice (private or public) and local councils providing the funding. "In other words, the funding will follow the child, not the other way round." This is already causing a good deal of debate. Is it really the privatisation of childcare, will low income families really have any choice, and will the local funding prove adequate?

If the SNP don't get it right on childcare, they not only fail a generation of working-age women, they fail an entire generation of children too. Childcare does not exist in isolation; reformation of this vital service benefits society as a whole. Without robust, realistic and consistent childcare solutions, the SNP will not make the impact on poverty that it hopes. Childcare is the structural support of a fully functional society. A broken system affects everyone – not just children and families.

Is it possible to fix these issues in the lifecycle of a government? Likely not. But if the SNP are serious, they will be using their time to lay the foundations of a more equal future for all citizens. That starts with make sure everyone, regardless of background or income, can be more than the fruit of their wombs.

This is far more than solving a childcare system. The real challenge is laying the foundations of for the next generation of women to believe in themselves. Will one government ever be capable of rising to that challenge?

Chapter 22

How might Scotland handle its taxation powers?

Wendy Bradley

It is a truth universally acknowledged that the UK tax system is over-complicated, and that the tax code underpinning it is one of the longest in the world. How should Scotland make use of the devolution of some taxation powers without risking the Scottish tax landscape resembling the old joke about gradually changing which side of the road we drive on, starting with just lorry drivers?

The taxes actually devolved to date are, sensibly, those concerned with land and buildings. This means they can be tied to a physical location in Scotland, so the questions of cross-border avoidance and/or arbitrage are minimised. The Land and Buildings Transaction Tax (LBTT) replaced UK Stamp Duty Land Tax, and Scottish Landfill Tax replaced the UK Aggregates Levy, both with a starting date of 1st April 2015. An Additional Dwelling Supplement – a charge on second homes and buy to let properties – was added to LBTT from 1 April 2016.

They both seem to be well-designed taxes, the slight differences between the Scottish and rest of UK designs being positive ones arrived at in consultation with the relevant industries.

How they are both administered is slightly more interesting: there is a new non-ministerial public body, Revenue Scotland, set up at the start of 2015 with a relatively modest 40 members of staff, mostly taken from the existing tax and legal professions, and it has governance and stakeholder arrangements very similar to those of HMRC. This is enough of a taxing authority to set some rules but not the kind of presence required to administer and collect the full set of taxes, and nothing like the 56,000 or so staff working in HMRC.

Contrast this with the administration of the Scottish Rate of Income Tax (SRIT), where responsibility will rest entirely with HMRC. SRIT will be paid into the Consolidated Fund alongside all other taxes collected by HMRC, and then an equivalent amount paid over to the Scottish government. HMRC has the mechanisms in place to collect

PAYE of course, from computer systems on which returns are made and captured to the banking and payment systems through which is paid. As well as collecting the money, HMRC and not Revenue Scotland will administer the SRIT and investigate any question of whether a person is a Scottish taxpayer or not.

As it says in the memorandum of understanding signed between HRMC and the Scottish government in 2013: "Any issues of dispute about the tax will be matters between Scottish taxpayers and HMRC. Scottish Ministers will be responsible for the tax rate but not for any other element of the tax nor for its administration."

The decision point in 2016 and beyond, then, is what to do about the rate of income tax and the Scottish Rate of Tax in particular. Although the Scottish Government has had the power to vary the rate of income tax in Scotland by up to 3p since 1998 (the Scottish Variable Rate) the power was never used (and there is some doubt whether the tax system had the capacity to administer it if it had been). Last year, however, Scottish taxpayers – and what precisely that means is an interesting question in itself – were notified by HMRC that they will pay the Scottish Rate of Income Tax (SRIT) on their PAYE and pension income from April 2016. Scottish taxpayers will have their UK tax reduced by 10p in the pound and the Government must decide whether the Scottish Rate Income Tax which is added back to replace it is the same as, less than or more than that 10p.

This is the Kobiyashi Maru of tax: an unwinnable exercise, politically. If the Government makes no change to the tax rate (leaving Scottish taxpayers charged exactly the same as other UK taxpayers) then the UK government will no doubt argue that there is no need for a devolved power at all. If they charge less, the amount they receive from the consolidated fund will be less than in previous years, but if they charge more then they risk being labelled "uncompetitive" and creating a new cottage industry in tax-inspired border-hopping

The rate change itself applies only to PAYE and pensions income, not to savings and dividend income. This leaves a gaping hole in the SRIT concept which will create opportunities for potential tax receipts to trickle away from Scottish coffers. Consider the use of personal service companies, with which many industries, particularly those working in IT and in the oil industry, are riddled as an alternative to direct employment relationships.

Under those circumstances a company is engaged to provide the services of Important Person, and the company is paid a fee for their services. The company is of course owned by owned by Important Person, or perhaps by Important Person and Their Spouse. Once that fee is lodged in the company, the company can then pay whatever salary and dividends it pleases, (subject to some legal limits and a longstanding tax anti-avoidance mechanism called IR35).

So you might want Star Speaker to deliver a lecture at your annual conference. It's arranged through her company Star Speaker Ltd and her fee is paid to Star Speaker Ltd. Star herself, being the boss, has an agreement that Star Speaker Ltd will pay her a salary of the minimum wage and as she is a Scottish taxpayer, 10p in every pound of the tax she pays on her minimum wage goes to the Scottish government ... but then at the end of the year when she finds the company has half a million pounds in profits, she happily pays herself and her spouse a dividend amounting to half a million and the tax on the dividend income is NOT subject to SRIT but to the UK-wide rate.

If the Scottish Government decided to put up the Scottish rate in order to get more income, or down to make Scotland more "competitive", how would the ratio of salary to dividend change, do we imagine?

As the tax year runs from 6th April one year to 5th April the next, we are already in the 2016/17 tax year and the rate of SRIT remains 10%: taxpayers with the letter "S" in front of their tax code (the identifying letter that shows that you're paying Scottish Rate of Income Tax – check your payslip) will pay exactly the same amount as they would if they weren't considered a Scottish tax payer.

In 2017, however, the Scottish Government will have the power not simply to change the rate of tax but the point at which the different rates bite. The SNP's policy is to keep the rate at which the higher, 40%, rate bites from rising as it will in the rest of the UK and to retain £43,001 as the starting point for higher rate tax, revaluing it by inflation each year. This is what's known as "fiscal drag". You can scarcely consider someone on £43,001 as a filthy plutocrat in these inflated days, but while English taxpayers won't be considered high earners till they reach £45,000 in 2017, Scotland's will suffer the 40% rate at £43,001 plus inflation. Scottish middle income earners will lose about £500 a year, but they won't notice.

If collecting tax is, as satirist Stephen Colbert suggested, all about "plucking the goose as to get the most feathers with the least hissing" then fiscal drag is a nice way of doing so – middle earners will lose about £500 which George Osborne is giving to English taxpayers by raising the 40% rate threshold, but it isn't money they have ever had in the first place, so perhaps is less painful and will produce less hissing.

Is this, however, what setting up Scottish independent taxation should be about? Looking at the detail of the fully devolved Land and Buildings Transaction Tax and Scottish Landfill Tax on the Revenue Scotland website I was struck at how complex they looked, how like their UK-wide equivalents. The next tax to be devolved to Scotland is Air Passenger Duty, planned for April 2018. This is the tax on air travel and the detail is all about whether to charge per plane or per passenger: should Scotland reduce or even abolish the tax altogether to encourage more travel and tourism, or is there a place for green taxes to discourage the less environmentally friendly forms of travel?

The danger, it seems to me, is that Scotland will advance step by step into as complex and convoluted a taxation system as the rest of the UK as the different areas are devolved piecemeal. A staff of 40 people in Revenue Scotland will be able to do little more than put a tartan gloss on the infrastructure already designed elsewhere and handed over with its rivets showing.

As with the old joke about asking directions, if you were designing a rational tax system you "wouldn't start from here". Is Scotland going to double the complexity of the UK tax system by adopting all the UK tax structures but with its own thresholds and tweaks and administrative improvements to the underlying structure but leaving the underlying structure intact? Will businesses and individuals have to calculate all their taxes twice, once for UK and once for Scottish (and perhaps again, ultimately, if Welsh and Northern Irish devolution lead to transfer of taxing powers there as well) and then work out which country should be the base of which activity? Or can Scotland do better?

One area where there might be scope for improvement is in the administration of taxes. As HMRC moves towards a batch processing system, replacing local tax offices with huge regional centres, doing away with face to face contact in favour of "self service" internet systems backed up with webinars and the occasional telephone helpline, perhaps there is scope for Scotland to go a different way? Imagine a network of regional government offices – so that Scottish citizens could go somewhere and talk to someone local who could point them towards their rights and responsibilities, show them how to fill in the forms for the taxes and for other transactions with their governments. Instead of two giant processing centres in Edinburgh and Glasgow the Scottish government could model its tax and service offering on the NHS and keep it local, accessible; remembering always that it is a public service?

We may not have wanted to start from here, but this is where we are. The question Scotland needs to be asking is, not where we start but where we finish? What is the endgame for a devolved Scottish taxing power? The same as before but with a tartan gloss, or something radically different and better? The decisions that are made in this Parliament will start us on the way.

Chapter 23

Building on LGBTIQ+ equality gains

Kirsty MacAlpine

The year 2020 will mark the twentieth anniversary of the 'Keep the Clause' campaign, the privately funded attempt to stop the repeal of Section 28 of the Local Government Act 1988. This clause stated that a local authority "shall not intentionally promote homosexuality or publish material with the intention of promoting homosexuality." It also prohibited the "promotion of teaching ... the acceptability of homosexuality as a pretended family relationship". The campaign, funded by Brian Souter, was fierce. Many readers will remember billboards emblazoned with slogans about protecting children from harm, and front-page headlines screaming about 'Gay Sex Lessons for Scots Schools' from some of the tabloid press.

I mention this as a marker for how far Scotland has come in a relatively short space of time. I was a young teenager in 2000 and, like many others, I could never have imagined that we would ever see a Scotland where the majority of parliamentary party leaders were gay or bisexual. Or that we would have seen some of these same leaders posing for the classic election day 'I'm walking to the polling station to vote' photo hand in hand with their partners like the photos of Kezia Dugdale and her partner Louise, and Ruth Davidson and her partner Jen; a perfect picture of normalcy.

Thirteen-year-old me, part of the Scottish Parliament generation who had attended the opening with her school classmates would never have thought that it could become the Parliament with the highest proportion of LGB politicians in the world, or that she would be in a party with the highest percentage of LGB elected Parliamentarians.

Now Scotland, for the second year running, has unofficially topped the list of countries in Europe with the best laws for LGBTI people with a 90 per cent rating. I say unofficially as we are not counted as our own country (yet). As part of the UK we drop to third with a rating of 81per cent.

All in all it looks like being an LGBTIQ+ person in Scotland in 2016 and 2017 is pretty rosy. And don't get me wrong it is better than it has ever been. But it isn't perfect, not by a long stretch.

We regularly hear of people being homophobically abused in public places across Scotland. One of the areas that we need to work on over the next term is strengthening hate crime legislation and clarifying reporting practices. I'd like to see more guidance about where to go if you have been abused and better signposting on websites and apps as well as clearer information in stations, stadia, restaurants, airports about who is the best person to talk to in their organisation to report what has happened, safe in the knowledge that they will be able to take appropriate action.

Talking of stadia, in the biggest sport in our country, football, there has never been a single out gay, male, professional player; this is also the case for rugby and tennis. It is theoretically possible that no gay man has ever played professional sport in the top sports in this country. But it is far more likely that no gay man has ever felt that the support would be there for them to publically come out. This isn't something that can be changed overnight. In fact it requires a wider change in attitudes across sporting culture at all levels removing the barriers that too many LGBTIQ+ people face when trying to play sport at all levels. The work of organisations such as LEAP Sports and the Equality Network who have started the Scottish LGBT Sports Charter is invaluable and should be supported, and enhanced, over the next five years of this Scottish Parliament.

Stonewall Scotland's flagship 'The School Report' makes for harrowing reading for our policy makers, over 1 in 4 LGBTIQ+ pupils in Scotland have attempted suicide because of homophobic bullying in schools and almost half do not feel as if they are achieving their best at school. In the run up to the elections the Time for Inclusive Education (TIE) campaign was born and in a relatively short space of time it has managed to get commitments from all the main parties to work with them in the coming years to move their inclusive education agenda forward. Nicola Sturgeon has made education one of her key priorities for the coming Parliamentary term and alongside closing the attainment gap, she should make the inclusiveness of our education the other benchmark that she uses to judge her government's success – this is work that cannot wait.

For older LGBTIQ+ people the integration of health and social care and a renewed focus on modernising public services must also come with appropriate education for all public sector workers, especially around potential prejudice in care or sheltered housing, or the impact that living 'in the closet' can have on people and their well-being. Older lesbians could also be affected by the changes to pensions that the 'Women Against State Pension Inequality' (WASPI) campaign has been working to change. Although that is Westminster legislation all parties in Scotland should be standing with these women in their fight for fairness.

The ban on sexually active gay men giving blood remains an absurdity, totally at odds with scientific advice and our want to be an equal country. The next Scottish Parliament should scrap this ban and instead use the screening processes already in place for all other blood for the blood of gay men too. There should also be a widening of access to Pre-exposure prophylaxis (more commonly known as PrEP) which can lower the chances of people at high risk of HIV getting the illness.

Recognition in law is one of our fundamental human rights but in Scotland we are failing transgender people with our binary laws. It was heartening to see almost all political parties agree with the Equality Network's manifesto aims of changing gender recognition law. Indeed prior to the 2016 election Nicola Sturgeon made a high profile announcement that she would shake up gender recognition laws and bring Scotland in line with international best practice in these areas. This legislation would allow for transgendered people to change their official documents, such as their birth certificate, without having to be seen by a psychiatric panel. Proposing and thereafter implementing this legislation would have little impact on the wider population but a huge impact on transgendered people who would be able to have their gender officially recognised. This is one of the key areas that the next Scottish Parliament can make real differences to their citizens' lives.

During the last Parliamentary session, the introduction of equal marriage was seen by many as the highlight of the term and proof that the Scottish Parliament can make big, bold decisions. Sitting in the public gallery on that cold February day in 2014 I could not have been more proud of our Parliament. While we have equality in marriage, there remains a curious inequality in civil partnerships and the Scottish Parliament should widen their availability to heterosexual couples too.

I mentioned earlier that this Parliament has the highest number of LGB Parliamentarians of any in the world. While that is to be hugely welcomed, the stubborn refusal for the gender gap between male and female MSPs to close is still a problem that needs to be addressed. The

SNP made strides in this with all women shortlists for constituency seats where sitting MSPs were standing down and as a result 75% of new SNP MSPs are women. However, numbers of candidates is not enough, The Scottish Greens are proof of this, they had a 50-50 candidate roster but only one out of six MSPs elected was a woman. We don't only need women candidates but they also need to be put in places on lists or in constituencies where they have a fair chance of winning! The number of disabled MSPs is even bleaker.

Political parties of all hues have to take stock, and take advice from the Women 50:50 campaign, and the One in Five campaign about how to support potential future politicians now so that when it comes to party members choosing candidates in four years' time, the tired arguments about 'best for the job' are (even more) moot because they have people who have been supported and honed for candidacy and can more than prove they are the best for the job, being put in to areas where they have a good chance of winning.

It is, after all, no coincidence that as the number of LGBTIQ+ MSPs in Scotland has grown, Scotland has become a better place for LGBTIQ+ people to live. This correlation will undoubtedly be the same for other under-represented or minority groups too. The current Scottish Parliament, and all political parties, needs to move forward with this now.

If the best thing to come out of the Scottish Parliament in the near future is to make progress on some of the issues outlined, and to lay the foundations for a more representative Chamber in 2021 with more diversity articulating different voices and making better, more considered laws for all our citizens, then that will be five years well spent.

Chapter 24

Humanism, Scotland and an unpredictable future

Tim Maguire

Predicting the future has always been a mug's game. The former chairman of IBM who said, "there is a world market for maybe five computers," was clearly wrong, but even when we get it right, as Macbeth found when Birnam Wood came to Dunsinane, the future is rarely as we had imagined it.

The past is an unreliable guide to the future. The first humanist marriage in Scotland took place forty years ago in 1976. Of course it wasn't legal, and I doubt anyone involved dreamed they would see humanist marriage come into law, but it did, in June 2005.

Not that many contemplated Brexit before June 2016. I also doubt that anyone back in 2005 could have envisaged a devolved Scotland with its own parliament, where not only would the leaders of the three main political parties be women, but that two of them would also be openly gay. Scotland is not yet what most humanists fervently want – a secular state – but it has undoubtedly become a much more tolerant, open, and diverse society.

With the exception of a secular state (and I'll come back to that later) I believe that most of Humanism's main objectives have already been achieved in Scotland. Free speech? Check. Human Rights? Check. Democracy? More than Westminster, certainly, but none of that was achieved by humanism. The real change that Humanism has made, and is continuing to make, is through its ceremonies.

Funerals are no longer sad, mournful occasions: they've become 'a celebration of life'. And in the ten years since humanist marriage has been legal, the people of Scotland have taken them to their hearts. This summer, the National Records Office is likely to confirm that 2015 was the year that humanist weddings overtook those of the Church of Scotland, to become the second most popular form of marriage in the country.

This is not mere point scoring: it's important. Marriage as an institution has been in decline in the British Isles for half a century, and there are more families with children living outside wedlock than in. Elsewhere in the UK, marriage continues to decline. Only in Scotland has it begun to rise, and that is directly attributable to the popularity of humanist weddings. What makes them so different?

One of the attractions is that couples are free to speak about their love in their own words. Another is that humanist celebrants don't tell couples what marriage means. Instead, we ask them to think deeply about it, and then tell their families and friends what it means to them. So every humanist marriage is, in a sense, a very personal redefinition of marriage, and that, I believe, is the key to their success.

Stable families make for stable societies, so this reinvigoration of the institution of marriage ought to be a cause for general celebration, but not everyone's so pleased by the rise of secular humanism. When Pope Benedict visited the UK in 2010, he likened it to Nazism, and rued the damage that 'the exclusion of God, religion and virtue from public life' had done in the last century.

It's easy to get worked up about the abuses of religion, and to accuse it, as Richard Dawkins and the late Christopher Hitchens have done, of being the root of all evil, but that is counter-productive, so I am glad to say that our response was remarkably restrained. Humanists didn't take to the streets in protest. Instead, we spent rather a lot of money on a 96-sheet billboard that said, "40% of Scots are good without god", a claim that provoked something of a stooshie at the time. Six years later, Benedict has gone and the most recent Social Attitudes Survey tells us that the percentage of godless has risen to 52 per cent, which is a remarkable thing, but the increase has less to do with our lone poster than with an ever-increasing disenchantment with organised religion.

Most people now describe themselves as non-religious, but few non-religious people describe themselves as humanists, perhaps because humanism is still an unfamiliar idea. After ten years of conducting humanist weddings, I am still struck that the vast majority of couples who ask me to marry them had never come across the H word until they met their wedding planner, who let them in on the secret that there is now an alternative to church and state.

Humanism is barely mentioned in RME classes, and indeed the possibility that people might be able to lead good and worthwhile lives guided only by compassion and reason is entirely ignored in Scottish education. I hope that when Humanist marriage replaces Presbyterian marriage at the top of the league tables, our politicians and educators will finally recognise that it's time to put Humanism on the curriculum.

Having said that, who will define what Humanism is and what humanists believe? Humanism is a broad church, but it has already suffered schisms, and it no longer speaks with one voice.

In 2005 when I joined it, the only organisation in existence was the Humanist Society of Scotland, a charity run by its members, but sadly it no longer exists. In its place is a new, professionally managed charitable company limited by guarantee called Humanist Society Scotland, alongside a good half dozen other organisations who have divergent ideas about how best to promote humanism.

Campaigning will always have its place, but I believe what the public wants most from Humanism are meaningful ceremonies that celebrate the most important moments in life, so that is our focus in the Caledonian Humanist Association. Rather than run political campaigns, we serve our communities. Unlike the HSS, we don't insist that couples join our organisation and pay an additional fee in order to get married. And rather than amassing a war chest, after covering our deliberately small administrative costs, we will give all our money away every year to local charities all over Scotland.

My advice to humanists over the next five years is, don't sweat the small stuff. Remember that The Great British Public is strangely protective towards the church to which they never go, and whose doctrines they no longer believe. Yes it is ridiculous in this day and age that there are still unelected religious representatives on the education committees of local councils, but nobody really cares, so don't bang on about it.

Instead, we need to work much harder to make the positive case for secularism, which is that it's the best way of bringing people of all faiths and none together. That means getting involved in inter-faith dialogue, and working with the churches on issues of mutual concern, like poverty, education, refugees, and equality. We should remember that the things we have in common are more important than those that divide us, and that secularism means accepting that others have a right to voice their opinions, even when we disagree with them. Similarly, humanists must speak out when bad things are done in the name of secularism, or risk losing not just the meaning of the word, but also our dream of a more equal, more tolerant world.

One last thought: it is almost an article of faith for humanists to work towards a secular state as a guarantor both of freedom of belief and freedom from the domination by any particular belief, but you only have to look at the USA and Bangladesh to see how a secular state doesn't always work in practice. When we try to predict the future, we should remember the law of unintended consequences.

The odds on Scotland becoming a secular state are even longer than they were on Leicester City winning the League, but I'd take a small bet that if it were to happen, we might look back in years to come on the UK's muddled, unwritten, but essentially benign and tolerant constitution, with its established church, and its bishops in the House of Lords and think that, after all, it may have been a blessing in disguise.

Chapter 25

Imagine and act for a more just Scotland

Richard Frazer

In 2015 over 10,000 people in every part of Scotland were asked to: 'Imagine ... it is 2035. Scotland is a fairer, more equal and more just society, in a fairer, more equal and more just world.' Then we asked people to say what one thing needed to happen in order for that hope to stand the best possible chance of becoming a reality.

The project was put in motion by the Church of Scotland, for whom I work. But it was essentially a community initiative. We set out on this task both because we were aware that people across Scotland were becoming more interested in shaping a different sort of future and because – from our own perspective – we believe that when churches speak out, they should do so not just on behalf of people but alongside people, and especially with attention to those whose voices are rarely heard.

The interest in political participation, while not solely about independence, has undoubtedly grown out of the independence referendum debate. For many of us is also – far more deeply – about striving for a society and world that more adequately reflects the sort of future the God we believe in hopes for and intends for all creation. This is one in which, in the words of an ancient prophet, we "act justly, love mercy and walk humbly with God" (Micah 6.8) and where, following the example of Jesus, we realise the central importance of struggling against poverty (Luke 6.20).

The seven core themes which emerged from the 'Imagining Scotland's Future' exercise will now shape how my own church engages not just with the Scottish Parliament for the next five years but also with wider society for at least the next decade. It will, we hope, also shape a significant part of our work and service in every community the length and breadth of our country.

These themes, which can be owned by people whether they are religious or not, are:

- Investing in our Young People
- Caring for Creation
- Economy Driven by Equality
- Health and Wellbeing
- Doing Politics Differently
- Flourishing Local Communities.

Each of these relates to what those who took part in this exercise consider should be some of the priorities of the Scottish parliament and government over the next few years. I will offer a Church of Scotland perspective on these, but in a way that I hope can be owned by those of different backgrounds.

The Scottish Government has given a very clear steer that it wants to make education a core priority of its agenda. For the church, **Investing in our Young People** is about significantly more than formal education but it most certainly includes it. While the current education system works for many young people, it is clear that others have been consistently left behind. It is the voices of some of the people we spoke to in a 'Speak Out' process whose views now shape our agenda of concerns. Georgina, for example, told us that, because of where she lived, the expectation was that she would work in beauty care or with children, despite the fact that she wanted to do neither. Kourtney has challenged politicians to ensure that every trainee teacher sits down with the young people in her community in order that they might understand just what it is like to grow up in poverty. Youth work, decimated by short sighted cuts over the last decade, is a crucial means of investing in young people.

Caring for Creation (in the Earth understood as gift) has been at the forefront of the Church of Scotland's mission for much of the last decade. With our partners in Eco-Congregations Scotland, with our own Climate Change Officer and with people across the world, we campaigned for the historic climate deal reached in Paris in December 2015. Over the next five years we want to hold the Scottish Government to account for the commitments that it made – and to encourage them to go further still. The reality is that the Scottish Government in the past has been stronger on rhetoric than action. But we need tangible change.

This issue is not just about global treaties. It is also about day-to-day living, like making sure that people have enough food to eat. In the past few years, many congregations across Scotland have set up and supported foodbanks. We celebrate the generosity which inspires people to give in this way, but we are appalled that in one of the richest countries of the world there is a food poverty epidemic. We heard from people just how hard things are – and the indignity of needing to stand in a line to be given a carrier bag of food. We urge that parliament and politicians come together to agree a plan which will lead to a radical reduction in the numbers of those who living with food insecurity.

Fundamental to this will be the promotion of an ***Economy Driven by Equality*** rather than one focused on growth for the sake of growth. That will mean growing the value of the Scottish Living Wage and ensuring that the new social security and tax raising powers which the Scottish Parliament now has are used primarily to tackle poverty and inequality.

Many of the people that spoke to us expressed considerable concern about the future of the National Health Service. We are clear that the NHS is one of the jewels of society. However, it also increasingly apparent that what we have is a National Illness Service as opposed to a National Health Service; one focused on dealing with disease as opposed to promoting health. It is becoming increasingly evident that this approach to health care is putting impossible pressure on the NHS. The only way in which the NHS can be sustained in the future is through a shift towards preventative health care/ promoting better diet and a greater investment in community health medicine/talking therapies and voluntary and communitarian initiatives of care and support.

Previous governments in Scotland have been very effective in identifying the problems and the need to move towards a prevention strategy that promotes the broader agenda of ***Health and Wellbeing***. This Parliament needs to have the courage really to invest in that agenda. It will require innovation and, in particular, closer co-operation with community groups, including faith groups.

One area where past Scottish governments and parliaments have acted positively has been in relation to the refugee catastrophe which we have seen unfolding on the borders of Europe. Churches and faith groups, in collaboration with many others, have consistently called for a far more generous attitude towards asylum seekers and refugees. Through people we talked to like Aimee, Parveen and Maqsood – people who have travelled to this country in fear of their lives – our communities have been deeply enriched. It used to be that ***Building***

Global Friendships meant looking to other parts of the world. Increasingly other parts of the world now live in this country and we are far richer for that. We hope that the new Parliament will continue this tradition of hospitality and advocacy as well as investing in the successful integration of new citizens.

Building global friendships, of course, is not just about immigration policy. It is also about international development and the active promotion of peace. While the renewal of the UK's nuclear weapons system is a reserved matter, we hope that the Scottish Parliament will continue to play a strong role in advocating for a world free from nuclear weapons. Our church and others can and will, of course work with the Westminster Parliament seeking to re-state its long held opposition to nuclear weapons

Constitutional politics has played a major part in political debate over the last five years in Scotland and – for better or for worse – there is every indication that it will do so for the next five, not least in the light of the Brexit vote in June. While there were elements of the 2014 referendum debate that some saw as divisive and damaging, the greatly increased interest in the democratic process which erupted out of it is to be celebrated.

It is up to us in the churches and others groups within civil society to test whether this new found interest is widespread and genuine, but we are sure it can only be sustained if people feel that their voices and opinions count and can make a difference. We are already ***Doing Politics Differently*** in Scotland and we want to see a continuing heightened level of participation in the democratic processes. There is a real opportunity for Scotland to move into a new phase of what it means to be a modern democracy, through for example, increased use of participatory budgeting, but this will require leadership from our politicians and a willingness deliberately to cede and share power rather than accumulate it.

Too much time over the last decade has been spent on the question of the relationship between Scotland the rest of the UK and too little on how we support ***Flourishing Local Communities***. The Community Empowerment Bill enacted during the last parliament gives an opportunity for local neighbourhoods to be more effectively in the driving seat for change. If this is to work for the currently most disadvantaged groups and places, there will be a need to ensure that proper resources and support are put in place. The deliberate prioritising of resourcing towards the economically very poorest communities has been a deliberate policy of the churches over much of the last twenty years – indeed over much of the last two thousand years – so we have an idea or two to offer about how we can best enable transformative organisations and movements to emerge.

Perhaps the core lesson which my own Church of Scotland has learnt as it has engaged in the process of listening to people over the last period is about the wisdom of people, particularly those who have been treated unjustly, unfairly and unequally. We have increasingly recognised that we cannot determine solutions without the direct involvement of the people most affected. Through the active work of Scotland's Poverty Truth Commission, we now recognise even more clearly that 'Nothing About Us, Without Us, is For Us' – to adapt the potent phrase that came out of South Africa. We hope that this is also a lesson that the Scottish Government and Parliament has learned and will continue to learn in the coming years.

Chapter 26

Religion and belief in Scotland

Matthew Ross

Adapting Denis Diderot, the political theorist Tom Nairn once wrote that "Scotland will be reborn the day the last minister is strangled with the last copy of the Sunday Post". It was a withering portrayal of religion as a force for atavistic social conservatism. Much has changed in the decades since Nairn penned his words, for the church and other faith groups, as well as for society, economics and politics. So I hope out of that we can form a more positive approach to how different beliefs, religious and non-religious, can help shape a changing Scotland.

It is worth looking at the changing landscape in considering this. Many church denominations report a considerably reduced and ageing membership. The decline of industry and manufacturing, the achievement of a Scottish Parliament with legislative competence, a referendum on independence, secularisation, immigration and the corresponding rise of other faith communities have changed Scotland in ways barely imaginable in earlier decades. Now we also face an uncertain European future. In trying to envisage Scotland in 2021, it seems highly likely that such trends will continue. Further dramatic developments (such as those arising from Brexit, or from a vote for independence in a second referendum) cannot be ruled out. Where stand religious communities in such upheavals? Where will be the place of religion and belief in Scotland in 2021?

Examples of structural change within the church can be striking – such as the impact of the Second Vatican Council on the Roman Catholic Church. In 1985 the General Assembly of the Church of Scotland voted to disassociate with the anti-Papal sections of the 17th century Westminster Confession of Faith; a move which may seem of little practical consequence to an increasingly secular society, but which but opened the door to ecumenical *rapprochement* and an increasing aversion to sectarianism by mainstream denominations.

Some denominations show a willingness to embrace further change. Such trends are particularly evident in the Church of Scotland, the United Reformed Church and the Scottish Episcopal Church –

including extensive debate at the national and local level. This is not without controversy, including defections by some theologically conservative members. Such theological divisions are illustrated by the often-bitter debate over sexuality that has divided many denominations. Consensual same-sex relations were decriminalised in Scotland on 1st February 1981, yet over three decades later arguments on homosexuality have dominated internal Church debate in several different denominations. This comes at the price of diversion of energy away from other key priorities – a diversion which a Church struggling for relevance in an increasingly secularised society can ill afford.

Sexual abuse scandals have had a catastrophic effect. As well as the trauma caused to individuals, the institutional church has been undermined both by initial response and public perception. The seriousness of the issue has resulted in once unimaginable responses, notably the appointment by the Catholic Bishops' Conference of Scotland of a former Moderator of the General Assembly of the Church of Scotland to conduct an investigation and write a report. This shows the development and maturity of ecumenical relations within Scotland, notably at the level of leadership. Given the growing levels of trust and the realisation that each denomination is too weak to continue to resource all areas of work individually, scope for ecumenical co-operation (including the sharing of expensive resources such as buildings) is likely to increase between 2016 and 2021. Declining attendances as well as increasing maintenance, insurance and energy costs are likely to result in the closure of church buildings.

As of 31st December 2015, the Church of Scotland had a communicant membership of 352,912 – a decline of 14,434 since the previous year. The recorded membership of the Kirk has been in continuous decline since the late 1950s. This contrasts with the census figures from 2001 and 2011, showing claimed affiliation with the Church of Scotland at approximately 1.7 million and 1.2 million respectively.

The concept of "believing without belonging" mirrors social change, but numerical decline in once powerful institutions in Scottish society is not confined to the Church. Membership of political parties (with the notable exception of the SNP and the Greens) trades unions and numerous voluntary groups has also been adversely affected. The 2021 census is likely to show further decline in formal membership, though membership of the Catholic Church would be anticipated to remain fairly constant through immigration from Poland (for which Brexit could have a considerable adverse impact).

Despite declining membership the churches are seeking to respond to social change, such as the growth of new ecumenical bodies such as Work Place Chaplaincy Scotland. Since 2012 the Church of Scotland's 'Go for it' fund has also facilitated innovative projects, often complementary to parish ministry.

The churches have also had to adapt to recent constitutional events. Virtually all of the mainstream denominations have been officially neutral (but far from uninterested) in both the 2015 independence referendum and the 2016 EU membership referendum. The General Assembly of the Church of Scotland has, voted to support EU membership. It has its Church and Society Council – the best-resourced agency working on public affairs of any church in Scotland and noted for its willingness to champion controversial issues, including longstanding opposition to nuclear weapons.

The future influence of the churches in the public sphere will increasingly be determined by the quality of their work. Secularisation means that they cannot expect their voice to be heard or respected unless the quality, nuance and distinctiveness of the argument is good. The clarity of such a message is greatly assisted, particularly in dialogue with government, by ecumenical and interfaith co-operation. The recent creation of Scottish Faiths Action for Refugees[*] is an example of practical co-operation for human flourishing.

Incomprehension by a sceptical, largely secular society is not confined to relations with Christianity, of course. Scotland has a rapidly growing Muslim community, no longer largely confined to adherents of Sunni Islam from Pakistan. Refugees from Syria will further increase Scotland's Muslim community, which will almost certainly have increased from approximately 25,000 in 2001 to six figures by 2021. There is a danger that relations with the Muslim community are seen primarily as problematic, with an emphasis on counter-terrorism and fear of ghettoisation. Can Scotland's politicians and civic society have a realistic dialogue – beyond platitudes and mere politeness – with the various, very diverse strands of Islam?

Scotland's Muslim communities have made great efforts at building relations with government and civil society. The Muslim Council of Scotland also plays an active role in Interfaith Scotland. The Scottish Ahlul Bayt Society, a Shia Islamic organisation, is active in promoting dialogue with political and civic society as well as other religious traditions, including holding well-attended events in the Scottish

---

[*] http://www.sfar.org.uk

Parliament.

2021 will mark the 100th anniversary of the legislation underpinning the status of the Church of Scotland. Although the legislation is unchanged, recent years have seen a greater emphasis on the Church of Scotland perceiving itself as "a national church" rather than "the national church" – with an emphasis on maintaining support to areas of economic deprivation and low population rather than retreating to the prosperous suburbs. Openness to increasing ecumenical co-operation is evident through the creation of Action of Churches Together in Scotland (1990) and the Scottish Churches Parliamentary Office (1999). Both organisations work closely together, notably in organising an annual meeting for church leaders with the First Minister.

Declining church membership and attendance is far from unique to Scotland. Similar trends can be seen throughout much of Europe and North America. The Lisbon Treaty of the European Union provides for dialogue between the EU institutions and religions as well as with non-religious bodies (such as humanist or secularist societies). Article 17 of the Treaty of the Functioning of the European Union states that:

1. The Union respects and does not prejudice the status under national law of churches and religious associations or communities in the Member States.

2. The Union equally respects the status under national law of philosophical and non-confessional organisations.

3. Recognising their identity and their specific contribution, the Union shall maintain an open, transparent and regular dialogue with these churches and organisations.

European Union law does not affect the legal status of churches (whether established or not) within the Member States. Nevertheless, the EU's own formal model for "open, regular and transparent" dialogue is effectively mirrored in Scotland – albeit without a legal basis. Should a formal legal basis be considered? Following the terror attacks in Brussels on 22nd March 2016, the debate on the separateness of sections of the Muslim community has been intense, but does this imply that religion is inevitably a "problem" for a secular norm? The denigration of all religion as problematic is as lazy as it is inaccurate. Diversity within religious traditions requires much greater understanding rather than simplistic labelling, such as Shia verses Sunni or Catholic versus Protestant. Religious values can offer a challenge to injustice, as with the Confessing Church in Germany during the Nazi era, but concepts such as Sharia are often perceived as sitting uneasily alongside secular norms. Such issues need further exploration by all faiths as well as by those whose life stance is non-religious.

The future of religion and belief in Scotland appears to be one of ever-greater diversity, with unresolved tensions between liberal and conservative sections of Christianity – sometimes within the same denomination – plus increased numbers of adherents of other faiths and the recognition that a large and seemingly increasing number of Scots (at least according to the last census) have no religious faith. A converse trend may be one of religious nominalism – "belonging without believing".

Right now, the constitutional future of Scotland is difficult to predict, yet any changes (or lack of change) will impact the whole of society, of which belief communities are an integral part. In such uncertain circumstances, dialogue is necessary for mutual respect, greater confidence and understanding – from which religion, in all its diversity, cannot be excluded.

Chapter 27

Women's equality in Scotland's parliament

Talat Yaqoob

Women's representation was a key political issue during the 2016 Scottish Parliament elections. Commentators told us that we might return to the dizzy heights of 2003 where we had almost 40per cent women MSPs in the debate chamber.

Women 50:50 has worked tirelessly from our creation in 2014, to make fair representation a political priority. Nicola Sturgeon signed up to our campaign and the SNP adopted all women shortlists for the first time in their history. Kezia Dugdale, co-founder of the Women 50:50 campaign and leader of Scottish Labour, who have a 20-year history of all women shortlists, went a step further, and ensured that there were at least 50 per cent women candidates across regions and constituencies.

The Scottish Greens, who have good form on gender equality, fell short of 50 per cent women candidates, but included strong support for quotas in their manifesto.

Despite all of this, election night back in May bought us no change whatsoever. Today, we have the same number of women MSPs as we did in the 2011 parliamentary term (and fewer than we have had previously). How did that happen?

Well firstly, the Scottish Conservatives won more seats than anyone had predicted, and this is the one party that has unequivocally rejected fair representation so far. In fact, a mere 16 per cent of their candidates in this election were women – a perfect example of the fact that simply having a woman leader is meaningless unless it is backed up by policy and practice that fights for women's social justice. Secondly, Scottish Labour's major losses impacted the number of women in parliament, as they have consistently had the highest overall percentage. Fewer Scottish Labour wins meant fewer women overall. Lastly, the Scottish Liberal Democrats, although small in number, returned only men in the 2016 election, having relegated the only woman with a chance of winning to second place on their list.

However, there still remains a majority support for fair representation. Four out of five party leaders or co-convenors support the Women 50:50 campaign and now is the time for this support to translate into action. What the May 2016 election revealed is that voluntary mechanisms and rhetoric only go so far. We need legislated change and we need all parties to comply. Women's representation cannot be left to the whim of whoever happens to be in charge of a party.

With a relatively new parliament in place, we need to continue to lobby for action and to push for those who support us to come through to make fair representation a reality.

But there is a misconception that we must address: namely, meritocracy. Quotas, despite what may be published about them, do not put gender before merit. They in fact promote women with the merit and ambition who otherwise would be overlooked or face barriers in getting to the places they deserve to be. Why is it that we do not question the merit on which men are elected? Do we actually believe that men, somehow naturally are 65per cent more talented? Of course not. True meritocracy does not exist in today's Scottish Parliament, but it can if we open the doors to more women.

Over the next five years, we have an opportunity to capitalise on the momentum women's organisations and Women 50:50 have created. Now more than ever, women's equality is a top priority, the word 'feminist' has never been used more in Scottish politics – but how do we make change for women's political equality? We need to fight a battle on multiple fronts if we are to overcome generations of institutionalised inequality. In this context, the following five issues need to be tackled:

1. Legislated candidate quotas

Voluntary mechanisms have taken us far, but not far enough. We need legislated candidate quotas. This means that every party would be mandated to put forward at least 50 per cent women candidates. The elected choice will be left to the voter, but from a much more representative ballot paper. This is the same measure used in eight European countries and is a fair way to create equilibrium for women in politics. It is to be hoped that over time, the measure would not be needed, but legislation is the only viable fast track to the equality that women should already have. The way in which it is implemented, however, requires full consultation with all parties and with equalities groups, as we must ensure that intersectionality is at the core of such legislation and that parties do not see this as a tick box, but instead put effort into placing women in winnable seats.

2. Media (mis)representation

Women face more scrutiny and criticism than anyone else in politics. The scrutiny is rarely of their policies, as it should be, but about their personal lives, their appearance and how they will manage their caring responsibilities (if they have any, if not, then the question is why they do not have any). Around the time of the May elections, the *Daily Mail* ran a "Downing Street Catwalk" with photos of the women in the UK cabinet. Nicola Sturgeon has been depicted in a tartan bikini riding a wrecking ball and Kezia Dugdale was described as an "unattractive accessory" to Jeremy Corbyn. With this level of very public sexism, we cannot be surprised that women do not come forward to put themselves in the spotlight and on the ballot paper. We need to push this Scottish Parliament to hold the media to account and to be vocal in calling out sexism in the press – no matter which woman, from which party, is being unfairly targeted.

3. Tackling sexism within political parties

People in glasshouses should not throw stones. Equally, parties with sexism within them (which is all of them, as microcosms of society) shouldn't think that passing legislation on women's representation means that the job is done. All parties need to review their internal practices and ensure that sexism is taken seriously. The language used by parliamentarians, whether in formal writing or social media, needs to be respectful of women. Training in equalities should come as standard for anyone considering representing the people of Scotland. Finally, all political parties need to set up women's training and development opportunities, reaching out to them, rather than assuming they will come along gradually – an inclusive and open system is needed, rather than the cloak and daggers approach taken too often and putting too many people off being engaged, particularly in larger parties.

4. Gender balanced committees within the Scottish Parliament

In the previous parliamentary session, there were a number of Scottish Parliament committees that were all male. One, in particular, was the

Public Petitions Committee. This meant issues from a diverse public being scrutinised by an unrepresentative group. An easy way to create gender equality across the parliament is to seek gender equality in all committees, or at the very least ensure there is gender balance between convenors and deputy convenors. A small act, but a big difference.

5. A women's caucus

Although American politics is not where many examples of women's equality come from, there is one notable aspect that would encourage cross party development on fair representation, and that is a women's caucus. It could work as a multi-party initiative, with women parliamentarians from all parties collaborating together to develop good practice within the parliament itself and pushing for better policy for women across Scotland. This would be one group who can make sure that women's representation and social justice is on the top of the agenda for every party; and also ensure that the issue is not played as a political football, but rather as an area of policy that everyone feels a responsibility towards.

These initiatives alone will not solve women's social injustice within five years. We cannot think that ingrained, generational inequality can be erased so easily. But it will put us on the right track to creating a more inclusive parliament and a fairer Scotland for women. Within this parliamentary term, we can and will push for significant change. All that is needed is for rhetoric to translate into action.

Finally, though this chapter has focussed on women's equality in parliament and in the representative functions of political parties, the challenge remains much wider. Women 50:50* is also concerned with our councils and with all public boards.

---

* http://www.women5050.org

Chapter 28

Co-operatives are vital for economic and social democracy

Mary Lockhart

The woman I met outside the café three days before the Scottish parliamentary elections in May 2016 was one of a group who had recently undertaken a Workers Education Association (WEA) course in local Politics. "Have you time for a coffee?" she asked, "I wanted to ask you about the election."

Ten minutes into the conversation over coffee that followed, she stopped me. "You keep talking about publicly owned and controlled public services and key industries," she said. "What do you mean? How can the people own anything? Businesses own companies."

An hour later we had discussed nationalisation, privatisation, Quangos, outsourcing, housing associations, the BBC, Scottish Government control over rail and ferry franchising, EU regulations and their impact on franchising and public procurement, what Labour and the SNP had in common, and where they differed, and who really owned Scotland's land, coastal waters, and natural resources. As I rose to go, she stopped me in my tracks

> "But what is the point of the Government nationalising anything if the next government can just privatise it again, whether the people want them to or not? You call it public ownership, but that doesn't mean things belong to the people, does it? It just means they belong to the Government. Which in the end is just the same as belonging to a company."

The principles of social and economic democracy have been seriously eroded throughout the UK, and with them a mainstream political drive towards public ownership. An economic orthodoxy which claims that the public sector is inherently wasteful and inefficient has passed virtually unchallenged. Successive Labour, Tory, and, in Scotland, SNP governments have continued a spiral of outsourcing, franchising, and other forms of privatisation, including the linking of construction contracts to long term maintenance to keep the appearance of public debt off the balance sheet.

There are few, if any public services which have not been affected – including in Scotland, where private companies provide management services to some local hospitals, and entire bolt on operating theatre suites, complete with nursing staff and equipment to allow NHS Trusts to meet their waiting list targets in others.

When the Scottish Government awarded the franchise to run the trains on Scotland's railways to Dutch National Railways UK operating arm Serco, many expressed outrage that Scotland's railways could be nationalised so long as the nationalisation was not Scottish. The Scottish Government has promised that it will, in future, permit Public Sector Organisations to bid for operating contracts under the new powers to the Scottish Parliament under the Smith Commission. This promise is to be welcomed. But the permission did not prevent the private company, Anglian Water, from successfully outbidding publicly owned Scottish Water for the contract to supply schools, hospitals, and other public buildings in Scotland.

There has been some disagreement as to whether there are steps which could be taken to avoid EU legislation which insists that once put out to franchise, bidding must be recommenced each time the contract runs out. Similar disagreement has existed as to the extent and inflexibility of EU procurement rules, and what exceptions on the grounds of the national strategic interest may be permitted. These issues have been given a new context and added urgency by the June 2016 Brexit vote and its impact on Scotland. But wherever this goes, the Scottish Government has said it is committed to public ownership, and a way must be found to turn the words of that commitment into robust reality.

I believe that over the next five years we have an opportunity to develop a strategy for accountable public ownership and control of public services and key industries which would strengthen the economy, and would simultaneously make Scotland a more democratic country.

Co-operatives are the most democratic form of public ownership, and the most difficult for any government to privatise, since permission must be given in a democratic ballot of the membership. Every political party in Scotland has nice things to say about co-ops; be they worker, consumer, consortium, or multi-stakeholder hybrid. In the financial sector, despite the deliberate elimination of many building societies from the high street in the Thatcherite 1980s, financial mutual remain largely trusted. Credit Unions as People's Banks are growing fast. Because their boards are elected rather than appointed, Housing Co-operatives are more in touch with their tenant members than is often the case with Housing Associations, and because the tenants are members, they are fully engaged in determining the facilities they need, the problems they need to resolve, and the communities they want to build.

Scotland indeed needs a fully-fledged Co-operative Development Agency. It should be discrete from Scottish Enterprise, under whose auspices Co-operative Development Scotland has become largely an advisory and support body for worker co-operatives, and a resource for business owners who want to sell to their employees on retiral.

The new Co-operative Development Agency should have a strategic arm, and should be integral to the Scottish Government's economic planning. New forms of co-operatives and mutuals are evolving, being developed, and achieving recognition by the International Co-operative Alliance, and the strategic arm of Scottish Co-operative Development Agency should take cogniscence of these, while working towards new forms of partnership co-operatives designed to meet Scotland's economic needs; and to take the place of private corporations requiring public subsidy to provide public services while paying dividends to shareholders.

Using the strategic findings of the Policy and Strategy Unit, the executive arm of the Scottish CDA should identify areas in which co-operatives can and should be set up to deliver economic, social, and community development.

Obvious social areas for the development of co-operative ownership and control are personal care, housing, and People's Credit Unions with an associated Investment Bank (about which Common Weal have produced a detailed proposal in October 2016). Currently, Co-operative Development Scotland is precluded from working in all but the first of these. This should be rectified.

On the economic side, there are also opportunities, and these go beyond having co-operatives ready to take on the ownership, management and running of expiring franchises, or key industries, manufacturing, and research. Already, people are willing to invest in co-operative renewables schemes, and have done so. During the second world war, people bought War Bonds. Today, a mutual could be established through which people could invest in a range of co-operatives, from energy to housing, from manufacturing turbines to installing solar panels on public buildings to generate and sell power to the grid.

In an era of determined imposition of austerity, and ideological imposition of cuts to public services and diminution of local democracy, the Scottish Government has the opportunity to reach beyond mitigation – but it will require vision, imagination and courage. Many of the people who supported a Yes vote in the referendum on Scottish Independence, who turned up in their thousands to attend meetings and who registered to vote for the first time, did so because of a sense that at last they had an opportunity for their voices to be heard, and their needs and aspirations to matter, and to be heard. They wanted to play a part in shaping the society in which they lived, and to feel that the way they voted would matter, and would continue to matter. They wanted to regain a real share in the power which they felt had been abrogated from them, and from their communities. Let down by governments, abused by banks and financial institutions, betrayed by the political elites, they began to have hope.

That hope needs to be nurtured, and I believe that the encouragement and support of co-operatives at every level will help build real democracy, and restore some sense of power to the people. Next time I meet my ex student from the WEA group, I want to be able to point her in the direction of the co-operatives which she, and every man woman and child in Scotland, part owns. And which no government can take away from us without our democratic consent.

Chapter 29

Sustainability and flourishing

Jan Bebbington[*]

On the matter of promoting sustainability and flourishing in our government's performance, the new Scottish administration faces epochal challenges. I would propose that three ideas should frame and shape the actions of the new Parliament in the coming years: the Anthropocene, capabilities for flourishing, and economic democracy.

Debates around "sustainable development" have been enlivened by the proposition that we are living in the Anthropocene. This is defined as an era where the impact of human actions on the earth rival that of geological processes.

It's uncontroversial to assert that human actions are affecting the global environment. For example, we often cite biodiversity loss, or disruption of the water cycle, or increasing greenhouse gas concentrations.

But the idea that these impacts constitute a new geological epoch is more arresting.

It may be news to you that, officially, we're not actually living in the Anthropocene yet. The decision that will recognise the Anthropocene as an epoch rests with the International Commission on Stratigraphy (who issued an interim report on this back in January 2016.)

What we need for that recognition is a 'golden spike' – some evidence in sediments, an ice core or the fossil record, that a global scale 'event' has taken place. This also has to be accompanied by an array of associated impacts, indicating changes to the Earth system happening at the same time as the spike.

It may help to show something that isn't a global spike. For example, the impact of copper smelting by the Romans is detectible in ice cores – but that wouldn't qualify as a spike, because it did not reflect a global phenomenon (as it was local to Europe). Nor was it associated with an array of other changes.

While there are several candidate dates for the start of the Anthropocene, the early 1960s appear to be favoured for identifying

---

[*] This article first appeared on Bella Caledonia earlier in 2016.

a major spike. This was the peak in radioactive markers arising from nuclear testing, which increased until 1963 when the Partial Test Ban Treaty was signed.

Another potential date is the 1950s, called in the eco-literature the 'great acceleration' – when population levels, resource use and pollution effects all increased exponentially.

Regardless of whether or not we end up naming our current time the Anthropocene from a technical point of view, the idea of the Anthropocene is likely to be influential. Part of this influence is cultural and social.

The election of a new Government, with the energy and impetus this brings, makes this a good time for a revisiting of national purpose. As the Anthropocene comes into (perhaps) formal recognition, we should take another look at what a just and safe economy, where all may flourish, could entail.

For example, how might we think about ourselves if 'we' become the clear agents of global environmental change? Does this encourage the hubris of massive projects to "geo-engineer" the planet? Or will it instil a sense of humility in humanity?

Likewise, deciding who exactly is the 'anthro' in the Anthropocene becomes a political and ideological question. Some people alive today (and historically) have had more substantive impacts on the earth than others. If we think too "universally" about "humanity" driving us to the Anthropocene, it might obscure how imbalanced some of these human contributions might be.

Living in the Anthropocene, then, represents the first challenge for the incoming Scottish Government. If our collective impacts are driving epoch-scale changes, then we should wish to be more proactive in countering that impact. Here are some creative ways forward.

For example, past ScotGov policies around zero waste have been internationally innovative. As is their recent shift in framing and thinking about waste and resource use, in terms of a circular economy. The Scottish Climate Change Act provides a good context for continuing and accelerating our ambitions to develop a low carbon economy. As the Paris Declaration is signed, the overall global shift in ambition needs to be matched by progress within Scotland.

More difficult for any government, however, is to be clear about what should cease in a low carbon future – especially where there are difficult trade-offs to be dealt with, particularly in terms of prosperity. The extent to which North Sea oil and gas might be left in the ground as unburnable, while wishing to sustain livelihoods in the oil-making region, is not an easy set of tensions to resolve.

Perhaps the most important first step is to explicitly recognise these as tensions.

Capabilities for flourishing

Living in the Anthropocene also raises the question of how we might flourish, in what are likely to be more trying times. Two thinkers in this context deserve highlighting: Amartya Sen and Martha Nussbaum. Both of these writers are concerned with how society should be structured so as to ensure that it is 'just' for its members.

Their work is called the Capabilities Approach (that is, they lay out what capabilities people need in order to flourish). This might sound prescriptive. But they are also clear that people will seek to flourish in many and various ways, according to what they value in life. (As an example of their flexibility, Nussbaum's work also deals with the issues of justice for non-human animals).

As we enter the Anthropocene, with its various accompanying stresses on natural, social and economic systems, the ability to ensure the capability of individuals to flourish is a central task. Rather than framing our task as a social contract – a compromise between classes or interests – the Capabilities Approach sets a base from which everyone can flourish. The idea of a guaranteed minimum income would fit into this framing.

Economic democracy

Whenever you think of what it means to flourish, the question of economics is not far away. Here economic democracy becomes important. A renewal of interest in what a democratic (and just) economy might entail comes from the consequences of the financial crisis of 2007/08, as well as the social/ecological impacts of economies.

There is much activity going on in this area. It includes workplace democracy (focused on workers' rights as well as employee/consumer/producer and community owned organisations). Also, the democratisation of finance (via credit unions; local banks; local currencies and trading systems; and crowd sourcing of funding for ventures). As well as broader financial processes (for example, participatory budgeting provides communities with the ability to influence local authority spending).

Across Scotland, there are numerous experiments with forms of economic democracy – participatory budgeting in Leith, community ownership of land/woodlands and a host of employee owned firms – and it's likely this will continue. I would argue for these types of organisation not to be seen as 'fringe' experiments far from the economic mainstream, but as pointers to what a just and democratic economic system might include.

A National Performance Framework that lets Scotland flourish

These three ideas might seem a long way away from the concerns of a relatively newly elected Government and Parliament, especially with the dominance of Brexit on the political landscape. I would argue, however, that they go to the heart of what the central purpose of government is.

Scotland's National Performance Framework states that the purpose of Government is to "focus Government and public services on creating a more successful country, with opportunities for all of Scotland to flourish". It is, therefore, a flourishing framework, even if it does not explicitly reference the Capabilities Approach.

Likewise, any flourishing is only achievable in the longer term if ecological integrity is maintained (in the face of the Anthropocene). The "purpose of Government" goes on to describe the means by which flourishing is to be achieved, that is through "increasing sustainable economic growth".

At this stage there is a disjuncture, with a lack of clarity about what economic growth would meet this description. The phrase looks like a grand oxymoron. We need a more explicit and nuanced position on what sort of economic activity might be fit for flourishing. A serious treatment of the social and environmental costs of its activities has to be revisited for the purpose of Government to be realised.

The next five years will take us past the year 2020, with all the hopes that are held for that date. By 2020 the first reduction target within the Scottish Climate Change Act will have to be met, and the EU's Biodiversity strategies also have key aims for that year – now under fresh scrutiny following the upheaval of the June 2016 referendum.

This is a good time for a revisiting of national purpose. As the Anthropocene comes into (perhaps) formal recognition, this is the right time to take another look at what a just and safe economy where all may flourish could entail.

Chapter 30

Towards an economy focused on wellbeing

Katherine Trebeck*

When will our politicians get serious about getting beyond GDP? Just after the Scottish parliamentary elections in May 2016, The Economist magazine caused some waves by recognising the flaws of Gross Domestic Product (GDP) as a measure of national progress. It's a welcome, if overdue, shift. Perhaps Scotland will now also allow itself to think the previously unthinkable too?

As we face the challenges of Brexit and other major political issues, will we have the capacity to think beyond the 'realistic' or the 'doable' to what is necessary (and indeed possible), even if this means upsetting some habits, some orthodoxy, and some vested interests? In fact, especially if it does! Could Scotland become a different kind of champion to the big corporation variety: one that leads the world in charting a different course, beyond GDP?

We can start by asking why we have an economic system configured in a way that rewards the powerful and gives power to those who already have the most.

This system and the politics that too often maintain it, rarely challenges the calls for more growth and it therefore dodges the apparently more challenging conversation about sharing the great wealth we already have more fairly.

We like to believe we enjoy a relatively enlightened government in Scotland and, to the extent that protecting the environment and the promotion of greater equality often get top line billing, we do so with some justification. But the environment and greater equality are positioned as on a par with GDP growth (or too often below it in the pecking order).

In this sense, rather than seeing growth as a means to an end (as it can be under the right circumstances, but not always), GDP growth remains the end in itself, albeit with some nice Scottish qualifiers ('inclusive growth' and 'sustainable growth').

---

* This article first appeared on Bella Caledonia earlier in 2016.

By continuing to value GDP growth so highly, our economic model pursues an approach to progress and development that demands more resources, more effort, more political manoeuvring, and more patience than need be. It is an inefficient approach to delivering good lives sustainably.

At its simplest, this 'long way around' to good lives entails using the spoils of growth to heal what we break, hurt, pollute, and damage in our quest for 'more'. Essentially the long road is 'end of play' redistribution, which simply places sticking plasters over the wounds caused during the course of events.

Scotland has long been awake to the notion of 'failure demand' (that is, spending driven by not getting things right in the first place), but it is arguably more extensive (in both UK and Scottish policies) than it seems at first glance. Take these examples:

- Tax credits for those in jobs which do not pay enough to live on

- Interventionist medical treatment for those alienated and stressed by the precariousness of this economy

- Welfare payments and food parcels for those cast aside by companies who downsize in their quest for short term shareholder value

- Flood defences and shelters for those whose homes are flooded as climate chaos worsens.

All this provision is undeniably vitally important for recipients in the short term. There is no doubt about that, especially when cuts face us with the alternative. But these measures are designed to heal and ameliorate, rather than prevent harm in the first place.

The 'long way around' approach is also environmentally unsustainable. It depends on a growing economy which is dangerously pushing beyond safe planetary boundaries. In many countries, this growth is premised on exploiting finite natural resources and has been described as 'neo-extractivist', dare I mention 'North Sea Oil'?.

By charting a different course Scotland will recognise that more is not always good. It will understand that the nature of economic growth as currently pursued may destroy the environment which is so important for economic and human wellbeing – in Scotland, and globally. It will be a course that no longer needs to make the 'business case' for addressing extreme economic inequality and protecting the environment. This is seen in so many assertions that reducing inequality is 'good for growth' or that protecting the planet will boost the economy.

Addressing inequality and protecting the planet will instead be embraced as important in their own right. And this perspective will critically and consistently ask what growth would do for people and planet, switching our focus to its quality and distribution. This means creating an economy that does more of the heavy lifting upfront. This economy will generate jobs that deliver basic needs like security and sufficiency of income, but also – importantly – psychological needs such as control, autonomy, self-esteem, and meaning.

Scotland is a place of heightened opportunity. It is an over-used cliché, but Scotland stands at a crossroads. With the greater powers over tax and welfare shifting to the Scottish Parliament, people are discussing what sort of country we want to live in and how Holyrood can help deliver it. The vote at UK level to exit the European Union has put this into even sharper relief.

Organisations and government are responding to 'democratic renewal' by recognising the need to really engage and involve our communities, rather than just hear from those who reply to traditional 'consultation' processes. There are some solid foundations for progress: Scotland has signed up to the Sustainable Development Goals; we have a National Performance Framework that is markedly better than GDP alone; we have the Business Pledge and the Fair Work Convention; we're investing in fostering the circular economy; and we've benefitted from an independent Poverty and Inequality Advisor.

Now is the time to put some teeth into those platforms. We also need to stare down those who demand a 'business case' before we take the action needed. Whether it's addressing extreme economic inequality, or making the entire economy circular, or going further in nudging GDP from its ill-deserved perch whilst putting in place a robust plan for meeting the SDGs.

We have to believe and act towards the vision that Scotland can embark on a new course and build an economic model that puts people and planet first.

Chapter 31

Beyond 'a greener Scotland'

Iain Black, Katherine Trebeck and Deirdre Shaw

Futurology in politics isn't for the feint hearted. Hands up who saw 56 SNP MPs coming, or indeed 31 Conservative and Unionist party MSPs? What about Brexit? So with this in mind, this chapter sets out a view on where Scotland is heading over the next five years (and beyond) with its view fixed on what would seem possible and what would be desirable to create a green, not just 'greener', Scotland – but with an awareness of the pace, scale and unpredictability of the change we face.

It starts from the assumption (let's be hopeful, eh?) that over the current parliamentary term, the Yes alliance parties, the SNP and the Scottish Greens, will find ways of working effectively together, most of the time. The most immediate source of the *possible* idea here are their specific manifesto promises and the hope that the Greens press hard to deliver their election promise to make the SNP a bolder government. It is not only possible and desirable but now essential that the centre of green politics is moved from climate change to the wider concept of sustainability (environmental, social and economic) as we are doing more damage than just changing the climate. Many of the policies described in this paper highlight this transition.

It needs to be remembered that all of the coal we burn, oil we use, iron we mine, in fact all the demand for the world's resources comes from our demands. These comprise those for government services and our demands as consumers. This chapter will focus on these in turn and explores the reality that for consumer demand to fall we have to invite that most unwanted of guests to the sustainable policy party – the ones that keeps talking about buying less stuff and who want to tackle our dysfunctional relationship with consumer goods. Sooner or later we will have to accept that to rely as heavily as we do on consumption taxes such as VAT and low paid retail work is incompatible with our need for a healthy environment and economy.

So what must Scotland do over the next five years? First, we must move from planning a greener Scotland, to planning a green one. When considering the perilous nature of our environment, aiming for greener means aiming for failure. We can be less polluting and use fewer resources, but without dramatic cuts by 2021 we will be just nine years away from when we're predicated to reach the point where we cannot put *any* more greenhouse gases (GHG) into the atmosphere and still keep global warming within two degrees. Two degrees warmer sounds like something we'd want for a Scottish summer. It's not. Two degrees is dangerous. Three degrees, (the more likely scenario) is the tipping point – the point we lose control.

So what about the policies we need enact to stay in control? Confident predictions can be made as to what is possible where there is manifesto agreement or where there are only small amounts of (green) water between the SNP and the Greens. The next five years will be marked by a post-fracking debate on energy policy, as the simple political reality of this parliament is that to allow these dangerous extraction techniques in Scotland, the SNP would first have to go against their manifesto pledge to ban it, "unless it can be proven beyond any doubt that there is no risk to health, communities or the environment" as overwhelming evidence already exists that it does. Secondly, they will have to get into bed with the Tories as they are the only party currently advocating the use of fracking. If they do that, the independence movement would also fracture and the SNP will have shot itself in the head. Fracking won't happen. The trajectory of policy on UCG ahead of the October 2016 SNP conference is another indicator of this.

Both the Greens and the SNP want 50 per cent of *all* energy coming from renewables by 2030, so we should expect that target to be adopted. The question can be posed – why not be bolder? It needs to be and countries like Germany, Denmark and Costa Rica show us it is possible. Sustainable adaptation and mitigation just like any change, needs investment and again the similarity between the SNP and Greens allows a confident prediction here; both talk about *Scottish renewable energy bonds* with the SNP wanting to 'explore them' and the Greens supporting them. Their introduction must be politically possible. The Greens also talk about local authorities issuing *low carbon infrastructure bonds,* both are good ideas not only for the environment, but as they challenge the neoliberal narrative of "I" that tells us that private ownership is better than public. So overall, funding our Green Scotland via community bonds looks possible and is desirable.

The SNP wants to investigate the creation of a government-owned energy company, the Greens want local ones. Depending on the scope of powers here, at least one of these solutions should be possible. Our bet is on the national one happening first (SNP centralism?), it would be great if both were available.

Both parties talk boldly about fuel poverty, one talks about eradicating it and the other ending it. Whether this is actually possible, like creating social justice, is a wider debate. What is possible from current party promises is bold action. With that comes the need for a timeframe and a budget, perhaps the Warm Homes Bill the SNP promises will provide these details. One of the unforeseen consequences of fuel efficient boilers and improved insulation is, however, that savings are often either reinvested in even more heat or they are invested in more consumer goods and, hence, create additional damage to our planet. These 'rebound' effects need to considered and is another reason for a deconsumerisation policy.

The next five years and beyond look hopeful for decarbonised transport. Regarding rail, the SNP talk about new stations: potentially at Reston, extending the borders line from Hawick to Carlisle, and using the now disused Longannet coal line. Their track record of delivery on new lines has been excellent so we should be hopeful of more success here. The Greens, of course, also talk about decarbonising transport and suggest Leven and Methil for new stations, they also want to duel the highland line. New stations reconnecting communities and reinvigorating local economies seems strongly possible here, though which particular ones is more opaque. Regarding who will be running the trains, the SNP promise to allow public sector operators to bid for future contracts, as Scottish ministers make the decision, it would seem possible that the Greens can push this further to where (as they want) the railways are brought back into public hands. The earliest that can happen now is 2022 however. There is more to decarbonised transport than trains and the SNP want ten per cent of everyday journeys to be made by bike, the Greens want ten per cent of the transport budget used to make active travel (walking and cycling) safer and, hence, to encourage it. The national figure is currently two per cent, by comparison Edinburgh council proposed to spend eight per cent in 2015/16. It is difficult to see how the SNP's target can be met with their budget. The Greens may push to find this money from the large road expansion budget.

Moving from the likely possible to the hopeful possible, the ambitions of Scotland's Yes parties around housing is an area for optimism. Recent history would suggest that the SNP will be successful in building their promised 50,000 new homes. Questions remain regarding whether these will create communities and what the environmental cost will be. Their manifesto does not say anything about the environmental standards to which these homes will conform (though existing standards provide a guide). A desirable target here is to construct them with world leading energy efficiency ratings and to include mandatory micro generation of electricity/heat (solar hot water, solar power, wind as locally appropriate). The Greens want new homes to be built with net zero carbon and current band C rating for existing homes. If the SNP take the Green's advice and buy the land at a rate reflecting the much lower *existing* use values rather than the *future* usage value then these superior environmental and build quality standards become more financially achievable. These bold, sustainable financing, housing and transport ideas combine to make possible some of the 200,000 well paid, high skilled jobs the Green party highlight can be created in a green economy.

The local environment around these new communities will also be improved if the government finally commit to a Scotland wide deposit return scheme covering glass, plastic and metal. The Greens want one covering glass, the SNP promise to give it more consideration. Litter is a sign of economic failure (something that had value now has none) and a sign of poor design, so over the next five years it would be pertinent to see governments shift the blame for its existence from the consumer to include the producer. Within 5 years with a Green party policy victory here, we could be living in a Scotland where you don't see aluminum cans or plastic or glass bottles lying on the ground, often near overflowing bins. If each is worth 10p, just watch how quickly local entrepreneurs will make these disappear. The next stage is the German model where uniform bottle sizes and shapes are mandated, making reuse easier and cheaper.

This talk of packaging helps us move to examining desirable ways of making Scotland sustainable by creating physical and psychological space where we can explore other ways of building our identity and gaining pleasure beyond buying stuff. An important change in the last three years in Scotland which facilitates this is the change in the language of government and societal ambition. Governments set their narrative via their speeches, press releases, manifestos and acts etc. The UK's version lauds private ownership over public, promotes

GDP as the central indicator of progress, and subsumes the rights of society and the planet to those of the economy. In Scotland we now talk about fairer, more prosperous and greener and words such as community, participation, shared ownership, local and empowerment are heard regularly and frequently from government. To help break our dangerous addiction to consumer goods, it would be desirable if this continued and followed through with a deliberate and sustained effort to use this language and so to embed a pro-society, pro-planet narrative throughout Scotland.

We also need to go further and control manipulative marketing and provide greater space for participation. Typically, when looking to reduce consumption, the onus is put on the consumer – they are told to recycle, turn down, switch off, put on a jumper, carry a bag. The onus should be placed back on the producer and government as these pro-environmental messages are drowned out by the state supported cacophony of messages telling us to consume. Consumers need space from identity based, symbol laden marketing practices that currently pervade our media and community landscape.

UK Advertising is 'controlled' by a voluntary, self-regulatory body, if we want a different form of relationship with consumer goods, we need our own, fully co-regulated authority. Currently advertisements must be "Legal, Decent, Honest and Truthful", we should add 'Does not undermine sense of personal or social self'. Via this regulator and existing planning powers, Scotland should instigate a complete ban on the advertising of goods and services *targeting* children and other vulnerable groups. This is not to say products cannot be produced for children but just that the messages promoting them must be focussed on those with the capacity to understand them for what they are. To help this, the type, amount and size of advertising allowed in civic and shared spaces should be controlled, Sao Paolo in Brazil has done this successfully. The sales of high fat, high sugar food and high sugar drinks should be banned from schools, libraries and other community-owned spaces. We could also look to control sponsorship arrangements between sporting, cultural and community groups and socially and personally damaging products like alcohol, gambling and high sugar drinks. Children in Scotland should not be cheering their heroes as they act as billboards for products that harm them.

Labels should contain the information regarding the resources used to make a product (water, energy, land clearance) and the waste products produced (CO_2 equivalent). We need progress toward including in the price of goods, the full cost of producing, maintaining and disposing of them. Tax payers currently foot the bill for the fly tipping of fridges, washing machines, sofas etc. Their purchase price should include the cost of disposal – we will see more progress towards this as the SNP and Green are both proponents of the circular economy which views all waste as a nutrient for another biological or technological process. Fresh impetus must be given to an international, GHG pollution cap and trading schemes.

Finally, as the previous ideas presented in this chapter have helped create the space for different ideas and relationships with consumption, we also need to ensure there is the physical and temporal space to allow families and friends to express and participate in relationship affirming, collective activities. The Community Empowerment Bill and Land Reform Bill, two of the most exciting agendas in Scotland today, can provide a step change in the availability of places to "be". To help this further we need to examine ways of reducing costs and administrative barriers (anyone who has tried to book a local authority hall will know what is meant here) and increasing skills levels.

David Cameron promised his 2010 UK government would be the 'greenest ever', but then consistently chose the dirty economy and low paid jobs over the planet and the potential of the green economy. Over the next five years, SNP and the Greens have a precious opportunity provided by parliamentary arithmetic to not just talk this good game but to combine and actually deliver significant progress on making Scotland a sustainable country. Their manifestos share many ambitions – in their targets, in how to make finance available, in how to heat and power homes, in transport and in who owns our land. When you look at this list it is a remarkable achievement that green politics has found its way so deeply into the mainstream, "party of government" SNP.

The next five years provide a greater opportunity for a de-facto Yes alliance in the parliament. If they both play nice and play the long game during the give-and-take required of government, they can move from the promises of mature, consensual, progressive politics made in so much Yes literature, to having a track record of doing it. A track record that will bind the Yes movement together and will build the confidence in it, of those soft No's we must persuade.

So if, sometime in the next five years Patrick Harvey is the cabinet secretary for Sustainability and expands its work to examine ways of changing our relationship with consumer goods, then considering what will have happened to get to this point, our environment will have won and independence politics will be much closer to winning.

Chapter 32

Rethinking criminal justice in Scotland

Mark Smith and Trish McCulloch

Crime in Scotland, as across most of the developed world, has fallen dramatically over the past decade, yet prison populations and community-based sanctions continue to rise. Scotland today imprisons more people than since records began. We have one of the highest rates of imprisonment in Western Europe.

Only England and Wales, Jersey and Gibraltar locked up a higher proportion of their people than Scotland. Even Spain and Portugal, with their recent histories of authoritarian regimes, have lower prison rates than we do. Ireland locks up around half the number of men and a third the number of women than Scotland. For many, the system is not working and is known to exacerbate many of the problems it seeks to address. Government reports from McLeish to Angiolini recognise the problem yet have had little impact on sentencing or on underlying trends in criminal justice practice.

With the advent of Conservative law and order policies in the 1970s crime became a political football. For a while, Scotland resisted some of the baser elements of these developments, hanging on to what commentators identify as greater penal welfarism. However, for much of the period since devolution and especially under Jack McConnell's watch, crime was identified as a key political issue. Progressive intentions were too readily shot down with accusations that proponents were being 'soft on crime'. More recently, there is some evidence of more thoughtful positions being struck. In the run-up to the 2016 Holyrood elections, the Howard League for Penal Reform organised an event involving the justice spokespersons from all of the main political parties around their vision and priorities for justice policy in the next Parliament. A consensus for change was evident across all of the parties.

Proposed reasons for change, however, can fall back on a continued reliance on managerial rationales, with talk of evidence, outcomes and cost. Of course, such considerations have their place, but they are not new and they have not delivered in changing attitudes or practices in respect of our continuing recourse to punishment and, in particular, to imprisonment. We appear to be stuck in recurring cycles of crime and punishment, in increasing prison numbers, in buckling community justice services, and in growing levels of public distrust or apathy towards justice reform.

At a point in our history when we are encouraged to imagine that we might live in a better nation, a fundamental examination of our justice system must be part of those (re)imaginings. Our current recourse to imprisonment is not only inefficient – it is wrong. Reasons to do things differently are not merely, or even primarily, managerial but are fundamentally ethical and indeed cultural. Change will require that we examine what it is within the Scottish psyche that makes us want to rush to a retributive and ultimately ineffective version of punishment.

Richard Holloway, the former Episcopal Bishop of Edinburgh, identifies a religious past that still hangs around our thinking about punishment like the haar off the North Sea. This legacy is based around a theological view of sin as willed disobedience of God's moral commandments. Premised on a notion of free will, disobedience requires to be punished. Within such an anthropology humans have no history to distort or determine their choices. Yet we ought to be only too aware that most of those caught up in the criminal justice system have encountered structural impediments, which have profoundly impacted on their capacities to make 'good' choices. We know that poverty and inequality are not only manifest in disparities of wealth and opportunity but that they distort an individual's sense of worth and belonging, which in turn, can lead to behaviours that are unthinking or uncaring (of self or others). Yet we continue to punish those who are victims of an unequal society. It can be hard to see any connection between what we do in criminal justice and Government priorities for a fairer, safer, stronger or healthier Scotland.

At a cultural level, our responses to crime perhaps reflect our continued national insecurities. Individually, but maybe also collectively, we seek security through the creation of binaries between ourselves and those others who don't think and act as we do. But the quest for security through imagining that we are somehow different from the other, the offender, is always tenuous and the demarcation lines inevitably blurred. This tendency towards stigmatising or 'othering' those who offend compromises efforts to promote citizenship, reintegration and social cohesion amongst these very same groups.

It is perhaps this fine line between the offender and the non-offender and the fear of dropping below that line that creates such a visceral popular reaction to criminality. And politicians understandably pick up on and respond to the emotive nature of much offending or at least its representation. One of the reasons policy makers might offer for failing to adopt a more radical approach to criminal justice policy is concern over how such policies might play with the public. They are, arguably, behind the curve on this. Surveys prior to the 2007 Scottish Election identified that crime was the foremost concern for 7 per cent of respondents. By 2011, this figure was down to 2 per cent. Moreover, the tabloid press and indeed the mainstream media more generally, have lost much of their power and influence, certainly among progressive voices in the new Scotland. A confident nation needs to be able to move beyond its residual insecurities. Politicians need to face down the atavistic demands of a baying but decaying mainstream media.

There are other signifiers of a need for change, which come out of the public sector reform agenda. Across the board, we are told that public services, or at least public service outcomes, are now a collaborative affair; they rest as much on the attitudes and actions of the people and communities who co-produce them, as they do on the attitudes and actions of those who once presumed to orchestrate them. Yet there are some sections of the public services that seem inured from this imperative to engage differently with individuals and communities. Criminal justice has remained, largely, the preserve of politicians, the police and the legal establishment, spurred on by a populist press. It needs to belong within a broader *civitas*, within which citizens and communities can play an active role in shaping, and sharing responsibility for, criminal justice responses and outcomes. And while a more democratic and participatory justice system does not necessarily make for a more progressive one, there are signs that the public are, or can be, more understanding and tolerant than they might be imagined to be.

There are growing examples of civil society claiming a role in criminal justice policy, the most obvious being the grassroots campaign led by Women For Independence (WfI), which influenced the Scottish Government's decision to cancel their proposed new women's prison at Greenock. Following on from this, WfI have initiated their Justice Watch campaign whereby women sit in on and observe court proceedings with a view to highlighting the futility and cost of them. Another initiative, Vox Liminis, harnesses the power of music-making to assist the reintegration of people with convictions into communities, using music to spark the imagination of those who struggle to otherwise engage in rehabilitative activity.

Relatedly, positive prison? Positive Futures is using the shared lived experience of people who are or have been subject to criminal justice sanctions to change the conversation around justice in Scotland. Their activity focusses on reducing the harms caused by crime, supporting reintegration and influencing change in social attitudes, policy and practice.

So where might we be in five years time? So long as we continue to believe that we can effect change in criminal justice practice through the elusive quest for more effective interventions or through managerial edict, then the likelihood is that we'll be in much the same place as we are now – wringing our hands over ever-increasing prison populations, intractable rates of reoffending and a divided Scotland. It is customary, in talk of public sector reform to speak of transformational change. Such change in the criminal justice system needs to focus on underlying value questions of what kind of society do we want Scotland to be. We need to imagine what a humane, progressive, and effective criminal justice system might look like, and we need to act to mobilise that vision. This might involve deliberation of values of citizenship, care, compassion, forgiveness and, ultimately, human flourishing. It might involve a more confident and connected articulation of what justice means in Scotland. It should certainly involve more civil engagement with these issues.

At the other end we need to be able to challenge those noisy elements of society who often claim progressive credentials but seek to identify ever more crimes that need to be prosecuted and punished. While few would seek to defend domestic or sexual violence we do need to ask whether prosecution and imprisonment is always the most imaginative or appropriate response we can come up with. We are at a point where, against the backdrop of falling crime identified above, 80 per cent of those appearing before the High Court do so for sexual offences, many committed decades ago. These are emotive issues where there can be a strong disincentive to question. But, if prison is ineffective and, as we argue here, very often wrong in and of itself, then it is equally wrong to begin to identify categories of crime for which prison becomes a default response. This represents the triumph of ideology over evidence.

Justice values cannot be imposed though. Rather, they need to bubble up, be debated, contested and mobilised by a wider set of actors than typically occurs in justice 'reform'. We need to move beyond the current consensus for change towards an irresistible programme for action, which will see tangible results in reducing the use of imprisonment and the emergence of more humane, participatory and effective responses to offending. If we are able to do so, we may, by 2021, have a criminal justice system we can be proud of and which defines us as the progressive nation we want to be.

Nation and Imagination

Chapter 33

Three dreams of modern Scottish nationalism: and what comes after?

Gerry Hassan

For the last fifty years, Scottish nationalism and the emergence of the SNP as a serious electoral force have shaped much of the political landscape. There have been three successive waves – 1967/74, 1988/92, and post-devolution Scotland particularly from 2007. First, it supplanted the Tories as the main opposition to Labour, then challenged Labour in its rotten burghs, and then surpassed Labour, leaving it marooned and marginalised.

The scale of some of this change has been pedestrian and slow: the SNP first breakthrough being Hamilton 1967 and the first national surge, February and October 1974. But some it has been phenomenal, with the SNP slender victory in 2007 and 2011 landslide transforming politics. The SNP replaced Labour as the dominant political force and natural party of government, Labour were reduced to the sidelines and withered, the indyref brought political discourse on to the SNP's favourite subject and terrain: independence and Scotland's voice.

Just as Hamilton fifty years ago changed so much, the SNP twin victories of 2007 and 2011 made everything else that came after possible. Looking back now nine years from the first triumph, it seems a very different world: then it felt as if 'a weight had been lifted from our shoulders', as if we had a second chance with devolution and the Parliament. Then four years later, a dismal Labour campaign was emphatically rejected and an unexpected SNP landside occurred. This was exciting, an opening, even, if over the top, 'a Scottish spring'.

These two moments were the foundational basis of the SNP's current ascendancy. They happened with the party as a clean broom, competent and confident, assured in its ability to be a government and stand up for Scotland. In short, everything Labour could not and would not be.

This takes us to more recent events, namely the indyref, 2015 tartan tsunami, and 2016 Scottish Parliament elections when the SNP won a historic third term. This is the triptych of Peak Nat – of the party at its height, at times carrying all before it. The SNP lost the indyref, but mobilised a part of the country which hadn't been reached in a generation; then swept the pro-union parties from literally every part of Scotland bar a few isolated pockets, and subsequently, increased their constituency vote in percent and numbers after nine years in office. Impressive, but success breeds new expectations and even entitlements, and the SNP reacted to each of these watersheds very differently from past triumphs.

The three peaks of the modern SNP

The 2014 indyref was a watershed in Scotland's political maturity. The forces of the union won the vote 55:45 but in the longer perspective, the forces of change shook the British establishment to its roots, disorientated the Labour Party, and came close enough to winning to make sure the status quo and union were not strengthened.

Yet, from these gains for the SNP and independence opinion, what has been the post-vote referendum response? First, in the immediate aftermath, neither Alex Salmond or Nicola Sturgeon spoke to the nation, instead choosing to talk to the 45%. Second, there was no proper post-mortem anywhere about how Yes lost: merely the continuation of the campaign momentum into subsequent elections. Nearly two years after the vote, no senior Nationalist politician has systematically addressed the shortcomings of the 2014 indy offer, examining where it was inadequate, looked at how to address it, or properly spoke to the motivations of the two million No voters.

The leading advocate of the 'no regrets'/'don't look back' approach has been Alex Salmond. He has blamed everyone and everything but himself and the flawed Yes offer. Thus, in the time since September 2014 he has continually carped about the biases of the BBC, the perfidy of the Vow, and the role of Gordon Brown and his late intervention in the campaign.

This isn't a defence of the role of the BBC, the Vow or Brown, but Salmond seems to think he has had the rightful victory that was his and the SNPs stolen from him. Thus, since September 2014 he has continually railed against the BBC, conducted a vendetta against the BBC's former Political Editor Nick Robinson, and argued based on the most flimsy evidence that the BBC was consciously and deliberately biased against the SNP and independence. Now the BBC didn't have a good referendum and had pro-union biases in some of its coverage, particularly some of the London-based reporting. But that doesn't amount to the charges Salmond levies against the whole corporation and its editorial line.

More important are two bigger points. First, this negates the problems in the Yes offer, from the currency, to Treasury/Bank of England position, European Union membership and more. Yes were happy to offer independence as apple pie and ice cream to everyone, to forgo hard choices, and instead, run a vote maximalising campaign, ignoring the basic contradictions in their offer. One fundamental was that while the SNP invoked a geo-political shifting of Scotland from Anglo-American capitalism to a more Nordic model, their indy offer would have entrenched a newly self-governing Scotland in the former, with few real strategic fiscal choices. All of this was ignored in the referendum and subsequently.

Second, the above limits haven't been fundamentally addressed since the indyref. This has big consequences. When Nicola Sturgeon and others talk about a new campaign for independence, what indy offer are they talking about? Reheating the 'cauld scones' of the 2014 indyref with all its contradictory Salmondnomics and worse? That offer is dead in the water and rightly so. Saying this doesn't make you an enemy of independence, but a believer in honesty.

Eight months after the indyref came the May 2015 general election – one in which the SNP as well as carrying nearly all before it in Scotland, played a central role in British debates. The party won 56 out of Scotland's 59 Westminster seats, reducing the three main opposition parties (Labour, Tory, Lib Dem) to one single seat each. The popular vote was slightly less overwhelming but impressive: 49.97% of the vote resulting in 95% of seats.

Post-election there were numerous assertions that the SNP and 'the 56' spoke for Scotland, some of which can be seen as over-enthusiasm and exuberance. Yet, the legal pursuit of Alistair Carmichael, the solitary Lib Dem MP, for his role as Secretary of State for Scotland and being dishonest about the Scotland Office memo leaked while understandable, gave the impression that Nationalists had a problem with opposition. That three opposition MPs were too many – considering the glee with which many went after Carmichael. There was no underwriting of the case against Carmichael by the SNP leadership, but as in many instances, there was no attempt to hold people back.

Finally, there were the SNP controversies of newly elected MPs,

Michelle Thomson and Natalie McGarry, both of whom were suspended from the party. Here the SNP leadership did act quickly, but the wider nationalist community seemed to be in mass denial. Actions which if a Labour or Tory politician had undertaken would be seen as a sin, were defended to the hilt: with SNP and pro-indy bloggers trying to deny there was any 'scandal' involved in either. (At the end of September 2016, Glasgow East MP McGarry was charged by police in connection with alleged fraud. On 15th September Police Scotland said:"There is no investigation into Michelle Thomson but there is an investigation into Christopher Hales, a 57-year-old solicitor who was struck off and whose services were used by Michelle Thomson for a number of property transactions and inquiries are still ongoing.")

Fast forward to May 2016 and the SNP's re-election as government. This, unlike previous contests, had been pre-costed as a SNP triumph and potentially second majority government. The SNP won and won well, but it didn't carry all before it: falling two seats short of an overall majority.

How did the party react to this? Not very well. Nicola Sturgeon spoke of 'a clear and unequivocal mandate' – which clearly this wasn't – and also that the party had won 'almost half the vote' – which 46.5% is a bit of a gap from. Senior nationalist politicians continued to cite from their script that they won over a million votes – the highest ever under devolution, and took every seat in six out of Scotland's seven cities. It all sounded a bit like Thatcher at her peak in the 1980s, or New Labour triumphalism: political class speak over-sell.

In the ensuing days numerous SNP politicians (Angus Robertson, Tommy Sheppard) tried to dismiss the Tory revival, pointing out that Ruth Davidson's 22.9% was lower than any achieved by Thatcher – missing that in her three UK triumphs her Scottish vote was significantly ahead of the SNP. The Tory vote was the highest seen since John Major won 25.6% in 1992: which amounts to a generational change, and the share of the vote the SNP won in pre-devolution times in 1992 and 1997, so not to be dismissed.

Worse were the complaints about the unfairness of the electoral system. Alex Salmond stated, "I won a majority on 45% of the vote five years ago and Nicola did not win a majority on 47% of the vote, which is quite astonishing – remarkable." He continued: "So you can get yourself into a situation if you cut it unlucky that you lose a range of list seats despite the fact you are topping the list vote by a very small margin in votes.' (LBC, 11th May 2016). Former Deputy Leader of the SNP, Jim Sillars, pointed out the outlier result given the D'Hondt system was 2011 when the SNP won a majority, while the 2016 showed the system working as it was meant to "designed to prevent a party winning a majority" (BBC Question Time, 12th May 2016).

There is in the above three scenarios a consistent pattern. It can be summarised as lack of generosity, absence of pluralism, inability to accept the voters' verdict, the politics of grievance (role of the Beeb, the Vow etc), and unwillingness to accept that the SNP are consistently a popular minority in Scotland and that non-SNP Scotland has even at Peak SNP (2015) remained a majority. The same characteristics often befall political parties at their most powerful as they turn inward and become out of touch: Thatcher 1987, New Labour post-1997 and Scottish Labour ad nauseam.

Scotland's dominant party system

Drawing from Tom Nairn's 'Three Dreams of Scottish Nationalism', his classic, questioning 1968 essay: what would be the story of modern nationalism today? It would be made up of first the motivation to destroy 'London Labour', second, give expression to anti-Tory Scotland, and third, the belief in a progressive, social democratic politics, and the SNP as the defenders of this. All three of these pillars are used to reinforce the idea that they are best aided by the pursuit and achievement of independence. This poses statehood as a means to an end, a contingent, and not something inherently superior on its own, but in reality, the distinction between means and ends has never been clearcut.

The SNP has historically seen itself as an outsider party, antiestablishment and not part of the cosy, closed networks of unionist and Labour Scotland. This gave the party when it came to power in 2007 an advantage: the freshness and populist touch of those who aren't political insiders. But slowly and inevitably, this dissipates with the passing of time and the rules of political gravity. It is interesting that the SNP have remained so popular nine years into office, aided by the leadership of Salmond and Sturgeon, and ineptitude of their opponents. But still much of the party has a problem with criticism of any kind: disputing whether it is now part of the 'establishment' and refusing to recognise any 'bad news' about policy choices.

One such area of dispute is whether SNP dominance counts as a 'one party state'. It can be rightly argued that Scotland isn't such a state, and that instead it is a dominant or pre-dominant party system.

Consistency isn't a strong point of some SNPers, as the deniers now are often many of the same people who used to call out Labour dominance as that of a 'one party state'. Rather than worry about the nomenclature of debate, we should focus on the substance, and Scotland's tradition of dominant party political systems.

A comparison between Labour at its peak and SNP at its peak in electoral representation shows a striking similar scale of dominance. Labour in 1999 won 115 of Scotland's 209 national representatives; the SNP today has 121 out of 194 representatives. Labour won 55% of representatives while their highest vote of the period was 45.6 per cent in 1997; the SNP have done even better with 62per cent of representatives achieved when their highest vote was 49.97% in 2015.

Table 1:
Labour Scotland 1999

	MPs	MSPs	MEPs	Total	%
Labour	56	56	3	115	55
SNP	6	35	2	43	21
Lib Dem	10	17	1	28	13
Conservatives	–	18	2	20	10
Others	–	3	–	3	1.5

Note: Based on most recent elections: 1997 UK, 1999 Scot Parl, 1999 European.

Table 2:
Nationalist Scotland 2016

	MPs	MSPs	MEPs	Total	%
SNP	56	63	2	121	62
Conservatives	1	31	1	33	17
Labour	1	24	2	27	14
Lib Dem	1	5	–	6	3
Greens	–	6	–	6	3
UKIP	–	–	1	1	0.5

Note: Based on most recent elections: 2014 European, 2015 UK, 2016 Scot Parl.

In both situations, the opposition parties are left scrambling around for the remainder of the crumbs. In 1999 this was the SNP, Lib Dems and Tories; today it is Tories, Labour, Lib Dems and Greens. One caveat is that this doesn't take account of Labour's predominance in local government in 1999, and the more pluralist politics today under STV – where only two councils have one party rule and both are Labour (Glasgow and North Lanarkshire). However, twenty years ago local government had a much bigger, important role in the nation, whereas today shorn of most council housing and after nine years of council tax freeze, it is much less important.

Nationalist Scotland isn't a majority and that matters

Some will say: welcome to the new establishment, just like the old establishment. Not quite yet. The SNP are still relative newcomers to the politics of power. They have not built up the politics of inter-generational cronyism and insider dealing which denoted Labour rule. But there are already warning signs that the party's instinctive touch and popular feel are being worn at the edges by the price of success and incumbency.

Scottish nationalism was never going to be enough on its own to make a new political dispensation. That was always clear. That is one reason it has since the 1980s adopted a distinctively centre-left message and politics, but the SNP has never unconditionally and unequivocally been a social democratic party, instead sitting centre-left and centrist with 'Big Tent' aspirations and politics.

After Labour Scotland's demise, the limits of nationalist Scotland were always going to appear. In three specific spikes of political engagement the SNP have in part called it wrong: the aftermath of the indyref, post-2015 and post-2016. A pattern of hubris, rubbing opponents up the wrong way, the emergence of an entitlement culture, and lack of willingness to recognise the boundaries of the appeal of your own project, paint in places an unattractive picture and ring the alarm bells for the future.

The SNP have contributed much positively to our politics in recent times, from the 1960s, post-devolution Scotland, and since it came to power in 2007. A Scottish politics without the SNP is hard to imagine, but it would be one much less attractive and pluralist, and more predictable and boring. A politics reduced to Labour, Tory and Lib Dems would be a profoundly dispiriting place: that of course was the Scotland and Britain of the 1950s. Imagine how parts of England have felt at times – only having the Greens as an attractive home of protest, and in many places of desperation, having to turn to UKIP to show their frustration and get the Westminster political classes to sit up and take notice.

It is essential for the SNP to recalibrate how does its politics nine years into office. It has to open up a bit, lets its hair down, and let go, recognising it is no longer the new kid on the block. The SNP isn't Scotland and nor is the SNP independence, or independence synonymous with the SNP.

The Scottish Nationalists were a breath of fresh air on the way up, now they have reached the top, a very different politics is required. Nationalist Scotland even at its peak hasn't commanded a majority of the vote. Non-Nationalist Scotland at the peak popularity of the SNP in 2015 still won a majority of the vote.

Many nationalists reading this will say what does any of this matter: losers complain, we are the masters now. It matters for two reasons – first, good politics, democracy and if the SNP is to renew in office as all long-term successful parties have to. But even more importantly, the SNP needs non-nationalist Scotland more than it needs the SNP.

When Labour decided to have the 1997 devolution referendum, central to its strategy to winning was that it recognised it couldn't win on its own vote. It knew it needed Lib Dem voters to win even a bare majority, and SNP voters for an emphatic margin. Everything else flowed from this. I know this directly as I wrote the 'Scotland Forward' external message strategy based on the equal need for Labour, SNP, Lib Dems and other voters. Any future indyref cannot be won by SNP voters on their own. Instead, it will take an alliance of Labour, Lib Dems, Greens and those of no party, and that means, as in 1997, developing a politics, messaging and strategy, which recognises the limits of the leading party: in this case the SNP and its reach. That is a tough ask for some politicians to undertake, but it is essential to winning a future indyref.

The SNP have taken us far. We always knew that nationalism – whether Scottish or British wasn't going to be enough. Social democracy, that oft cited description of our politics, is on its knees across Europe, and we haven't solved the modern dilemmas which impale others. The new left of the 1968 generation never lived up to its hype, while neoliberalism, despite never being openly advocated in Scotland, has influenced all the mainstream parties, but is now openly discredited and associated with zombie capitalism, apart from in its core post-democratic political and corporate elites.

This leaves radical democrats, egalitarians and those from the left tradition, knowing that we have to invent a new political tradition. That isn't something the SNP or Scotland can do on its own, but we can play a small part in, if we recognise the failings of the political traditions which have defined us. Scotland's future will look very different from today and that is something we should welcome and embrace.

This isn't a clarion call to 'work as if you live in the early days of a better nation' which always sounded very Scottish, purposeful, and possibly orchestrated with an element of coercion. Instead, let's 'act as if' we already are independent – which necessitates seriousness, radicalism, play, irreverence and standing up to groupthink and orthodoxies – wherever they come from – the SNP included. For this we require a politics which allows for dreaming, but recognises its inherent failings, if as is so often the case, action and words aren't connected. So let's dream of a better nation, but focus on the detail and fuzzy, messy realities of modern Scotland.

Chapter 34

Scotland in postcolonial perspective

Michael Marten

Postcolonial thinking can be understood in two broad ways: there is what I tend to call a postcolonial *moment*, which is the actual ending of colonial control of a territory (e.g. India removing the British and becoming independent in 1947), and a postcolonial *movement*, which points to a mode of thinking and action that opposes colonialism specifically but also more generally domination and control. The latter therefore includes various movements that have arisen before, during and after periods of colonisation.

In thinking about Scotland in a postcolonial perspective, we need to begin by highlighting Scotland's colonial past. Scotland – as part of Britain – played an integral role in the largest empire the world has ever seen, controlling huge swathes of the planet and brutally exploiting resources and people in the furtherance of imperial aims from the 1707 union onwards, and in particular from the early 19th to the early 20th centuries (and having mentioned the union, we should recall that the union itself came about in part because of Scotland's failed attempt at colonialism in present-day Panama with the Darien Scheme). A disproportionately high number of Scots served in various British colonial functions, and though for many this can in part be explained by deprivation and a lack of opportunities at home, coupled with a good education and an appetite for the adventurism that might be experienced abroad, Scots still carry as part of their – often unacknowledged – heritage, a key role in the oppression of large numbers of people around the world. This almost always involved taking resources for use by the Empire, whether minerals, foods, manufactured goods, or even human slaves (remembering that Robert Burns would have been involved in slavery in the West Indies had his fortunes at home not suddenly improved).

It is too easy for Scots in contemporary times, especially those seeking independence from Westminster rule, to argue that this history is part of the *British* state's heritage and can therefore be safely ignored. But many Scottish families will have ancestors who served the Empire, many of our cities were built through the exploitation of imperial riches (as many street names show), and in some cases, substantial family wealth originates with imperial involvement: Empire is therefore very much a part of our heritage and contemporary context. Equally, many people overseas will understand Scots as a part of the British Empire, even if Scottish involvement (e.g. missionary schools and hospitals) is at times viewed more benignly than wider British control (which is often seen in military and economic terms).

We therefore need to be aware of our own part in this history if we are to engage with the rest of the world beyond the (in the meantime somewhat dis-United) Kingdom. This is even more the case since Britain as a state is so clearly wedded to militarism and imperial adventurism in its dealings with the wider world, echoing an attitude that in many regards has not moved on substantially from the days of the Empire: Tony Blair's illegal war on Iraq in 2003 is emblematic in this regard.

It is partly in objecting to this that many people during the 2014 referendum campaign argued that an independent Scotland could and should embody a different kind of foreign policy to that of the British state. The argument went that Scotland could offer a role more akin to that of the Scandinavian countries, with a greater interest in active global peacemaking, poverty alleviation, and international development. An independent Scotland would not enter into illegal wars to control oil or other resources, but would engage constructively in situations of conflict and poverty.

The present Scottish government does not, of course, have most of the powers required for such levels of autonomous engagement, but all governments since 1999 have sought to play an active role overseas insofar as the confines of the devolution settlement allows. Most recently, Humza Yousaf, as Minister for Europe and International Development in the 2011-2015 SNP-majority government, supported an ongoing relationship with Malawi through the Scotland-Malawi Partnership (initiated in 2004 under First Minister Jack McConnell of the Labour-Liberal Democrat government*), and especially after visiting Greece in autumn 2015, bringing pressure to bear on the UK government in relation to Europe's moral crisis over refugees, and much more. This kind of engagement can, I think, justly be described as postcolonial, in that it emerges from a way of thinking about the world and acting in it that seeks to oppose and even undo structures

---

* http://www.scotland-malawipartnership.org

of domination in order to enable all people, whether in Scotland or connected to Scotland, to take control over their lives, to have agency.

So what might a postcolonial approach from the new Scottish parliament for 2016-2021 look like?

The pro-independence parties have a majority in Holyrood (63 Scottish National Party, six Scottish Green Party, both parties being internationalist left in outlook and ethos), even if the SNP no longer has a majority on its own. With the Conservative and Unionist Party as the second party in the parliament (albeit a distant second), it may be that the Labour Party in particular moves from an "opposition for opposition's sake" position against the SNP to a more progressive stance that allows it to cooperate with the SNP/Greens on areas of common interest, especially if they do not appear to touch on the constitutional question directly which is obviously still a contentious internal issue for Labour. Labour might therefore join the broad internationalist left SNP/Green majority (perhaps even with the Liberal Democrat Party), meaning interest in international justice questions would clearly be supported by an overwhelming majority of MSPs in the parliament. (There is, of course, no reason to assume the Conservatives would support such an approach, tied as they are to the Conservative government in Westminster and their policies, representing precisely the kind of foreign policy so strongly criticised by many Scots; an alignment as outlined here would clearly marginalise the Conservatives still further, however).

It is important, of course, that Alasdair Allan, Yousaf's successor in the ministerial role (renamed Minister for International Development and Europe) carries forward the kind of engagement that he has been pursuing, but even beyond that, there is scope for the Scottish government to become more engaged overseas.

For example, the success of the Scotland-Malawi Partnership in bringing people from Malawi to Scotland and sending Scots to Malawi to teach and study has enriched many in both countries. Scotland has a long connection to Malawi: colonised by the British in 1891 and finally gaining full independence in 1964, many Scots played a role in the colonial rule, but also in the independence movement and the liberation of Malawi (often as church missionaries). The Partnership represents a positive way for Scotland to move from the postcolonial *moment* to the wider postcolonial *movement*, and it would be encouraging if something broadly similar could emerge in relation to other countries with which Scotland already has connections: a very obvious candidate would be India. As with Malawi, many Scots went to India in the colonial era (including as missionaries to work in schools and clinics), and there are still many connections between the two countries. However, as a result of the Westminster Conservatives' race-based immigration policies (a reserved matter), ever fewer Indians are now coming to Britain to study (for example). This has been widely reported in the *Times Higher Education* and elsewhere, and is causing considerable concern for universities, including in Scotland. Finding creative ways to work around such restrictions to enable more positive interactions to develop between Indians and Scots in India and in Scotland would be a very positive step.

But there is also something more to this postcolonial movement that relates to the kind of country many Scots want their country to be: the day after the May 2016 election, ten members of the UN Office of the Special Envoy's Syrian Advisory Board arrived and spent four days in Scotland, including meetings at the parliament, looking at ways to help Syrian women with peacemaking and conflict resolution skills. Staffan de Mistura, the UN Special Envoy explained the choice of Scotland: "The very special case of Scotland – currently with its own parliament and its own strong gender balance in government and the fact that the First Minister and two opposition leaders are women – were key motivating factors in helping set this up." This revealing statement should make Scots proud: it is a comment not only on the way we *do* politics, but the way we *are* in our politics, even without independence: "even when you are not independent you do still have a very specific message to give that has international resonance, and you should do so", de Mistura commented. (David Pratt, 'UN's top diplomat: Scotland is perfect setting for Syrian peace initiative', *Sunday Herald,* 15th May, 2016.)

It is in this kind of area that Scotland can also perhaps offer more than Westminster, even without independence. Scotland's politics is by no means perfect, whether in terms of gender representation (it is high time the SNP introduced quotas for candidate selection, for example) or ethnic diversity (again, some form of quota might be helpful), but there is undoubtedly a recognition that something different is happening in Scotland in the here and now. Working to improve our democratic system, by utilising the tremendous levels of engagement that the independence debate produced is clearly important for its own sake. The comments from the UN Special Envoy suggest we should be encouraging our government to do more in this regard, not least to be a more positive influence in the world than many perceive the Westminster government to be. This really is about *being* the change we want to see happening.

But this is not simply about the government doing something, removed from the people. The "firm democratic credentials" that are so lauded by the UN Special Envoy originate with us, the people, engaging in politics, prompting and pushing our politicians to act. Whether this be Women for Independence in January 2015 successfully campaigning against the government's plans to open a large women's prison in Inverclyde, the SNP's members challenging the party leadership on land reform in October 2015, or the voters in May 2016 returning a pro-independence government that was not just an SNP-majority government, it is of paramount importance that we act. As Scottish citizens, the postcolonial movement that we want our recently elected parliament to engage in comes about in part through our local actions, as well as in international interests that many of us have. The slogan 'think globally, act locally' has clear resonances in bringing about a government and country that understands itself as having a positive role in a postcolonial world.

Chapter 35

No settled will: what next?

Stuart Fairweather

Everyday life dominates the existence of most of the people most of the time. The media told us early in 2016 that it was a boring Scottish parliament election campaign. Holyrood 2016 was not the referendum of 2014, or for that matter the EU referendum of June 2016 (generally judged to be a dreadful campaign leading to an 'exciting' result).

The May 2016 poll saw Nicola Sturgeon endorsed as First Minister. The voting system and the votes cast mean we have a plural parliament with six parties represented. Scottish voters spread their bets and ensured no party has 'overall control'. That said the SNP's 63 MSPs – just two short of a majority – are a powerful block. Taken alongside the six Greens, they create a balance in favour of independence.

The Conservatives 31, Labour 24 and Liberal Democrats 5 give the 'unionist parties' a significant voice but only if they speak with one voice. The workings of the parliament are proving to be more complex, of course.

The dominant messages from the results are that the SNP continue to do well but cannot be complacent. The Tories have managed to unite conservative and overtly unionist voters behind them. This has hurt Labour, who were not in good shape to begin with. The Greens and the Liberals are each able to play a role dependent on arithmetic and alliances.

All these parliamentary parties would do well to remember that almost two million Scots did not vote; many poor, many young. Those seduced by the "both votes SNP" strategy were pushed towards "wasting" their votes. If the objective was to elect the maximum number of pro-independence MSPs then this tactic was futile. Ironically for the left, unionist voters appeared to make use of the voting system without too much fuss. Labour, Liberal, and even SNP voters in some parts of the country, gave the Tories their list vote for a range of reasons relating to the union. The Conservatives brought together those that never want to see a referendum under any circumstances with those that remain unsure. In constituencies a tactical approach was employed to support the best placed unionist. This worked on fifteen occasions, with local factors, particularly in the Northern Isles being a consideration.

While the result could have been different, one outcome is that the regional list vote has now become extremely competitive for all parties other than the dominant SNP. Another aspect of the Scottish elections is that Labour seems squeezed. They appear to have very limited ability to build constituencies beyond their core vote. Their message changed for this election. They tried to sound more left-wing but were not believed with voters sticking with the SNP or choosing to support the Greens.

More urgent for Labour perhaps is the way they appear to have become "trapped" in the unionist camp. The record of Blairism and the experience of Better Together mean that many progressive voters are reluctant to listen to arguments from born-again social democrats. It is not clear how the Corbyn ascendancy at a UK level, and the struggles around that, make things better or easier.

In spite of a late sprint to the centre ground, the SNP are still seen by many as more authentic defenders of the Scottish variant of the social democracy. How authentic this is highly debatable. The Greens are the only party in parliament to come anywhere near to challenging the dominant position that is being taken; one of trying to hold on to the appearance of defending a Scottish welfare state whilst passing on a Westminster austerity agenda. The democratic left in its various forms needs to build an infrastructure and alliances to oppose this. This is the real priority.

Individuals in parliament and members of the SNP and Greens need to be encouraged to develop a progressive policy agenda. The internal democracy of these parties and their relationship to workers and hard-hit communities needs to be put to the test. Labour politicians that are serious about opposition to continued cuts across the public sector should be welcomed too. But it is unlikely that many of those strongly connected to Holyrood's political parties will be able to find the space to consistently oppose austerity.

Resistance to cuts is more likely to be found in the communities experiencing constant economic emergency and amongst those providing services. While this will not be automatic there have been some signs of an opposition building. The STUC (Scottish Trade Union Congress) has been asked by its members to take action against the next round of local government budget cuts and this is where pressure could be brought to bear on the Scottish Parliament and in turn the instigators of austerity at Westminster. This approach could do something to re-kindle the mass participation of the 2014 referendum period.

To do this, two aspects of the continuing election calendar need to be negotiated. Firstly, the European referendum result needs to be responded to in a way that does not derail the opposition to ongoing austerity. Secondly, thought needs to be focused clearly on the local government elections of May 2017.

May 2017 will see elections for all of Scotland's 32 councils. These elections, using single-transferable vote (STV), are the nearest to where people live out their lives and use services. Voters need to understand how to use the system. Who will support this learning? The established parties, including the SNP, did not take the lead in promoting voter registration during the referendum campaign. The established parties, where they did canvass, did not engage people in meaningful conversation. They simply collected data about voting. Those that oppose austerity need to return to this experience and launch a campaign that increases the number of informed voters, that increases the number of working-class people voting, and increases those voting against austerity. Holding off for a UK general election in 2020 is a wait too long. Acting now will build the forces for resisting further onslaughts.

Can Labour in Scotland contribute to this through the People's Assembly? Perhaps at the margins in some geographies but the official party looks set to move off in another direction and lacks the authenticity that comes from supporting Scotland's democratic advance.

Can the Greens reach out into working-class communities? To date the record is very limited and their parliamentary party look like providing another focus. But there are possibilities here.

The SNP are more complex and their 'legendary' discipline and reach across the country makes things more difficult. The search for legitimacy in office is likely to overshadow action on the ground. The election results for RISE were not encouraging. A rethink will be needed.

Beyond those above there are limited numbers of campaigners already engaged in action against the cuts, but again the experience of the referendum was that things can quickly grow over a relatively short period of time.

The women and men that took part in the 2014 referendum campaign have not gone away. The most progressive and productive elements of the campaign clearly linked anti-austerity and independence. It will rapidly become clear that voting "both votes SNP" alone will only produce limited results in furthering either cause.

So the approach to next May's elections will go a long way to determining what can be achieved over the next five years. Our parliament, our political parties and people in their everyday lives need to recognise that accepting ongoing cuts from London will not benefit Scotland.

Chapter 36

Grassroots political campaigning and the challenge to parties

Jane Denholm and Tam McTurk[*]

In the midst of writing this, the title that came to our minds was 'Ingliston no more.' Here's why. On the early morning of 19th September 2014, the Conservatives and Labour celebrated dependency together, quite deliriously, at the independence referendum count in Ingliston. We were spared such scenes at the Edinburgh International Conference Centre on the morning of Friday 8th May 2015, but you have to suspect that a glass or two was raised in Scottish Tory HQ when it became clear they had a UK-wide majority. On the early morning of 6 May 2016, Tories, Labour and Lib Dems celebrated separate victories in three Edinburgh constituencies at the Holyrood count in Ingliston.

This is the reality you face as a grassroots activist in the SNP and the wider Yes movement in Edinburgh and the Lothians. Yes, there are moments of joy, but the bigger picture is patchy, at best.

Campaigning and electioneering can be intensely rewarding, especially in a fantastically diverse area like Leith. Yes Edinburgh North and Leith (YENL) was multi-party, vibrant and innovative. The SNP campaign teams for Westminster 2015 and Holyrood 2016 were enthusiastic, dedicated and hard working. The Greens and RISE are highly visible on our local streets too. But then come the counts....

On all three occasions the hard work paid off in the polling districts we worked but the gratifying knowledge that we had done our bit was overwhelmed by the national result in 2014, tempered by the UK Tory majority in 2015 and our celebration was somewhat subdued in May 2016 by results elsewhere in Edinburgh.

The inevitable lesson

There are lessons in this for every level of the wider independence movement as well as the SNP. One is that nothing is inevitable in politics and Scottish politics is no exception.

---

[*] This is a personal perspective on local election and party campaigning. Written by two SNP members, it revolves around that particular party, but in the context of preparing for any future independence referendum in Scotland. It is likely to find resonance in other parties.

Of course the SNP and the Yes movement have done phenomenally well in recent years and the party continues to do so. The problem is that we set ourselves incredibly high ambitions – reviving a nation and making it socially just, environmentally friendly, prosperous and free from WMDs.

Compare and contrast that vision with the reality of London Conservative rule and the magnitude of what lies ahead is hard to ignore.

Disconnect

At ground level in Leith, in the aftermath of electoral struggle, there was and is little sense that the reason we are still so far from these goals is the fault of any one pro-independence party, individual or group in the Yes movement, no appetite for a blame game and yet more re-runs of the list-vote argument. That way madness lies.

Disconnect is a popular phrase, verging on the overused, in political discourse. Despite living in a digital age and all the communications options that entails, we were caught in a bubble, especially in 2014 and 2016, psychologically unprepared for what was happening elsewhere in the country and the city and no warnings were being passed down – or along – the chain.

Being active in a region of the country that has been less open to the independence message and the SNP message than Glasgow or Dundee, for example, has been a chastening experience and turns the mind to the nature of campaigning, especially at grassroots level, in the 21st century in Scotland. Any future analysis has to include the perspective of the door knockers, leafleters and other dedicated activists – both new and old – not just those of the commentariat, elected officials, spin doctors and leaders.

In recent campaigns it has sometimes felt as if we are reinventing wheels instead of complementing each other at the different levels of the campaign. The higher echelons need to learn to seek out and listen to the messages being passed up the chain and also to pass relevant and timely information back down it.

For example, we were acutely aware that the EU and pensions were issues in Edinburgh North and Leith during the Indyref campaign. Little of use filtered through from Yes campaign HQ in Hope Street, which seemed to think we should be saying – "Oh you're worried about your pension, here's a leaflet with a picture of two bairns on bikes". When we realised we were on our own, we researched, wrote and printed our own leaflets on a range of key issues. And that was great and empowering and we shared them with other groups. But the point is that there was simply no interest in hearing, never mind a mechanism for passing such messages up the line.

Similarly, notwithstanding the merits or otherwise of the act, the photograph of the SNP party leader holding *The Sun* newspaper, during the 2016 campaign, led to many supporters getting themselves bogged down in an excruciating morass of denials and justifications that raged across social media to the glee of unionist opponents. All it would have taken were a few timely words from the leadership, to at least clarify the facts as they saw them and offer reassurance to those for whom this was a significant concern.

The reality of twenty-first century grassroots activism is a mix of door knocking, running stalls and events and one-on-one conversations with people online as well as on doorsteps, often with committed, aware and informed opponents.

Volunteers can't keep up to speed with everything. They don't need the kind of detailed briefings and lines supplied to candidates, but activists need information at their fingertips, and preferably today, not tomorrow. Individual activist interactions on social media are just as much a part of digital engagement as any excellent video produced centrally.

Put bluntly activists need to be regarded as an intelligent resource, not simply always as canvassing fodder. And two-way communication need to be recognised as vital and to become the norm.

Nuts and bolts

Experience in Leith over the last few years suggests there has been a certain amount of fumbling-around-in-the-dark innovation, a certain amount of reinventing multiple wheels and a lot of doing things the way that they've always been done. None of this adds up to a 'new way of doing politics' designed to realise the latent potential of local activists in the digital age.

This not a criticism of the grassroots. We are where we are only because SNP activists have knocked doors relentlessly for decades, and being told where to go at many of them. It is, however, a criticism of the leadership of Yes Scotland, and also a piece of comradely counsel to the SNP leadership that it needs to think about and address, urgently.

Time and motion?

Hard pressed local election campaigns run exclusively by volunteers always face difficult choices. There's no time to study what they are doing as they do it. The electoral timetable grinds on inexorably and the imperative inevitably becomes just to get things done. And those things are the aye been.

This shouldn't be considered good enough in this day and age. Activists need help to decide how to plan campaigns based on the number of people available to do the work – time and motion studies if you like. Which forms of voter contact are the most productive? How does the time spent leafleting 100 doors compare to the time spent canvassing 10 doors? How do both of them compare with spending time organising a local rally or a street stall? Is it worth stuffing leaflets into addressed envelopes or are they just as effective without? And how do all traditional activities compare with digital campaigning?

All activities that might reasonably be classed as 'fun' tend to drop off the agenda in the interests of targeting scarce activist resources on traditional activities such as canvassing. National, evidence-based guidance on what is proven to work and what isn't, is badly lacking.

As a party, the SNP needs to help make its local teams as professional and modern as a team of volunteers can be expected to be. Apart from winning elections in the future it will serve as good preparation for any future Indyref campaign. The recent Depute Leader campaign helpfully highlighted the need for support and organisation, as well as more effective member participation in decision-making in a party that has grown from 25,000 members to 120,000 in a remarkably short space of time.

The numbers game

Locally, in Edinburgh North and Leith, SNP membership has also grown exponentially and is now approximately five times higher than the local Yes figure ever was. The local branches of the other Yes parties have also grown. So is everything set to go with a huge campaign next time around? Hardly. The painful truth is that when history came knocking the first time around a lot of people weren't sufficiently motivated to get involved and to date there are no solid indications that this has changed. On a somewhat simplistic level, approximately 100,000 people should have little problem making contact with 3–4 million voters over a period of 4–5 years. For 10,000 people it would a lot more difficult.

Internal organisation

The influx of members post-referendum was as unprecedented as it was unexpected and the election timetable since then has given local branches and HQ little time to work out how to cope with it. This needs to be addressed now, and not just for the sake of the party. Tens of thousands of new members joined the SNP because they support independence just as much, if not more in many cases, than because they support the party. They have not metamorphosed *en masse* into campaigning or electioneering activists. The vast majority of them show little interest in sitting through monthly business meetings at branch level either.

How do we get more people engaged and how can the grassroots and the leadership talk and work together more effectively? One approach would be for the SNP to conduct an open exercise aimed at fundamental reform of its internal structures and activities. Not because the party hasn't been successful, but because they were designed for a different era. At the October 2016 SNP conference a motion along these lines was passed. It is important that it is delivered.

Over the next couple of years, it would be great to see bold new attempts to find a new national structure for how we organise and what we do, preferably one that allows for local conditions to be taken into account so we can organise in actual communities rather than only along constituency and ward boundaries.

Peak Blair to Dugdale doldrums

In the context of the need for two-way communications, it is fascinating to watch what looks to many to be the twitching corpse of Scottish Labour 2016 and compare it with the height of New Labour success in 1997. So many lessons can be learned from that long political decline. Among the biggest are that the Labour Party changed nothing internally, made no attempt to do things differently, stopped listening to each other at various levels of their organisation and took their supporters for granted to pander to an imagined group of electors. The fact that they still behave like ferrets in a sack just makes it even more tragi-comic

The mood music at all levels of in the SNP at the moment seems to be to learn from the past and to keep our eyes firmly on the prize. It would be good to see some real discussion about how we can put flesh on the bones and make that happen.

Shibboleth shaking

Leaving aside national tactical and strategic questions, it's time for some new thinking about what we do and how we do it. This will involve awkward questions about what activities are the most productive and shibboleths will be shaken in the process. Some will not like it but if it we do it now while the SNP and the wider Yes movement have so much goodwill to draw on, we'll be in good shape for the next Indyref whenever it comes.

Chapter 37

The threat of a good example: a view from south of the border

Bernadette Meaden

In 1985 Oxfam published a report entitled *Nicaragua: The Threat of A Good Example?* Oxfam found that, in spite of problems and limitations, the Sandinista government around that time was "exceptional in the strength of that government's commitment ... to improving the condition of the people and encouraging their active participation in the development process." The Sandinistas took radical measures to address inequality in land ownership, and to extend the provision of healthcare and education to poor peasant families.

As far as the United States was concerned, this could not be allowed to continue, and President Ronald Reagan set out to destroy the Sandinistas, using military and economic means. But why did the world's dominant superpower see tiny Nicaragua as a threat? Perhaps it was the fact that whilst many US citizens lived in fear of needing medical treatment they couldn't afford, the Sandinistas were establishing a National Unified Health System, giving even the poorest people access to government-funded health care. They were building an alternative to free market capitalism that looked effective, fair, and popular. And as Noam Chomsky explained, 'The weaker and poorer a country is, the more dangerous it is as an example. If a tiny, poor country ... can succeed in bringing about a better life for its people, some other place that has more resources will ask, "why not us?"

Now, admittedly the SNP are not exactly the Sandinistas, and Nicola Sturgeon is no revolutionary leader. But the political culture in your country has manifested bursts of energy and hope of real significance, and my personal hope is that, in seeking its own way forward, Scotland will be an example on England's doorstep of a country successfully taking a more progressive and egalitarian path, and thereby making such policies less easy to dismiss here in England. In a sort of poetic reversal of Margaret Thatcher trialing the hated poll tax in Scotland, we could in future see progressive policies being implemented in

Scotland and, hopefully, English voters asking, "Why not us?".

Currently in England, the political debate is largely contained within the narrow parameters of what a right wing dominated press deems allowable. Any idea not considered acceptable by billionaire tax-avoiding newspaper proprietors is branded as the product of an extreme, outlandish, and potentially dangerous 'loony left' or deemed 'Corbynism' in a pejorative, backward looking way. The lurch to right and to anti-migrant prejudice and policy after the Brexit vote has made things even worse in this respect. The broadcast media (sadly, often including the BBC) dutifully takes its cue from these newspapers, or from Conservative Central Office, ensuring that any radical policy proposals which see the light of day are soon buried beneath a combination of scorn and contempt.

We are constantly told that the English are naturally conservative, and will never support progressive policies. But in 2014, over 400,000 people took an online survey in which they were asked to vote for policies with no indication of the party they came from. Green Party policies came top, closely followed by Labour, with Lib Dems third, Conservatives fourth and UKIP last. Of course this is hardly scientific and the participants were self-selecting, but policies like taking the railways back into public ownership consistently get strong support in conventional opinion polls. When not mediated by establishment and corporate media, and viewed on their own merits, what might be deemed more radical policies are probably not as unpopular as we have been led to believe, even in England. A recent survey (October 2016) suggested that when more progressive Labour policies are presented to people without their source being identified, the reception is better, suggesting that branding and image play a significant part in popular political receptivity.

All this is why the General Election campaign of 2015, when the Conservative party, enthusiastically assisted by their friends in the press, portrayed a Labour/SNP coalition as some kind of doomsday scenario, was such a frustrating experience. Those of us who would have been very happy to see the SNP lending some anti-Tory muscle and courage to Blairite Labour would have welcomed the development. Even more depressing was the fact that this fearmongering, somehow, resonated with English voters and enabled a Conservative majority.

Perhaps a section of the English electorate project onto civic

Scottish nationalism the negative connotations that often accompany the sort of colonial-style nationalism espoused by UKIP and more right wing Conservatives. But Scottish nationalism, as far as I can see, does not stray into jingoism, does not define itself in terms of superiority to others, and is about what it stands for rather than what it is against. To me, it looks to be more about loving where you live and wanting to make it the best country it can be, in peaceful co-operation with other countries, not in any attempt to dominate others. (This, of course, has also produced some resentment towards "uppity Scotland" in other sections of the electorate in England.)

Scotland's distinct political culture should of course not be seen as offering a naïve panacea for progressives south of the border. But the ways in which Holyrood has diverged from Westminster, in retaining free education, free prescriptions, etc., all demonstrate a continuing faith in the idea of a comprehensive and supportive welfare state and social security for all. Meanwhile, for those of us in England who have watched the unfolding disaster of welfare reform causing terrible harm to the most disadvantaged people in society, to hear a politician with actual power, like the Scottish Social Justice Secretary, talking about abolishing the Bedroom Tax and the dignity of people who rely on benefits, is something we can only dream of.

Admittedly the SNP government has yet to make some of the bold and radical moves many of its supporters would like to see, but the very fact that there is room to debate them rationally, in public, without them being dismissed as the product of a lunatic fringe gives cause for hope. There appears to be a wider intellectual space in Scotland, in this respect at least. And while some measures adopted at Holyrood may have been relatively small, they indicate a much more positive mindset than the one that currently prevails in Westminster, where the forces of reaction are resurgent following the EU referendum vote. The announcement that the Scottish government would provide 'baby boxes' for every new born child, as in Finland, was a promising indication of a generosity of spirit and egalitarian approach entirely absent when the Westminster government tells us we are all in this together, but then acts to target and push aside disabled people, those on low incomes and many others.

Perhaps one of the most encouraging results of the 2016 Holyrood elections, from my vantage point, was the election of the Scottish Green Party's Andy Wightman. He is an expert in land ownership and land reform far less known in England than Scotland, and articulately advocates policies that pose a serious challenge to the interests of wealthy landowners. His book *The Poor Had No Lawyers* has been a real encouragement to people like me.

It is almost impossible to imagine a candidate like Wightman being elected in England. Long before he reached the ballot one would imagine that a media campaign would have attempted to destroy his character, and represent his policy proposals as a threat to civilisation as we know it. This has also happened to those pushing for a more radical stance from Labour, too. Yet the way land is owned, used, and taxed (or not taxed) is a major contributor to the dysfunctional property market and hence the housing crisis we are now experiencing in England. If any significant land reform can be enacted in Scotland, it could demonstrate to Generation Rent that things do not always have to stay as they are, property does not inevitably have to accumulate in fewer and fewer hands. Land Value Tax, anyone?

Of course, underpinning all this is the way the Scottish Parliament is elected, which is a big improvement on the anachronistic system Westminster still stubbornly clings to. There must be nothing more disheartening for a politically engaged person than casting your vote in a safe seat, when you know that effectively your vote will be wasted, and you will have no impact on the result locally or nationally. We may deplore low turnouts, but who can blame people for not voting in these circumstances? The Additional Member System adopted for Holyrood may not be perfect, but it reaches a result that far more accurately reflects the views of the population, and is light years ahead of first past the post.

Henry Ford said, "My best friend is the one who brings out the best in me". As their political systems and instincts diverge, I very much hope that Scotland can be such a best friend to those of us seeking progressive change in England.

Chapter 38

Global action beyond nation and identity: a view from the Balkans

Milja Radovic

In the midst of heated debates over the future of Europe and Brexit, the question of the role and place of Scotland in both the UK and to-day's Europe remains open. Make no mistake: Europe is in crisis, democracy is in crisis. The right and the extreme right are resurgent once again. The lurch towards anti-migrant policies in the UK and the mean-spirited response to refugees is one clear symptom of this.

I have been in Scotland long enough to learn about the pitfalls of the bulky bureaucracy upon which the whole system relies, and to see in which direction several matters such as health and education are slowly unfolding. I have been here long enough also to be able to compare, understand and repeat "the lessons learnt from Yugoslavia" – especially when it comes to the issue of nationalism, understandably a very sensitive matter for me. Scottish nationalism, wrapped on a day-to-day basis in a misty vision presenting itself as 'civic nationalism', is of a 'left' orientation when it comes to welfare state.

Civic or not, the outcome of the 2014 referendum was that a majority in Scotland preferred to stay in the UK, threatened as they were by economic crisis and the collapse or exodus of business. I am not an economic expert, and I certainly have no intention of offering a simplified view on the complex issues facing Scotland's constitutional future. However, it is worth remembering what holds citizens back from more radical political ideas and actions – regardless of their decisions or views on whether to stay or leave the UK – is a fear of international business abandoning the place. This same fear has kept international financial institutions in power in many other countries, under different conditions.

Here we come to the real problem. Regardless of whether we speak in terms of progressive dreams of Scotland's independence, or of general left approaches to matters like the NHS, social programmes, benefits and free education, what is really lacking is a larger momentum towards radical political action and collective civic consciousness. Scotland is still trapped in the games of global neoliberal politics and of the transnational financial institutions, about which the majority of citizens remain uninformed, buttressed by silence in other quarters. So the bureaucratic wheels keep turning, regardless. But the truth is that democracy in Scotland has been infected by the neoliberal disease on multiple levels.

Let me here recall just one example, of which I have personal experience. Universities (where education is still tuition free in Scotland, differently from England) are becoming more like corporations run by skilful managers. Increasingly, their prime value is determined by the price and worth as determined through the market. According to a University and Collage Union (UCU) survey, by 2013 the University of Edinburgh had already become the largest user of zero hour contracts with over 2,712 academics working on this type of contract. The same university was the first in the UK to introduce the new 'staff monitoring' policy. Our universities are introducing through the back door the sort of 'anti-terror' policies whereby staff, researchers and students are monitored, and are also required to monitor each other. In this climate of fear, any form of radicalism may become grounds for suspicion. In the pre-crisis world I believed that universities were there to form the innovative thinkers, not mere customers and servants of the market. This is less and less the case.

If the future of higher education is uncertain, so is that of the NHS and the welfare system. Scotland is trying to go in a different direction on these issues, but it is not immune from what is happening in the UK or in other parts of Europe and the world. Brexit or not, the elephant of neoliberal corporatism is already in the room. So where do we go next?

The priority has to be radical politics of the kind that recognises this global challenge and aims for the restoration of democracy, freedom of information, equality and economic recovery – effectively a continuous divorce from those neoliberal practices which serve the elite. The seeds of Diem 25 (the Democracy in Europe Movement 2025) have, in it own words, "been planted in several countries" as a network aiming to reform the European Union's existing institutions in order to create a 'full-fledged democracy with a sovereign Parliament respecting national self-determination and sharing power with national Parliaments, regional assemblies and municipal councils".[*]

---

[*] https://diem25.org/manifesto-long

Founder Yanis Varoufakis argues that the core challenge is renovation and replacement of institutions, not mere amelioration.

Radical politics should also mean a greater sense of solidarity and cooperation among citizens – abandoning the parochial mentality of 'tick box' bureaucracy, and looking at the real issues that the businesses who threaten to leave us, and their political guardians, have brought to the daily existence of those forced to live with the consequences of austerity. That is, all those who have to listen to motivational speeches from the UK government and others on how to get back to work through insecure zero hour contracts and the like. Unless we challenge these narratives at the deepest level (that is what the word 'radical' means) many caught in this situation will end up pointing at "foreigners" as the ones to be held responsible and blamed, as has been illustrated all too powerfully in the aftermath of the Brexit vote.

The issue here is not simply to challenge politicians and the media, for the real solution lies with citizens who through solidarity and working together, both at the grassroots level and through the appropriate institution, aim to restore democracy and divorce it from rapacious capitalism. In other words to take the power back – to coin a phrase which has been used for very different purposes recently!

If we do not find a way to do this, the existing dominant order will keep on running like Bong Joon-ho's train in the science fiction film *Snowpiercer* – with humanity trapped and cowed by a catastrophic global remedy which actually worsened the crisis it was meant to solve.

The role and place of Scotland could be to step outside – but only in this sense – from the practices that are strangling her, the UK and Europe right now. This is the kind of constructive dissent promoted by the likes of Diem 25 (mentioned above), whose aim is to reinvigorate the idea of Europe as a union of people governed with democratic consent rather than what the movement fears the current EU has been heading towards: a superstate ruled by technocrats issuing unaccountable edicts.

Chapter 39

The class factor in the independence question

James Maxwell

At the 2014 independence referendum, turnout in East Renfrewshire, one of Scotland's leafiest constituencies, was 90 per cent. By contrast, in Glasgow and Dundee, the two poorest cities in the country, it was 75 per cent and 79 per cent respectively. East Renfrewshire voted overwhelmingly in favour of the Union. Glasgow and Dundee backed independence.

Nine months later, at the UK general election, 54 per cent of voters turned-out in Glasgow North East, the bulk of them to elect SNP candidate Anne McLaughlin as their MP. Meanwhile, in Edinburgh South, where Labour's Ian Murray fought-off the SNP's advance, there was a 74 per cent turnout.

This pattern was repeated in the May 2016 Holyrood election. Average turnout in the 14 constituencies that elected pro-Union MSPs was 61 per cent, six per cent higher than the overall national turnout. Conversely, some of the lowest turnouts occurred in the SNP's Glasgow heartlands: 44 per cent in Maryhill and Springburn, 45 per cent in Pollok, and 46 per cent in Shettleston.

You don't need a degree in psephology to see what's going on here. The trend couldn't be clearer. Wealthier Scots vote in higher numbers. They are also statistically more likely to support the Union and, in turn, a unionist party. Poorer Scots are less likely to vote but more likely to support both independence and the SNP.

The Yes campaign, then, faces a problem. The SNP will be able to maintain its dominant status at the next two elections, in 2020 and 2021, because the unionist vote is split, unevenly, between three parties, the Tories, Labour and the Liberal Democrats. But in a referendum, there are only two options: Yes and No. Supporters of the UK won't have to divvy-up their ballots between Ruth and Kez. They will come out en masse, East Renfrewshire-style, to defend the Union.

Unionist Scotland, in other words, is a relatively solid, coherent bloc built around a motivated and prosperous electorate, not a scattering of diverse political interests. It's easy to forget that in the scrum of an election campaign, when everyone's howling at one another from a dozen different angles.

So, how might the SNP respond? Can the unionist firewall be vaulted? The most obvious strategy would be to boost turnout in poorer areas. The SNP has 120,000 members, active and well-attended local branches, and significant resources. It is a formidable electoral machine. This autumn, Nicola Sturgeon launched a new initiative to broaden support for independence, revolving around a National Survey. It would make sense to also look at a mass voter registration drive, with efforts focused on those communities where levels of political disengagement are rising.

At the same time, Sturgeon will have to target the softer sections of unionist opinion. A sustained majority for independence won't be possible unless a chunk of the No voting public changes its mind. The good news is that Ruth Davidson could end-up doing a lot of work for the Yes campaign in this respect. Just as the surge in nationalism has hardened support for the Tories, so too might the Tory surge harden support for nationalism, particularly among beleaguered left-leaning Labour voters who have seen their party's prospects in Scotland collapse and don't expect Jeremy Corbyn to win the next UK general election. Under Davidson, the centre of unionist gravity will shift (further) to the right, leaving unionism's dwindling band of leftwing stragglers in an even more isolated position.

How carefully, if at all, is the SNP considering any of this? Back in 2014, neither the SNP nor Yes Scotland seemed remotely interested in addressing the specific social and class barriers that stood in the way of independence. Their plan was to develop as wide a coalition for Yes as possible, in the hope that it would inch them over the line on polling day. The result was a bungled pitch that lacked ideological consistency.

Since 2014, there has been an assumption among Yes campaigners that another referendum is inevitable, which is probably correct, and that a Yes vote is guaranteed, which definitely is not. True, backing for independence has gradually ticked up over the past 20 months. But the East Renfrewshire problem is very real, and it isn't going away. The Yes campaign should start mapping a path around it, sooner rather than later.

Chapter 40

(Re)imagining Scotland's future

Doug Gay

Let me begin in a place which, for some, may seem odd or surprising. Ancient culture. "Where there is no vision, the people perish." So runs Proverbs 28.19 in the King James version of the Bible. Proverbs belongs to what is known as the Wisdom literature of the Hebrew scriptures, a range of disparate texts mixing insights from Ancient Israel's legal and prophetic traditions, with elements of comedy, lament, fable and parable. From the eroticism of the Song of Songs, through the cynicism of Ecclesiastes, to the troubled theodicy of Job, their influence hallows and haunts Western culture, not least the drama, art and literature of Scotland.

Manifestos are meant to make vision manifest; to show and tell the future we could have if power was used in one way or another. But production of 'the vision thing' needs to call on the imagination of more than politicians and political parties. The work of imagining Scotland's future needs to be ecumenical, plural and dialogical: ecumenical because different parties and communities need to find common ground, plural because we are enriched by a range of voices and perspectives and dialogical because politics in its broadest sense involves a vigorous civic conversation about the common good.

As a theologian shaped by the Reformed and Calvinist traditions, I have been struck by some observations the Canadian Catholic philosopher Charles Taylor makes about the influence of the Reformed tradition in Europe. He notes how it combined an often severe and austere vision of human limitations and flaws with an extraordinary confidence in the possibility of reforming and reshaping human society. Nothing in me is nostalgic for what Michael Marra called 'chain up the swings' religion. I am as willing to acknowledge the Kirk's share of responsibility for a swathe of damaging repressions and depressions, cultural blind spots and social prejudices as I am determined we move on from them. But there may yet be something compelling about the synergy (even *antisyzygy*?) Taylor names, which melds together humility and bold ambition, realism and high ideals, pessimism about self-interest and passion for change.

After the crash of 2008/9, when I was part of the Kirk's Special Commission on The Purposes of Economic Activity, we named four key goals: to end poverty, to reduce inequality, to promote mutuality, to ensure sustainability. Those would still be four points of the moral compass I want to see guide economic policy between now and 2021. I am encouraged by their ecumenical potential to offer a way of mapping common ground between Scottish Labour, the Lib Dems, the Scottish Greens, RISE and the SNP. The devil, I recognise, is in the detailed iteration of policies which move us closer to achieving these goals.

Here is where the work of political imagination so often polarises. Those more pessimistic about human nature, we could call them 'Augustinian', are easily tempted to embrace a conservatism which in its lack of ambition for reform, becomes decadent and self-serving. Those hot for transforming the world, we could call them 'Franciscan', are easily tempted to embrace a radicalism, which in its lack of capacity to win popular support and power, becomes irrelevant and self-deluding.

The space between these low and high roads might therefore seem the obvious ground to make for, but there are dangers here too. For those of us who like the idea of an ecumenical big tent, the legacy of the New Labour project and of the Liberal Democrats in coalition is a chilling realisation that a triangulation too far, leads to cynicism and outrage among those we disappoint and, I reckon, a degree of self-disgust at the compromises we made to secure power. As a member of the SNP, I am committed to the big project of building support for a Yes vote from 45 per cent to over 60 per cent, but I am stung like others, by criticism of the cautious centrism of our 2016 manifesto. There is a real fear of over triangulation, of being too cautious in power and then regretting the missed opportunities. The prize of building a broad consensus in support of independence is not separable for me, from the goal of building a similar consensus in favour of creating a more equal society.

The *dialogical* work of shaping political imagination calls for spirited conversations around key sites of public policy. Here I consider how conversations around some economic sites might be developed in the next five years.

Developing the social market

Writing of the need for government intervention in markets, the moral theologian Oliver O'Donovan (recently retired from New College, Edinburgh) argues that "markets do not regulate themselves. They adjust themselves, but like the brutish and short-sighted Leviathans they are, they trample people beneath their feet while they do so". Reimagining the Scottish economy as a properly regulated social market economy requires among other things:

> First, a persuasive and discriminating defence and promotion of the role of the public sector as regulator, registrar, investor, owner and incentiviser.

Successive governments at Westminster (and in some instances at Holyrood) share blame for weak and indeed, craven *regulation* of financial services pre 2008; for failures to insist on transparency in *registering* ownership of land, wealth and companies and for the sleekit and reckless promotion of PFI as a way of moving public expenditure off book.

There has also been shameless ideological prejudice against public *investment* and *ownership*, pursued to absurd extremes of hypocrisy and inconsistency. Consider the monstrous irony of Conservative agreement to a nuclear station at Hinkley Point, to be built by the French state, while being part financed and owned by the Chinese state. Or take the bizarre post-privatisation spectacle of Scotrail being run by Dutch state rail company Abellio.

Progress towards a more sustainable economy has also been hampered by the reluctance of the Treasury/Finance Directorate to make more effective use of fiscal sticks and carrots to *incentivise* change. The successful examples of the switch to lead free petrol, landfill taxes, and the levy on plastic bags beg questions about why the stick of repricing environmentally damaging behaviour is not more widely used. The success of subsidy regimes for renewable energy show carrots working effectively.

> Second, an inclusive myth busting account of wealth creation and a new pro-social vision of incorporation.

Parties of the broad left usually lose rhetorical wars over being pro-business, to their electoral cost. Countering this and convincing voters the economy will flourish in our hands calls for a sharper focus on deconstructing the language of wealth creation, but also requires a smarter and more creative economic offer. Current patterns of incorporation show a poverty of ethical imagination. In return for its grant of legal personality to a business enterprise, society can ask for much more. It must ask for transparency of ownership and proper payment of taxes from all companies. It should also offer much greater fiscal recognition of pro-social behaviour. Companies which are some or all of the following: owned or part-owned by employees or customers (whether co-ops, fan-owned football clubs or John Lewis style mutuals), committed to fair trade and high environmental standards, paying living wages and restricting ratios of highest paid to lowest paid workers, should be eligible for lower rates of corporation tax. We need to reward pro-social economic activity which helps to create a more mutual society. Fiscal incentives offer state led, but not 'statist' ways of doing this.

Third, a tax and welfare offer which can command wide support and drive progress towards greater equality.

I am sympathetic to what Richard Murphy calls 'the joy of tax' and my heart warmed to Yes campaigners promoting Nordic visions of high tax, high welfare societies. I also recognise this is not an easy sell to electorates. Blame neoliberal hegemonies or media scares or some such, but even low-income voters who would clearly benefit, are often resistant to high tax proposals. This is a classic example of where some virtuous rather than vicious triangulation is needed. Charles Taylor uses the term 'social imaginaries' to describe broad, largely unconscious mental mapping of our life worlds. In the twentieth century, national insurance (paying your stamp) offered populations one such memorable map which they took to heart?).

Today we need new ways of imagining tax which command broad support and resist a race to the bottom. We need rhetorically and imaginatively strong ways of mediating between the low tax, small government offer of the right and the high tax, big government offer of the left. It may be an eccentric suggestion, but I think we have neglected the symbolic and metaphorical dimensions of tax and welfare policy making to our cost. Pennies up and down or threshold and allowance tweaking may be less important than working on simple, memorable and symbolic ratios and proportions, which are given a clear ethical coding: those with broadest shoulders etc. Parties of the left need to beware of empty gestures and pyrrhic victories on (high) tax rates, which fire up the core but leave the wider electorate (including many low income voters) cold and suspicious.

The tax debates of the 2016 Holyrood campaign, around Income Tax, Council Tax, Land Value Tax and (the not yet devolved but surely coming soon) Corporation Tax, along with the extreme political nervousness around change, underline the fact that we need to take on the civic work of renewing our collective imagination about tax. This in order to use the powers we have between now and 2021 and to prepare for those which are yet to come.

Where there is no vision, the people perish. Martin Luther King's vision of 'the beloved community', which has much to say to Scotland today, was one of economic justice and inclusion. Here's to five years of Augustinian and Franciscan progress towards that.

Not Chapter 41

New Leaves – a poem

Alison Phipps*

They grew on a
mature birch tree,
silvering through
winter, budding
in spring.

They breathed out
green air
but those who
walked in their
shade knew
not of the
heart-wood, saw not
its dark rings.

And only once
the winds blew
did they
flame into ashes
sharing pale
hope with a
whitening earth.

So turn each one
over,
trace out the bones,
crack the spine open,
and wait.

Afterword

The practicalities of 'getting radical'

Simon Barrow

The results of the Scottish Parliament elections on 5th May 2016 had just come in when this collection was being put together. Our idea was not so much to solicit responses to the result of that poll, but (based on an awareness of the new parliamentary balance of power) to use the occasion to cast a visionary eye forward for Scotland – something that is difficult to do in the rough and tumble of daily politics. The shadow confronting all of us at that time was the UK referendum on membership of the European Union on 23rd June (see Smith and Gow's chapters). The dominant consensus was that Remain would win by a whisker, in spite of a poor, negative campaign at the UK level. When the shockwave of the 52:48 Brexit result hit, I was in the US, staying with friends who have strong French and Italian family connections. The vote to leave the EU was a stunning moment – a possibility which many of us had contemplated intellectually, but had barely begun to fathom emotionally and politically.

Encountering disjuncture

My next thought, as someone born in England and domiciled there for most of my life, was a sense of relief that I was now returning to my new home, Scotland, which had voted to Remain 62:38 nationally and with a majority across all 32 council districts. Then came the sense of democratic outrage that one of the 'family of nations' that supposedly makes up the United Kingdom could face economic and social damage, chaos and upheaval as a result of a decision we did not vote for, occasioned by a Westminster government we voted overwhelmingly against, and in the face of an entrenched right-wing hegemony delivered by a voting system which disenfranchises millions of people.

"Brexit changes everything," one commentator declared apocalyptically two days after the EU referendum. This is true. But, at the time of writing, five months later, it is still not anywhere near being clear what Brexit means in practice, how it will proceed, and what will rise and fall in its wake. Scotland's First Minister continues to play her cards, including the possibility of a further independence referendum, carefully and shrewdly. Before and immediately after the June poll, the dominant speculation was that a Brexit vote in the UK that was rejected north of the border would almost inevitably lead to the United Kingdom losing Scotland. Even Tony Blair seemed to believe this. Now the terrain looks much more complicated and uncertain. Prime Minister Theresa May appears as determined to achieve a sharp Brexit as she is to keep together a Kingdom for which the term United feels less and less applicable in anything other than a forced sense. Scotland's day as a self-governing nation may still be coming, but when that will be and what it will look like is very much up for negotiation.

Which is where *Scotland 2021* comes in. What we have done in this volume is focus on the immediate and long-term challenges that will continue to press Scotland whatever happens to our political topographies over the next few years – since no settlement (Scotland out of the EU but in the UK, Scotland in the EU and out of the UK, or anything besides or between) is going to take hold in any kind of future whose levers of change are graspable right now. Moreover, the kind of constitutional and political settlement that will work best for Scotland, and indeed for our neighbours and friends near and far, will not be shaped by ignoring the key issues of economy, environment, education, health, social care, justice, international relations (and more) that we examine in their Scottish dimension in this book. Rather, looking at what is changeable in the short-run, from the perspective of a hopeful vision of a better future, seems the best way to shape our sense of what Scotland can and should be with far greater powers, or full independence. Or, indeed, what strategies will be needed if neither is forthcoming in the way we might want. Because, contrary to much propaganda from those who wish to maintain the present UK system at all costs (the UK being just one temporal way of arranging governance in the British isles, please note), the issue of our constitutional future is not properly understood in terms of tribal identity politics and the reassertion of cultural symbols. It is more fundamentally about whether another Scotland, another Europe and another world are possible.

Envisioning a different future

The contributors to *Scotland 2021* may vary on a number of things (including political allegiance, issues about religion or belief and, in some cases, the question of independence), but what unites them is a desire for what can rightly be called radical change towards economic, social and political democracy; towards environmental sustainability; towards equality and decent life chances for all; towards an internationalist future free of weapons of mass destruction; and towards a country and world that recognises and includes the talents and needs of all, not least those currently disabled by society and by the recent dominance of the austerity agenda.

So how do we translate these radical visions into practical politics? That is the task each of our writers, in different ways, seeks to tackle in setting forward proposals and hopes for the next five years of Scotland's journey. Part of the clue to a workable answer therefore lies in examining the step-changes that can be made in specific policy areas, guided by a picture of the differences we want to make. In some cases that can be clearly articulated in a measurable, realisable way. 50:50 gender representation in our parliament and in other major public bodies, for example (Yaqoob). In other cases the goal (moving in the direction of a carbon free energy future – Black, Trebeck and Shaw) may be accepted, but the steps to achieving it and the acceptability or otherwise of compromises along the way will be hotly disputed. And all the time, in a democracy, what is desirable and what is possible are being persuaded, pressed, bargained and negotiated within a public sphere that includes many different aspirations, and where the dominance of concentrated wealth, entrenched privilege, large corporations and plutocratic politics is always holding us back. We have to go deeper.

Therefore "getting radical" (in this positive sense) requires, I would suggest, three qualities which are often overlooked:

- The capacity to nourish the kind of the security that gives people the courage to change

- Willingness to adapt flexibly to the challenge of the political environment, but in a principled way, and

- An ability to act humanely by developing transformative relationships as well as policies and practices.

Let me flesh out those headline ideas with reference to some of the issues touched on in Scotland 2021, and then note a few concerns that did not make it into these pages, but which will be explored online alongside this book.

Rethinking radicalism: roots and routes

First, security and change. This goes to the core meaning of the term 'radical', which is often (mis)used these days as a cipher for wild or violent extremism, but actually comes from the Latin, *radix*, meaning source, root or foundation. To be truly radical is not to reject our past and our inheritance, but to take the best what is has bequeathed us into the different conditions of a new era. This entails nurturing a sense of shared security that makes change less threatening and more inviting. It encourages the kind of practical solidarities that strengthen us both to let go of what has been (where that is necessary) and to embrace what can be (where that is beneficial).

True radicalism, in other words, is about making a connection between the actual communities people find themselves living in (with all their joys and sorrows) and the 'imagined communities' that enable a move to something better, more satisfying, more just and more inclusive. 'Imagined communities' is the concept developed by Benedict Anderson (in his book of that name from 1983) to argue that a nation is a community socially constructed, imagined by the people who perceive themselves as part of that collective. It is essentially a narrative, a story that gives us a sense of belonging and achieving together. Scotland is one such story – or, more accurately, set of stories. The question (one which indirectly arises in many of the preceding chapters) is who gets to tell the story, who is included or excluded, what sustains it, and where it is going?

At present, many of the stories that shape the UK are based on fear of 'the other'. Some, like austerity, demonising claimants and those on the margins, are told in order to preserve an unequal balance of power. Others, like the rhetoric of anti-immigration, are about ways of getting people to blame their neighbours rather than to address injustices in the distribution of wealth and resources which leave us fighting each other rather than working together to change an unequal system. "Getting radical" in this context entails propagating an alternative, popular vision of the future that restores the connections between people, enabling us to embrace difference and let go of prejudice – together with some workable examples of how it can happen. This is what the case for a future Scotland needs to be about. Unless it is positive and inviting it will not persuade. At the same time, it must address people's fears, but on the basis of a *visionary realism* rather than the kind of cultural and political 'cannae do' which creates a gulf between what is and what can be.

The German theologian Jurgen Moltmann once pointed out that the whole point about a *qualitatively* different future is that, by its nature (being qualitatively different) it cannot be adequately described and mapped out on premises wholly determined by the present. There will always be something 'more' about it. Its realisation requires bold experimentation, rather than passive accommodation. For a 'realism' that prescribes present terms as the only ones possible is not, in fact, realism. It is ideologically disguised pessimism. Likewise, idealism (the willingness to imagine the future differently, and to allow that to shape current choices) is not necessarily un-realistic – unless it refuses to acknowledge the human need for security in the midst of change, or unless it refuses to deal with the contingency and fallibility of life and of human beings as we seek to move forward together. "Getting radical" means asking *what kind of reality* lies at the foundations of any 'realism' that is being advocated against the possibility of something better, and how that reality can be addressed. This in turn requires the ability to face down obstacles in the process of forging proposals for reform which recognise (in the way they are formulated) where we are, where we want to get to, and where the bridges for a secure crossing are to be found or built. This is what I would designate as 'visionary realism'.

The poetry and prose of politics

There are plenty of examples of this in the preceding chapters about where Scotland needs to go over the next five years: working towards a major cultural shift on childcare (Moyes); strengthening the case for cooperatives as a bridge to real economic democracy (Lockhart); the reimagining and reshaping of our justice system (McCulloch and Smith); rejuvenating democracy (Fairweather); an economy based on wellbeing that measures things differently (Trebeck); making tax policy wily and creative (Bradley); acting together for gender justice (Orr); enabling the participation and wisdom of disabled people in politics (Szymkoviak and others); a new approach to asylum seekers and refugees (Alsaba); putting health back into our hands (Kapilashrami, Marsden, Robertson); sustainability for human flourishing (Bebbington); urban land reform (Bunce, Marsden, Allan); regenerating arts and culture, starting with the local (Cooper); choices facing higher education (Chalmers); reconsidering the print and broadcast media environment (Holleran); building on LGBTIQ+ equality gains (MacAlpine), negotiating an energised public square open to civic engagement by people of different beliefs (Maguire, Frazer, Ross), and others. In each case you will find, to a greater or lesser extent, a mixture of envisaging something better, addressing challenges and proposing tangible moves forward.

The second of the three qualities I identified for "getting radical" is also at play in these contributions: the willingness to adapt flexibly to the circumstances of the moment, but in a principled way. The late Mario Cuomo talked about the inevitability of 'campaigning in poetry and governing in prose', and the Italian PCI in the 1960s and 1970s conceived of a 'historic compromise' in terms of possible coalition with the Christian Democrats. Politics is, in one respect, the art of compromise and the practice of prose. But compromise can and should retain a flavor of what it is a step-towards, and prose can embrace and be changed by the poetic in stating its case. We have very deliberately ended the third section of *Scotland 2021* with a poem (Phipps) for that very reason. By contrast, the era of Blair, in particular, ushered in (or perhaps crystalised) a technocratic managerialism and PR cynicism within politics and public life which has infected too much of our despairing commentary and cramped expectation through to today.

In very different ways, and without seeking to compare their politics and their contexts, Nicola Sturgeon, Caroline Lucas, Jeremy Corbyn and Leanne Wood are all recognised politicians from different parties who exhibit an ability to connect with people (some more widely and successfully than others) in a way that demonstrates that involvement in the political process can retain an edge of genuine motivation for change. Since our view of politics is neither begun nor ended by political parties (though Bill Gilby, Maggie Chapman, Connor Beaten, Ian Dommett and Emily St Denny are among those contributors to *Scotland 2021* who deal ably with that important landscape), it needs to be said that grassroots movements, while often heavily focused on nurturing hope and lobbying for causes, also need to connect their frontier vision with the prose of politics and of everyday life – where most people are not concerned with such matters – in order to make an impact. This is a challenge coming out from initiatives like Common Weal and the quest to create an effective, ideas-rich environment for change (McAlpine). In a different way, it is also what lies within the detail of Alasdair Davidson's question about whether Scotland can become a Nordic nation, and Doug Gay's intriguing juxtaposing of 'Augustinian' and 'Franciscan' ways of progressing public goals.

Perhaps nowhere is the rub of poetry and prose felt more keenly than in matters of international policy, mapped out by Adam Ramsay. Here the temptation to be mired in anaesthetising diplomacy and geopolitical manoevering is so strong that only a clear-sighted alternative narrative will ward off some of the worst aspects of armed pragmatism. Even then, it's tough. Remember Robin Cook's 'ethical foreign policy' and the mockery the very attempt to conceive it was subjected to? At present Scotland does not wield the powers of global diplomacy with anything like the weight of a nation state, but its influence can still be positive, for example, in the European debate and in the firm stand the SNP, the Greens and to an extent Labour in Scotland (considerably emboldened by the hard work CND and other peace movements) have taken against Trident and nuclear weapons. In order to discover the kind of positive orientation in the world that enables tough questions to be tackled with principle, we need to think of Scotland in a consciously postcolonial way (Marten) and to face up to those dominant global forces which press hard on romanticised versions of independence (Radovic) – in the same way as they confront the realities of class (Maxwell) and re-situate talk of 'taking back control' (in a way inimical to the dangerous populist rightism of a Donald Trump, say) in a consciously progressive framework, enabling us to recall how powerful 'the threat of a good example' (Meaden) can still be in a torn and anguished world.

Humanity and relationships making for change

In all of our striving for better communities locally, nationally and globally, there are, as Joyce MacMillan says, 'reasons to be cheerful, or not' for self-styled progressives in the political arena. Her focus is on change in and for Scotland, and she identifies this as "a moment for civil society to stir itself again" to ensure that Scotland doesn't slide backward after the stirrings of the 2014 referendum. This touches on the third characteristic of a positively radical politics that I wish to point to: the ability to act humanely by developing transformative relationships as well as transformative policies and practices.

It is easy to think of 'civil society' in abstract, organisational terms – campaigns, NGOs, charities, unions, community initiatives, faith bodies, secular groups, enablement networks, alliances, cultural enterprises, and so on. Equally, what was once the 'voluntary sector' can easily be professionalised to a degree that it becomes just another part of the apparatus of governance and maintenance. So also 'volunteering' can be a way of making up for cuts in statutory provision, rather than a way of connecting people beyond the formalism and consumerism of much contemporary existence. But what we should never forget is that 'civic life' and 'civil society' are at heart about people and relating, and therefore contain within the best of the activities they support the capacity to restore humanity and relationship to the bureaucracy and infrastructure of 'a society of strangers'. That is, to challenge the way of seeing and doing which makes people instrumental rather than focal to a lot of social, political and economic activity.

So radicalism capable of making worthwhile change will take the human dimension and the precariousness of human endeavours seriously. That might be a matter of looking at political campaigning from the street level, where it is about contact between ordinary people's lives and the tactical desire for votes and allegiance (Denholm and McTurk), or it might be about the dreams that inhabit our political philosophies or ideas (Hassan) and what happens to them in the rough and tumble of political machination. It will be about much more than this, of course. Both Humanists and different faith groups mentioned in four of the 40 chapters of Scotland 2021 are among those who belong to consciously 'moral communities': groups of people who come together to advocate a way of life, a way of believing (not necessarily religious), a way of seeing the world and a way of acting with which they wish to engage others. What would parliaments and public bodies look like if those forming and leading them felt the need to incorporate an element of moral community in their operation? Would it really allow the DWP and related contractors to go on treating disabled and sick people in an often heartless and dehumanising way? Or politicians to produce policies without adequate regard to the human scaling and impact of what is being implemented? There is a whole dimension of politics which we are apt to forget here, and which is closely related to the sharing and locating of power as close as possible to those who need to be involved in it and who are effected by it (the subsidiarity principle).

This humanising is also possible, and indeed vital, in the contestation of ideas and the taking of large decisions, like the independence one for Scotland. Nicola Sturgeon was honest and emotionally literate enough in her October 2016 SNP conference speech to say that the sense of loss she felt as the EU referendum result came in helped her to understand better how some No voters in 2014 might have felt had they lost. That is a point picked up in practical terms by the passionately pro-Yes Irvine Welsh ("don't hate No voters, but challenge those who do") in his chapter about big picture change for Scotland. It is a chapter in which he remains typically trenchant overall, because being considerate towards our humanity doesn't mean being anodyne.

Finally, it is important to acknowledge that not everything that was intended for this book got in. The good news here is that we have some material that can and will grow around the *Scotland 2021* project. In particular, I conducted fascinating interviews with health professional Dr Catherine Harkin (about how the agenda around wellbeing, health policy and the NHS needs to be developed, extended and reframed in Scotland, related to chapter 17) and with Moni Tagore (an independence and SNP activist who brings a cross-cultural perspective to his own involvement in Scottish politics). At one point we were also going to include an article by Polly Jones of Global Justice Now on TTIP (a text slightly overtaken by events given the delay in publication, but something that definitely requires continual monitoring and action). There were additional discussions with Maureen McGonigle, founder of Scottish Women in Sport, and Paul Goodwin, co-founder and organiser of the Scottish Football Supporters Association (SFSA), about the central role of sport in Scotland's past, preset and future. We would also wish to reference the vital work of financial journalist Ian Fraser, whose revealing book on RBS, *Shredded,* casts important light on the need for thoroughgoing reform of the banking and finance sector in Scotland and beyond. Equally, we want to recognise the importance of the housing debate in Scotland, the subject of a recent book and a forthcoming policy paper from Ekklesia. I might also have been interested in examining the question of confederalism (the idea of self-governing nations collaborating together) as an alternative to the UK as a political framework for these islands, something I think could strengthen the remit of Scottish independence considerably, as well as offering political space for allies in other parts of Britain. But those are for another time, and for our websites.

Engaging with change agency

These, then, are some of the larger challenges that might be seen to come out of the invitation in Scotland 2021 to continue to cast a visionary but practical eye on Scotland over the next few years – not so much in the constitutional and Brexit dimensions of the unfolding future, but in the large issues, the minute particulars and the bridges between the two that need to be explored in every area of public policy. Among other things, this will also involve looking further at the architecture and process of political change: from community engagement, to campaigning, to research, to policy formation, to lobbying, to parliamentary procedure, to legislation, to implementation, to monitoring (and right round the circle again). That, of course, is a book in itself!

Contributors

Hamish Allan is active in Common Weal Edinburgh North and Leith. He has also been involved in independence and Green campaigning.

Khuloud Alsaba is a Researcher and Public Health Advocate with the Syrian Center for Policy Research (http://scpr-syria.org) and is based at the University of Edinburgh where she did her doctoral research.

Simon Barrow is Director of the public policy think tank *Ekklesia*. He has been active in journalism, politics, adult education and ecumenism for many years. He lives in Leith, having moved to Scotland in 2010. He is also a member of the Iona Community, is on the NUJ Ethics Council, and is Chair of the Scottish Football Supporters Association (SFSA).

Connor Beaton works as a journalist. He is member and former candidate in the Scottish Socialist Party, and is supporter and activist with RISE.

Jan Bebbington is Professor of Accounting and Sustainable Development at the University of St Andrews.

Wendy Bradley is a retired senior tax inspector currently undertaking doctoral research into tax simplification and better regulation. She was nominated as tax blogger of the year in 2016 (https://tiintax.com). She writes on science fiction as well as on tax and tax policy. She lives in Sheffield.

Lee Bunce is active in Common Weal Edinburgh North and Leith. He also works in the Careers Service at the University of Edinburgh.

Doug Chalmers is Senior Lecturer in Media and Journalism at Glasgow Caledonian University and President of the University and College Union Scotland. He is also involved in Democratic Left.

Maggie Chapman is Co-Convenor of the Scottish Green Party. She was a councillor for the Leith Walk ward of Edinburgh Council from 2007–2015 and represented the Scottish Greens on the Smith Commission. She is the Rector of the University of Aberdeen, having been elected in 2014.

Neil Cooper is a writer and critic on theatre, music and art. He is Theatre Critic for the Herald newspaper and active in the NUJ. His work is archived at http://coffeetablenotes.blogspot.co.uk

Alistair Davidson is a member of the Bella Caledonia editorial team. He is a member of the SNP, a democratic socialist, and on the advisory board of Open Rights Group Scotland. He writes regularly on politics and policy.

Jane Denholm has been running Critical Thinking, a public policy consultancy specialising in further and higher education, training and skills since 2003. She is active in the SNP, works with a parliamentarian, and has been an election agent.

Stuart Fairweather is Convenor of Democratic Left in Scotland (na Deamocrataich Chli an Alba). He is an active trade unionist and Dundee branch Chair of Unite.

Richard Frazer is convener of the Church of Scotland's Church and Society Council. He is Parish Minister of Greyfriars Church in central Edinburgh, and Chair of the Grassmarket Community Project.

Doug Gay is a lecturer in Practical Theology at the University of Glasgow. He is a Church of Scotland minister, who has lived and worked for many years in the East Ends of Glasgow and of London and is now based in Glasgow's West End. He is the author of *Honey From the Lion – Christianity and the Ethics of Nationalism*, SCM, London, 2014.

Bill Gilby is Chair of Edinburgh Northern and Leith Labour Party, and former director of the executive office of programmes for Unison. He has been an active campaigner on a range of issues, including cross-party opposition to Trident.

David Gow edits http://sceptical.scot. He is also editor of Social Europe and a former European Business Editor and Germany Correspondent for the Guardian.

Gerry Hassan is a writer, academic, media commentator and Research Fellow in cultural policy at the University of the West of Scotland. He is also an associate fellow with IPPR Scotland. His latest book is *Scotland the Bold* (Freight Books, November 2016). He has also recently edited *SNP Leaders* with James Mitchell.

Paul Holleran is National Organiser in Scotland for the National Union of Journalists (NUJ). He has considerable experience and involvement in media issues.

Anuj Kapilashrami is Lecturer in Global Public Health and Programme Director for the MSc in Global Health and Public Policy at the University of Edinburgh.

Mary Lockhart is the recently elected Labour Councillor for the Fife ward of The Lochs. She has been a stalwart trade unionist for many years, a former chair of the Cooperative Party, and has been a vocal supporter of Scottish independence.

Tim Maguire took an Honours degree in history from Edinburgh University in 1977. His first job was at a strip theatre in Soho, and it's been downhill ever since, he reckons. After a twenty-five year career as a producer and director, Tim became a humanist celebrant in 2005, and he firmly believes it's the most rewarding work he's ever done.

Sara Marsden researches public health policy at the University of Edinburgh. She was previously Development Manager for the Public Health & Wellbeing team at the Care Quality Commission. She convenes Common Weal Edinburgh North and Leith and is active in the Scottish Green Party.

Kirsty MacAlpine is originally from the Highlands and now works as a Policy Officer in Glasgow. She was one of the co-founders of YES LGBT and is involved in Out for Independence.

Michael Marten is currently working for the Iona Community. He has been a Visiting Research Fellow at Heythrop College, University of London, and is based in rural Stirlingshire. A historian and theorist focusing on Scotland's role in the British Empire and particularly in the Middle East, he has a long-standing interest in postcolonialism, nationalism and gender questions. He is an Ekklesia associate and board member.

James Maxwell is a widely published Scottish political journalist and contributor to Bella Caledonia. He has written for the New Statesman among many other publications.

Robin McAlpine is Director of Common Weal, the think-and-do tank. He started out in journalism and moved on to work in political media relations for 20 years. His new book (2016) is *Determination: How Scotland can win independence by 2021*.

Trish McCulloch is senior lecturer and Social Work Lead at University of Dundee.

Joyce McMillan is political columnist and theatre critic writing mainly for *The Scotsman*. She lives and works in Edinburgh and is Chair of the Edinburgh Freelance Branch of the NUJ.

Tam McTurk is a professional translator and is Director of Citadel Translations Ltd. He has been strongly involved in the independence movement, the SNP and other left-wing causes.

Bernadette Meaden is a writer on politics, social policy, welfare and disability issues. She is an Associate of Ekklesia, and has been strongly influenced by Christian Socialism, liberation theology and the Catholic Worker movement.

Vonny Moyes is an arts journalist and social activist. She has a weekly columnist in The National, is a regular media commentator and is head of digital communications for an environment agency.

Alison Phipps is Professor of Languages and Intercultural Studies (Creativity Culture and Faith) at the University of Glasgow. She is Co-Convener of Glasgow Refugee, Asylum and Migration Network. She is a poet, and a member of the Iona Community.

Lesley Orr is an academic, feminist, researcher and activist for gender justice. She works at New College in the University of Edinburgh for the Centre for Theology and Public Issues. In 2015 she was announced in the Herald as Scotland's Woman of Influence.

Milja Radovic is an author, academic and researcher on film, media arts, visual culture, citizenship, activism, religion and nationhood. Her book *Transnational Cinema and Ideology* was published by Routledge in 2014.

Adam Ramsay is the Co-Editor of *openDemocracyUK* and also works with *Bright Green*. He recently moved from Oxford to Edinburgh. He was previously a full-time campaigner with *People & Planet*.

Tony Robertson is Lecturer in Public Health at the University of Stirling.

Matthew Ross has been General Secretary of Action of Churches Together in Scotland (ACTS). The official ecumenical body, since 2014. He is a minister of the Church of Scotland.

Deirdre Shaw is Professor of Marketing and Consumer Research (Management) at the University of Glasgow.

Mike Small is editor of *Bella Caledonia*. A social ecologist, activist, writer and publisher, he is originally from Aberdeen. His several books include a study on pioneering urban planner Patrick Geddes.

Alyn Smith is an SNP Member of the European Parliament for Scotland. He was first elected in 2004 and re-elected in 2009 and 2014. A lawyer by profession, he serves as a full member of the Foreign Affairs Committee, remaining a voice in agriculture as alternate member of the Agriculture and Rural Development Committee (http://www.alynsmith.eu).

Mark Smith is senior lecturer and Head of School at University of Edinburgh.

Emily St Denny a researcher at the Public Policy Institute for Wales, based at the University of Cardiff, where she work on policy-making in Wales, especially in areas such as health and social policy. She previously had a research fellowship at the Centre on Constitutional Change, University of Edinburgh, where she investigated the policy-making process in Scotland.

Jamie Szymkowiak is founder of the cross-party *One in Five* campaign to encourage, empower and increase political participation among disabled people in Scotland. He is also an SNP staffer and is Convenor of the SNP Disabled Members Group committee.

Katherine Trebeck is Senior Researcher with Oxfam GB Global Research Team, an Honorary Professor at the University of the West of Scotland, and an Honorary Senior Research Fellow at the University of Strathclyde.

Niahm Webster supports Scottish based projects for *The Democratic Society*. Previously she worked at the Scottish Parliament in a political communications role. Her studies at the University of Glasgow University of Glasgow focused on public law, the EU and democracy.

Irvine Welsh is an internationally known writer of novels, stories and stage and screenplays. He has completed ten novels and four short-story collections since *Trainspotting* in 1993. http://www.irvinewelsh.net

Talat Yaqoob is Co-Founder of *Women 50:50*, the campaign for 50 per cent representation of women in the Scottish Parliament. She works for women in STEM, and is a writer and intersectional feminist.

BELLA CALEDONIA

About Bella Caledonia

Bella Caledonia is an online magazine, combining political and cultural commentary, that explores ideas of independence, self-determination and autonomy.

Named after a character in novelist Alasdair Gray's *Poor Things* (1992), it was formed in 2007 by Mike Small and Kevin Williamson.

It is not aligned to any one political party but believes in self-determination for Scotland. "Only then will a country disfigured by poverty and inequality be re-born ... It's time to get above ourselves."

The editor is Mike Small and the Gaelic and Scots editors are Ruairidh Maciver, Daibhidh Rothach and Rona Dhòmhnallach, Billy Kay, Matthew Fitt and Janet Paisley.

To write for us send your ideas to: bellasletters@yahoo.co.uk

Follow us on twitter: @bellacaledonia

Or, if you'd prefer, write to us at:
Bella Caledonia
Creative Exchange
29 Constitution Street
Leith EH6 7BS

About Ekklesia

Based in Edinburgh and London, Ekklesia is an independent, not-for-profit think tank that directs its work towards issues involving the changing role of beliefs and values in public life.

We advocate transformative ideas and solutions to societal challenges based on a strong commitment to social justice, inclusion, nonviolence, environmental action, participatory democracy and a creative exchange among those of different convictions (religious and otherwise).

Ekklesia is committed to promoting – alongside others – new models of mutual economy, conflict transformation, social power, restorative justice, community engagement and political renewal.

We are also working to encourage alternative perspectives on humanitarian challenges in a globalised world, not least a positive, affirming approach to migration.

During the 2014 Scottish independence referendum Ekklesia commented and reported on the case for 'interdependent independence', subsidiarity, the radical aspirations of the Yes movement, and the possibilities of a confederal future for the nations, peoples and regions of these islands.

Overall, we are concerned with the policy, practice and philosophy of moving beyond 'top-down' politics, economics and systems of belief.

This means that, while we are a political think-tank rooted in a nonconformist Christian outlook, we are keen to work with people of many backgrounds, both 'religious' and 'non-religious', who share common values and approaches.

Ekklesia's reports, analysis and commentary can be accessed via our website here: www.ekklesia.co.uk

The Ferret

Become a media mogul!

The Ferret is Scotland's first investigative journalism platform. Non-aligned and not-for-profit, we are dedicated to nosing up the trouser of power to hold the rich and the powerful to account. We are a democratic co-operative, beholden to no-one but our readers and writers.

When we launched in July 2015, we asked readers what we should investigate. Since then we have helped influence and change policy with a series of exclusive, in-depth, multi-media reports on fracking, surveillance and asylum – and there's much more to come. We don't accept adverts and we don't have any big corporate donors, so we are very reliant on our growing number of subscribers to fund our work. We would be delighted if you could join us.

You can see our stories at https://theferret.scot and learn more about who we are at https://theferret.scot/about-us

A subscription only costs £3 a month, and we are offering readers of this book a special deal. If you sign-up for a monthly subscription using the discount code TROUSERSOFPOWER then you'll get your first month absolutely free. Join here: http://bit.ly/ferretsub

Lightning Source UK Ltd.
Milton Keynes UK
UKOW03f0757060317
295952UK00001B/59/P